SYLVANUS MARSTON

For Harvey —
May you enjoy this
walk back in time.
With all best wishes,

Kathleen
10/24/08

SYLVANUS MARSTON

PASADENA'S QUINTESSENTIAL ARCHITECT

— ❖ —

KATHLEEN TUTTLE

Foreword by Kevin Starr
Afterword by Keith Palmer Marston

HENNESSEY + INGALLS
SANTA MONICA
2001

The author and the publisher would like to extend their special thanks to the Pasadena Historical Museum, where the Marston Collection is housed, for its kindness and enthusiasm which helped make this book a reality.

First published 2001 by

Hennessey + Ingalls
1254 3rd Street Promenade
Santa Monica CA 90401

©Hennessey + Ingalls 2001

ISBN 0-940512-19-X

California Architecture and Architects, No. 19

Printed in USA
Designed by Andrea Reibsamen

Library of Congress Cataloging-in-Publication Data

Tuttle, Kathleen, 1953-
    Sylvanus Marston : Pasadena's quintessential architect / Kathleen Tuttle ; foreword by
Kevin Starr ; afterword by Keith Marston.
        p. cm. -- (California architecture and architects ; 19)
    Includes bibliographical references and index.
    ISBN 0-940512-19-X
    1. Marston, Sylvanus Boardman, born. 2.
Architects--California--Pasadena--Biography. 3. Regionalism in
architecture--California--Pasadena. I. title. II. California architecture and architects ;
no. 19.

NA737.M432 T88 2001
720'.?92--dc21   2001039362

This book is dedicated
to the memory of my father,
Burt Joseph Tuttle;
and to my lodestars in this effort -
my mother, Gil, and John

If it is evil to care too much
for things that have neither mind nor heart,
then I am evil. For in the house where I was born,
I cared about the tiles around the fireplace,
the oak banister broad enough to slide down,
even the dumbwaiter, which carried up the trays
for those of us in bed with the measles....

~~Harriet Doerr, *The Tiger in the Grass*, 1995

Contents

Foreword – Kevin Starr   xi

Chronology   xiv

1 Shaping Influences   1

2 A Winter Colony   15

3 Embrace of the Arts and Crafts   31

4 Revival Architecture   49

5 The New Regional Idiom   73

6 The Nicholson House: China in Pasadena   91

7 Designing Community   97

Conclusion   115

Afterword – Keith Palmer Marston   117

Acknowledgements   119

List of Structures   123

Photographic Credits   141

Frequently Used Citations   143

Notes   145

Index   159

Foreword

Dr. Kevin Starr
State Librarian of California

Fᴿᴏᴹ ᴏɴᴇ ᴘᴇʀsᴘᴇᴄᴛɪᴠᴇ, ɪᴛ ɪs ɴᴏᴛ sᴜʀᴘʀɪsɪɴɢ ᴛʜᴀᴛ Sʏʟᴠᴀɴᴜs Mᴀʀsᴛᴏɴ should only now be receiving in this exhaustively researched, elegantly written, superbly illustrated book the recognition his career so richly deserves. Southern California, after all, in the creative decades of Marston's life abounded in talented architects who, from Santa Barbara to San Diego, were establishing a tradition that continues to delight us today by its scholarship, gracefulness, range, and variety. There were more good architects in those days than there subsequently have been good architectural historians to write a monograph that is each of these architect's due. The problem of proper recognition is even further compounded in the case of the architects of Pasadena during the first four decades of the twentieth century; for one can make a convincing case that Pasadena was the epicenter of all this architectural creativity. True, Marston has always been recognized as the inventor of the bungalow-court in his design for the St. Francis Court in Pasadena; yet rarely did commentary extend beyond this important but severely abbreviated recognition.

But now, thanks to the path-breaking researches of architectural historian Kathleen Tuttle, Sylvanus Marston is finally receiving the monographic recognition he deserves. Because of this ambitious study, Marston now stands revealed as an architect who in his lineage and sensibility, his education and eclectic tastes, together with his commitment to Pasadena as both an opportunity and an inspiration for fine architecture, more than holds his own among his distinguished contemporaries.

As Tuttle chronicles Marston's career and achievement, in fact, the case can be made that Marston is the quintessential Pasadena architect of his era: the one architect who most intuitively responded to the upper-middle-class aspirations of a distinctive Southern California city, in so many ways a colony of the Midwest and the East, with an architecture that helped Pasadenans recover the historicity that, subliminally at least, they feared they had lost in their move to a new region. All distinguished Southern California architects of this era, of course, were effective storytellers. Now we know that Sylvanus Marston was among the best of them in using architecture to re-center transplanted Easterners and Midwesterners in their new surroundings.

Like Pasadena itself, Sylvanus Marston had personal roots in the Anglo-American East: in Marston's case, in Maine from which his grandfather had migrated to San Francisco in 1858; and in Cornell University School of Architecture in Ithaca, New York, where Marston absorbed the taste, spirit, and exacting scholarship of the Beaux Arts tradition. He was, however, an original Pasadenan: arriving before cityhood at the age of four months to a place that deliberately saw itself as bringing the best of the Anglo-American East and Midwest to the Southland. He also attended Pomona College, an institution founded by New England Congregationalists.

Tuttle's monograph abounds in the telling details of Sylvanus Marston's Pasadena identity: his love of tennis and the outdoor life, for one thing; his memberships in the Pasadena Athletic Club and the Midwick Country Club, where he was among the founders; his stable marriage and family life, his regular and prudent habits, his solid business connections and life-long friendships, his statewide and local service in architectural organizations, including a two-time presidency of the Southern California Chapter of the AIA; and above all else, the range, tastes, and scholarly exactitude of his oeuvre, which earned him elevation to Fellow in the AIA in the last decade of his career.

There has always been something more than a little academic, even bookish, about Pasadena. For a variety of reasons Pasadenans were an erudite people. Their old American origins and elevated social and economic class lead to an abundance of leisure and a certain high-minded Protestantism. Pasadenans were very self-conscious about culture, very much in the mode of what Harvard philosopher George Santayana described as the genteel tradition. They chose, very deliberately, to define themselves as Pasadenans when they moved to Southern California. Santa Barbara, which was also emerging in this period, was more clearly a resort. Pasadena, by contrast, embraced an esthetic and ethos of wealth and culture as well as resort life. Soon, with the establishment of the Mount Wilson Observatory by the Carnegie Institution and the California Institute of Technology (both calling upon the distinctive talents of astronomer George Ellery Hale), together with Henry and Arabella Huntington's library and art gallery in nearby San Marino, genteel bookishness evolved into an institutionalized academic culture. Pasadena has become one of the most vital of academic and art museum centers in the United States, and the headquarters of a prestigious Federal Appellate Court.

A city such as this called for a certain kind of architecture: an architecture at once in dialogue with the great traditions of the past, yet possessed as well of a certain sunny informality lightening its orthodoxy of design. And this is exactly what Sylvanus Marston did over his thirty-plus-year career: move gracefully through the decades in a succession of styles—Bungalow, Craftsman, Palladian Villa, Spanish Colonial Revival, English Country Gothic, Seventeenth-Century French. In commission after commission, Marston offered his clients the narrative, scholarship, centering, and taste so characteristic of Pasadena. In one instance, the Grace Nicholson house (1924), now the Pacific Asia Museum, Marston showed himself a master of Chinese, although even here a measure of sunny Mediterranean informality can be detected in Marston's otherwise exacting Sino-statement.

Marston's invention of the bungalow court idea in 1908 with the St. Francis Court underscores the fact that he did not exercise his profession exclusively on behalf of wealthy clients. His was a practice involving schools, libraries, and retail businesses, even a cemetery, as well as grand mansions. And of course, being a Pasadena architect, Marston became involved in the design of hotels—bungalows for the Hotel Maryland and the Vista del Arroyo Hotel as well as cottages at the Huntington Hotel. Pasadena, like so many other architecturally distinguished cities in the Southland, remained in significant measure a winter resort for the affluent into the World War II era when these same cities and their hotels became convalescent centers for sick and wounded soldiers, sailors, airmen, and marines.

Whether Marston was turning his attention to a majestic mansion or to a small public library, he managed to introduce character and simple beauty into his otherwise scholarly designs. Marston's work, in other words, while scholarly, is never pompous or grandiloquent. Nor is it merely reduplicative. There is in Marston's best designs a certain lightness amidst the scholarship, a certain easy scenic visualization amidst the formality. His best work is colorful and possessed of charm, but it is never coy or self-regarding. Marston's craft was in pursuit of the genteel tradition: accurate and orthodox, but also reaching for certain refined emotional effects.

Architecture, we must remember, is a part of the everyday world. The best architecture applied on a human scale–introducing character, dignity, and taste to residences and communities–ennobles private lives and lifts the public's spirit. Such were Marston's gifts.

Whether or not Marston achieved any single "masterpiece" remains an open question. What this monograph testifies to is the meeting and matching of an architect and his city, his discerning clientele, and his community, through decades of prodigious and acclaimed work. From this perspective, Sylvanus Marston, as revealed by Kathleen Tuttle, not only invented the bungalow court, he demonstrated through hundreds of other structures as well the interpretive and sustaining power of unaffected elegance.

Marston, Van Pelt & Maybury

1883	Marston was born on August 16
1902-1903	Marston attended Pomona College
1907	Marston received his B. Arch. degree from Cornell University
1908	Marston became a licensed architect
1910-1912	Van Pelt worked as a draftsman for Marston during winters spent in Pasadena
1913	Van Pelt became Marston's chief draftsman
1914	Marston & Van Pelt was formed
1915	Maybury became a draftsman for Marston & Van Pelt
1918-1920	Marston spent nine months in France during WWI with the Foyer du Soldat (a branch of the the YMCA) attached to the French Army; Maybury left the firm in 1918
1921	Maybury returned to the firm as an associate
1923	Marston, Van Pelt & Maybury was formed
1927	Van Pelt left the firm
1927-1940	The firm became Marston & Maybury
1941	Marston & Maybury dissolved; Marston joined the war effort as an on-sight supervising architect with the U.S. Army Corps of Engineers
1942	Marston was elected to Fellow in the American Institute of Architects
1946	Marston died on November 16

Shaping Influences

Sᴠᴌᴠᴀɴᴜs Bᴏᴀʀᴅᴍᴀɴ Mᴀʀsᴛᴏɴ ᴡᴀs ʙᴏʀɴ ɪɴ 1883 in the Victorian nineteenth century when people still depended on gas lamps and the horse and buggy. He graduated from Pasadena High School before the Kitty Hawk flight and Theodore Roosevelt's presidency, at a time when ice and milk were delivered door-to-door. Mary Pickford hadn't yet set foot in Hollywood, much less met Douglas Fairbanks. Marston's professional training occurred in an era when design drawings–ink on linen–were considered works of art.

This book about Marston's life and architectural achievements tells many stories. In the same manner that a photographer chooses a subject and then adjusts the lens to capture different depths of field, this book, too, alternates between the personal and the panoramic. Presented here is Sylvanus Marston's story: his family, Pasadena upbringing, and architectural training, and a comprehensive survey of his distinctive professional portfolio.

Pasadena's and Southern California's development form the backdrop for Marston's life and work. The brooks and tributaries of his clients' lives fed into the rich channel that is Pasadena's history. A special effort has been made to view Marston's buildings through the eyes of that bygone era by examining local newspapers, architectural journals, and other contemporary sources.

Marston and the Region's Architectural Milieu

Sylvanus Marston, called "Van" by many of his friends, belonged to a special coterie of architects. When he joined the local architectural establishment in 1909,[1] his peers were a small and uncommonly talented group of approximately eighty men from Los Angeles, Pasadena, and the surrounding areas who constituted the Southern California Chapter of the American Institute of Architects (AIA). They had started their practices when the field was young and struggling for professional recognition in the West. Throughout his career, Marston was an active participant and in time a leader in the local AIA chapter. Other early members included Myron Hunt, Elmer Grey, Frederick Roehrig, Sum-

1.1 Sylvanus B. Marston, c., 1915

ner P. Hunt; Charles and Henry Greene, Robert Farquhar, Stiles O. Clements, Octavius Morgan, Albert C. Martin, Sumner M. Spaulding, Arthur B. Benton, and John Parkinson.[2] Ceramicist Ernest Batchelder (from the Pasadena Architectural League), L. C. Mullgardt of San Francisco, along with Irving J. Gill and Richard S. Requa of San Diego were occasional guests at monthly AIA meetings.[3] These men dominated the architectural landscape during Southern California's formative decades.

Marston and his colleagues were devoted to the development of their profession. AIA chapter meetings usually featured a speaker:[4] Myron Hunt on Italian gardens; "Don Carlos Lummis" (Charles F. Lummis) on his experiences as Los Angeles Librarian from 1905-1911; and Ernest Batchelder, who "spoke interestingly of his experiences in England among the art craft workers." One meeting was focused on the Los Angeles Architectural Club because it "has been invaluable in helping the architectural draughtsman of the city through the many problems of 'esquisse' [sketch] work in the Atelier." The club would soon "start sketch and water-color classes."[5]

The members valued design precedent. In 1910, they adopted a resolution urging the conservation of the California missions: "The buildings of the Franciscan Missions of California are among the most remarkable of the architectural remains of the Colonial period of the United States....This Chapter...seeks to conserve these examples of buildings, erected of native materials, largely by unskilled labor, under conditions of almost complete isolation from civilization, yet still possessed of an architectural character which commands respect and admiration of the ablest critics amongst the architects of to-day."

They also were consummate students. In July 1920 the chapter sponsored a weekend retreat at the Grove of El Capitan Ranch, on the coast about eighteen miles above Santa Barbara. According to the chapter minutes, twenty-one members in addition to Marston attended, men such as Reginald Johnson, Henry Mather Greene, Winsor Soule, Henry Withey, Harwood Hewitt, Alfred W. Rea, Edwin Bergstrom, and Octavius Morgan.[7] They slept in tents; Boy Scouts were on hand to cut wood, carry gear, and do other chores. The minutes describe in colorful detail the group spending an afternoon traveling by car caravan to Montecito to view several magnificent estates: "El Fureidis," a Roman villa "of marked individual character" designed by Bertram Goodhue on the forty-acre estate of J. M. Gillespie; "Arcady," the 200-acre estate owned by George O. Knapp; the Peabody House called "Solana" designed by Francis T. Underhill; the Lolita Armour Estate "El Mirador;" and the Bothin House with its "most ingenuous open-air theater" built for a San Francisco industrialist as a winter retreat. More than seventy years later, these still are considered some of the area's finest residences.

The day ended with an open-air banquet followed by a chapter meeting around a large campfire of oak logs. Albert C. Martin, Jr., who inherited the practice of his notable father, recalls that the profession was very different back then–structured, cohesive, even a little cliquish and exclusive: "It was like a fraternity."[8]

The Firm's Public Face

Only a handful of large architectural firms in Southern California existed in those days. In such firms, which included Marston, Van Pelt & Maybury, architects tended to specialize. This raises the question of each partner's contribution in Marston's firm. It is a difficult question to answer conclusively seven decades later. Compounding this handicap, only forty-three of the firm's 1,000 drawings remain, with few showing any partners' initials.

All three partners–Marston, Van Pelt, and Maybury–were strong in design. Maybury was a leading draftsman in the firm. By his own account, his contributions to the firm's designs were predominantly in the public and commercial category, with a few notable exceptions.[9] Maybury also published articles about some of the firm's public commissions.[10] His emphasis on the non-residential may have come about because he was the office's specifications writer,[11] a talent especially crucial for work on the more monumental buildings. Maybury's design role likely broadened after Van Pelt left in 1927, and the firm became Marston & Maybury. We know that in the 1930s Maybury had significant direct involvement with the firm's clientele.[12]

Van Pelt's sensitivity and attention to detail resulted in his having wide latitude to direct the manner in which a project's working drawings would develop. More than any other architect at the firm, Van Pelt worked with Marston to resolve any remaining design issues as a project came to fruition. The 1963 nomination letters for his elevation to AIA Fellow written by leading area architects make it clear, even discounting the hyperbole common to such letters, that Van Pelt was very gifted artistically and excelled at "relating buildings to their surroundings."[13] He was said to understand the architecture of the period, to exhibit a "sensitive approach and simple artistry," and to create with an eye to "design and function." Van Pelt's primary focus was on residential, not public structures.[14] By personality and inclination, Van Pelt could not have led the firm,[15] nor did he, with a few exceptions, have much contact with clients. Yet, his contribution to the firm was substantial.

Sylvanus Marston was the firm's principle architect. He had the paramount role and was adept at working with the people he hired and managing the different talents involved in a given commission. The success of the firm pivoted around his understanding of the client and the range of appropriate architectural possibilities. Architect Robert Bennett has said, based on his personal experience with Marston: "He really studied the person, gleaned all that he could, assessed the conditions that entered into the problem, and produced what was desired" by combining his interpretation with their demands.[16] As one architectural journal put it in 1929: "The architect must be sufficiently familiar with human desire to read between spoken words the unexpressed wish."[17] As client and architect spoke, Marston would produce sketches for a proposed design. He would then give the preliminary sketches to Van Pelt and draftsmen in order for them to develop a set of working drawings. Marston and Van Pelt would mull over and play with the drawings until they arrived at the right effect.[18]

With perhaps thirty different jobs in progress at any given time, Marston had to rely on the technical and artistic abilities of his staff,[19] as did other notable architects of the period, such as Wallace Neff.[20] The early conceptual sketch, decisions about design classification, larger judgments relating to a proposed design's appropriateness to site, and, if relevant, its relation to other public and commercial construction, fell to Marston. As the principle architect, Marston had to be adept at translating the drawings into clear images for the client.

Marston's prominence, according to Albert C. Martin, Jr., would not have been coincidental. He "would have to be very sophisticated, highly educated…to command the posture of the most prominent architect….He must be able to speak to clients in architectural terms and earn their trust."[21] Of all the factors, "the college system was the important thing in marking one as an architect," according to Martin.[22] Marston served as the firm's public persona; in 1925, for instance, he unveiled its proposed plans for the Pasadena Athletic Club at a 200-person formal banquet at the Huntington Hotel.[23] His dignified and informed design vocabulary was rooted in the historicism he was taught in his Beaux Arts education at Cornell.[24]

For the head of a large firm, Marston's involvement with a given commission was unusually extensive. He was the firm's contact with the engineers and the builders and was frequently on-site during a project's construction.[25] Keith Marston recalls the time his father was overseeing completion of a school commission and apparently "had his nose in so many nooks and crannies that a construction worker threatened to dump a bucket of cement over his head if he didn't get out of the way."[26]

Marston's active involvement in the profession led to his election as head of the State Association of California Architects (1939),[27] a two-term presidency of the Southern California Chapter of the AIA, and elevation to AIA Fellow (1942) as a result of "distinguished service to architecture and the excellence of the work of the firm of Marston and Maybury."[28]

A Kaleidoscope of Images

"Art for art's sake is good for the artist, but art for the people is better," wrote architect Charles Sumner Greene in 1907.[29] Architects often achieve distinction through the design of controversial buildings for architecture's sake. Developing a "signature" style, imposing a design agenda, or discovering a new architectural form are the dogged pursuits of many. By disposition and professional philosophy, Marston differed from this approach. Rather than designing to embellish his reputation or to augment his portfolio in particular ways, he avidly sought to discern the clients' desires and formulate the proposals that reflected these expressed wishes, but with outcomes often uncommon in their beauty. This was one of Marston's greatest talents as an architect and why, ironically, he might be less well known than he should be.

This ability no doubt is related to Marston's second great virtue: his mastery of an astonishing array of design styles. Few, if any, architects in Pasadena could match Marston's broad repertoire. After listening to his clients one by one, his designs for them became as varied as they were. Especially with Marston's residential commissions, the genesis of the design often can be ascertained by knowing the client, for Marston succeeded in translating his clients' personal imaginings into tangible designs.

His results often reflected the great historical periods or the traditions of one or another European country. When blending more than one style, the firm invariably introduced its own unique interpretation.

The firm designed nearly 1,000 structures, in styles ranging from the Arts and Crafts simplicity of bungalows to the opulence and sometimes extravagance of the Spanish mansions. Marston's renown for his ability to reinvent historically correct interpretations of many design styles, from the Prairie bungalow to English Tudor, to Spanish Baroque, to French Chateau, to the Chinese Palace, involved "definite originality which excites interest and attention."[30]

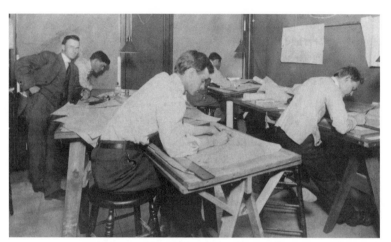

1.2 Photograph of Marston's office staff c. 1913. Pictured here are: Herbert E. Mackie, Burgo Purcell, G. Van Pelt (in far corner), S.B. Marston (standing) and J.C. Bennett.

Stylistic diversity was not accomplished seriatim, but often simultaneously. Consider the year 1924. The firm was busy that year preparing plans for a Chinese Palace, an imposing French manor, a Mediterranean-Italianate residence, a Neoclassical estate, and a Colonial Revival house in the Adam style.

This versatility was found not only in domestic designs but was incorporated into the firm's considerable public and commercial portfolio. Marston, Van Pelt & Maybury created award-winning public libraries, mercantile buildings, beautiful churches, public and private schools, banks, country clubs, resort hotels and their celebrated bungalows, as well as mausoleums, university buildings, YMCAs, and a community theater.

Marston's clients were both the mighty and the multitudes. In his first decade of practice, he designed small bungalows selling for $2,000 and $3,000 each as well as palatial residences costing $50,000. The larger houses were commissioned by heirs to the Libbey-Owens-Ford Glass Company fortune and the Scripps newspaper empire, among others. But Marston also designed for a frugal congregational minister turned academic and for a young man from the East who moved to Pasadena in a last desperate attempt to be cured of tuberculosis. Marston's design of attractive, affordable residences throughout his career distinguishes him from some of his peers who preferred to work only for the wealthy.[31]

The secret of the Marston firm's success was the simplicity of its designs. They avoided showiness, yet later won awards from the Pasadena Junior Philharmonic "Showcase House of Design" competition. In a 1916 article on West Coast architecture that included a Marston house, author and architect John Galen Howard discussed meritorious architecture in words that reflect the work of Marston's firm: "Quiet restraint, directness of expression, absence of ornament used for its own sake, beauty of effect derived solely from the essentials of the program.[32]

DIFFICULT DECISIONS HAD TO BE MADE concerning which of Marston's commissions would be covered in the main text and which would be presented only in the list of structures. Clearly, if a structure had unique architectural features or unusual historical significance it would receive textual attention. Sometimes the final decision was driven by an interest in the persons who had originally or subsequently lived in the house. I also have made a particular effort to feature each of the very wide range of architectural styles Marston developed.

Marston's additions and renovations to existing structures have been omitted from the text. The

Beaux Arts Fenyes Mansion at 170 S. Orange Grove, for instance, was designed by Robert Farquhar in 1905. In 1910, Eva Scott Fenyes engaged Marston to design an addition, an "art studio" where she planned to hold her Friday salon for Pasadena's cultural elite.[33] While the resulting addition is still regarded as the most splendid aspect of what is now the Pasadena Historical Museum, this was not a project covered in the text because it was Marston's renovation of another architect's existing structure.

Still other projects were omitted from discussion because of space limitations (however, all of Marston's known works appear in the list of structures at the end of the book). For instance, in 1921, Marston designed the Mountain Meadows Country Club where "San Dimas society often played golf."[34] He also drew plans for numerous structures, residential and commercial, in the Claremont-Pomona area, and several ocean-front beach houses in Laguna Beach and on Balboa Island for clients from Pasadena. In Santa Barbara, he designed several private residences as well as the award-winning Carrillo Hotel, touted as being "nothing garish, nothing ornate...no grinning faces or posing chiseled figures–just plain beauty."[35] Marston also designed a house in a twenty-acre tract called Armsley Square, an exclusive Ontario residential area developed by John S. Armstrong, owner of Armstrong Nurseries. Marston's residential work extended to Palm Springs, Mt. Baldy, Lake Arrowhead, and as far north as Los Gatos, Big Sur, and Santa Cruz.

Sylvanus Marston: Architect Within the Inner Circle

During the first two decades of the twentieth century one could not leaf through any of the leading architectural periodicals without noting the conspicuous presence of Sylvanus Marston and his firm. This was a function of the firm's exceptional design sense and its remarkable productivity. Marston's firm caught the public's attention and continually gratified its shifting design taste.

Sylvanus Marston was the quintessential Pasadena architect. Four months shy of having been born there and arriving before the city was incorporated, he became a part of a snug inner circle of the well-connected. Marston began his practice in Pasadena in 1908. In January of that year he had received his license, appearing before the California State Board of Architecture to present his credentials. Board members in attendance included John P. Krempel, Octavius Morgan, William S. Hebbard, and Frederick L. Roehrig.[36] Marston presented the drawings he had prepared of a house for a Cornell professor, and he described them as having been done as part of his course work at Cornell.[37] In addition, he highlighted his two years' office experience.[38] Marston was granted a license on the basis of his college education and his practical experience, without having to take a written examination.[39]

Marston's official sanction from this distinguished panel of pioneering California architects was an auspicious start. Octavius Morgan had been the first president of the Southern California Chapter of the AIA when it organized in 1894.[40] He received license No. 1 in 1900[41] and led the prominent Los Angeles firm of Morgan, Walls and Clements. Roehrig graduated from Cornell and, among other notable buildings, designed the Hotel Green on Raymond Avenue. Hebbard, who also studied at Cornell, was an eminent San Diego architect who at one time practiced with Irving Gill.[42]

Marston's mention to the state board of his office experience of "about two years" probably referred to summer jobs while home from Cornell. We know that Marston worked for Myron Hunt during some of that time.[43] Keith Marston, who considered his father a proficient wood-worker as well as an architect, also believes his father held a job as a carpenter for Greene and Greene during the period of his architectural studies.[44]

Athletic, popular, Ivy League-educated, conservative, and gentlemanly, Marston's easy entry into elite social and business circles–crucial to his professional success–was unsurprising. He was a founding member in 1912 of the Midwick Country Club, the most exclusive of the half-dozen or so county clubs then in existence. He usually lunched at his favorite spot, the Overland Club.[45] It was sequestered in a grand old bungalow on Garfield between Green and Colorado Streets, backing up on the Pasadena Athletic Club and not far from Marston's South Euclid Avenue office.[46] It was private, prestigious, "cozy and exclusive," and for men only. "You couldn't be on the time-clock and belong; it was for company owners and presidents," noted Paul Orban, Jr.,[47] whose lumber merchant father was a long-time member.

Marston's professional reputation and dignified bearing undoubtedly turned more than one club contact into client, yet even without such connections his personality would have led him to such associations. His son vividly remembers when the family pulled into a new town for gas or food on car trips in the 1920s. They often had to wrest Sylvanus from a clique of town elders who had gathered to discuss the events of the day. There was Marston, new to the town, exchanging stories and assessing the landscape.[48] He was social, magnetically attracted to the action, and liked the company of other influential men, but he was not loquacious. Rather, he was genteel, confident, affable, and sincere.[49]

The Partners: Van Pelt and Maybury

Marston's partners, Van Pelt and Maybury, apparently shared Marston's cultured and refined mien. Neither completed his architectural education through to obtaining a degree, but both men possessed a combination of extensive practical experience and brief but quality educations.

Garrett Beekman Van Pelt, Jr. was Marston's partner by 1914, but their association probably began in 1910.[50] Van Pelt's 1912 application for a state license indicates that his current employer was S. B. Marston, that he was "head draftsman" during the "past 3 winters."[51] It seems most likely that their association was initiated in 1910, for that is the earliest year showing the presence of Van Pelt's relatives in Pasadena.[52] Moreover, in Van Pelt's 1916 application for membership in the AIA, he refers to having been in practice for six years, reinforcing 1910 as the beginning of his ties with Marston.[53]

Born in 1879 in Milwaukee, Wisconsin, Van Pelt was thirty-one years old when he came to Pasadena with his mother, Sarah Lavinia (White) Van Pelt, or "Vinnie," during the winters of 1910, 1911, and 1912. They moved to Pasadena permanently in 1913 because Mrs. Van Pelt wanted to live near her brother,

1.3 Garrett Van Pelt on the far left, c. 1930

Frederic, and because "Pasadena was the place to be."[54] Walter White, Van Pelt's first cousin once removed, remembers that Garrett was an only child; a sister had died in childhood.[55] His father "disappeared" very early,[56] and nothing is known about him except that his ancestors named New York's exclusive residential street Beekman Place.[57]

Van Pelt never married. He and his mother lived together for much of his adult life, first in an old Victorian house at 488 S. Madison Avenue, and then at a house Van Pelt designed in 1926 located at 1212 S. El Molino Avenue.

There is a dearth of information about Van Pelt, making his cousin Walter White's memories all the more important. Concerning his physical bearing, Van Pelt was just under 5'7", slender, and dapper.[58] He always wore sport coats, never suits.[59] Walter recalls that Garrett waxed his moustache. "He'd twirl it," said Walter.[60] After Van Pelt had left the Marston firm in 1927 he grew a goatee. Walter remembered Garrett as temperamental and not very easy-going.[61] "He was not the front man in the firm, by any means. He kept to himself."[62] Walter's memories of Van Pelt as artist and architect are clear. "Garrett loved drawing. He would draw even as a very elderly man."[63]

Van Pelt listed in his state licensing and AIA applications attendance for one year, 1900-1901, at the Chicago School of Architecture.[64] In the 1928-29 *Who's Who In California,* he indicated that his education was at "Chicago Art Inst., Armour Inst. of Chicago," now the Illinois Institute of Technology.[65]

Near the end of his life when Van Pelt was being considered for elevation to Fellow in the AIA, he noted in a letter to architect Wallace Neff: "It has always been a cause of chagrin that my health never allowed me to attend an accredited school beyond a freshman year. Nowadays, one would not think of becoming an architect without a degree; you may imagine how sensitive I am."[66] No one that I have located knows of the health problem to which Van Pelt refers.

After his year of schooling in Chicago, Van Pelt returned to Milwaukee to work for about eighteen months as a draftsman for the prominent firm of Ferry & Clas;[67] Southern California architect Elmer Grey (from the Midwest) also had worked for that firm. Then Van Pelt became head draftsman for five and one-half years at Brust & Philipp, which became the largest architectural firm in Wisconsin.[68]

Of all Van Pelt's experiences, his foreign travels contributed most profoundly to his architectural expression. During fifteen months abroad beginning in 1906, Van Pelt spent time in Paris and Rome "measuring and studying with [a] tutor."[69] He and his mother took other trips to Europe after that.[70] Van Pelt also traveled extensively in Mexico, and in 1926 he wrote a book, *Old Architecture in Southern Mexico*, based on his travels.[71]

Van Pelt returned to Europe again in 1930, inviting then-recent Cornell architecture school graduate (and eventual Southern California architect) Robert E. Alexander to join him for an extensive three-month tour of France, Spain, and Italy.[72] Recalled Alexander: "It was a fantastic opportunity.... He knew Europe like the back of his hand." Alexander's father bought a Model A Ford roadster, which Alexander and Van Pelt took across on the steamship *Bremen*.[73]

During these early years, Marston's staff besides Van Pelt included one employee, Cyril Bennett, who had worked for Greene and Greene[74] for three summers,[75] and then switched over to Marston for six years, from 1909 until 1914 when he opened up his own firm.[76] Bennett began as a draftsman and office boy, and moved up to become the office manager.[77] When one considers that Bennett's eventual firm of Bennett & Haskell became Pasadena's other large architectural partnership in the 1920s, Marston's professional influence in the region obviously was strong. It was Bennett's departure in 1914 that probably led to Van Pelt's elevation to partner.

Edgar Wood Maybury was born in 1889 in Winona, Minnesota, and was the third generation of architects in the family.[78] He attended the University of California at Berkeley for two and one-half years (circa 1913-1914) where he specialized in architectural design under Professor John Galen Howard.[79] He also engaged in a self-study course under the Society of Beaux Arts Architects curriculum.[80]

Maybury's practical experience was extensive. Before enrolling at Berkeley, he worked for three years as an assistant for prominent New York City architect Donn Barber.[81] Maybury's daughter recalls her father telling her that he lived at the YMCA in Manhattan and attended church and went to its Sunday School which was taught by John D. Rockefeller. One day Maybury was invited to Rockefeller's house in the country where he watched infant Nelson Rockefeller crawling around on the floor.[82]

1.4 Edgar Maybury, c. 1920s

During his time at Berkeley, Maybury spent two years as a draftsman on the Oakland City Hall project. That work was supervised by John J. Donovan, later the Northern California AIA Chapter President.[83] Professor Howard, Barber, and Donovan all recommended Maybury for licensure in California,[84] which he achieved in 1915, the year he began as a draftsman for Marston & Van Pelt.[85] Except from 1918-1920 when Maybury worked locally for Reginald Johnson and also opened a branch office for him in Phoenix,[86] he was an associate, and by 1923 a partner, at Marston's firm. He practiced there until World War II, when Marston & Maybury dissolved.

Maybury is described as an attractive-looking man who was 5'9" in height, and lean. He was sociable, with an unmistakable hearty laugh, and very well-liked.[87] He and his wife had two children. Daughter Marjorie, who married Ogden Kellogg of the Scripps newspaper family, has said of her father that his sensitive nature aided him both artistically and in establishing wonderful relations with clients.[88]

It was a pioneering time for Marston and his partners to enter the profession: a formal course of architectural study through to a degree was a new development in California and nationally.[89] At the turn of the century, only nine professional architectural schools existed in the United States with a total enrollment of a mere 384 students. Many practitioners who at the time referred to themselves as architects had in fact no formal training.[90]

Yankee Marstons in Early California

Sylvanus Marston was drawn early to architecture through the influence of his Maine-born builder-grandfather, Phineas Marston.

Like many early California settlers, Sylvanus Marston's family journeyed to the West from New England during the Gold Rush. No fewer than 70,000 persons came to California from the East in 1849.[91] Sylvanus Marston's great-uncle and the man he was named for–Sylvanus Boardman Marston–was among them. On November 1, 1849, Marston the elder sailed from Bangor, Maine, headed for San Francisco by way of Cape Horn. During the voyage he kept a log that meticulously chronicles the voyage of the ship and its 66 passengers and crew.[92] Marston must have taken some delight in his entry of April 28, 1850: "At 2 1/4 P.M. discovered land about 20 miles distant–supposed to be the islands near the entrance of the Bay."[93]

Sylvanus Marston's great-uncle worked as a builder in San Francisco and became a member of the city's infamous Vigilance Committee of 1856.[94] His move west prompted his brother Phineas to follow. Phineas F. Marston was born in Danville (now Auburn), Maine in 1813.[95] He got his start as a skilled carpenter and eventually became a builder, managing projects that took him to the far reaches of the state.[96] In 1843, he settled permanently in Bangor, where he and his wife had five children. He was one of the city's prominent citizens. Along with the other local leaders, Marston had his own pew at the Unitarian Church.[97] When the church burned to the ground in 1851, the elders chose Phineas to superintend the new construction.[98] Marston's rebuilt Unitarian Church with its squared clock tower was officially dedicated in 1853 and still stands high on a knoll as a symbol of Bangor's mid-nineteenth century wealth and its aspirations for architectural distinction.[99]

The elegant Bangor house that Phineas built in 1852 is located at 56 Madison Street. It is a large, two-storied white clapboard with a sizable attached carriage house. Its indoor plumbing was then a symbol of affluence. Described as a "conservative and polished essay in Italianate style," the dwelling is considered "one of the finest complexes of this kind to survive in Bangor."[100]

Phineas Marston moved his family in 1858 to the Pacific Coast to join Sylvanus, his favorite of the five brothers.[101] The family sailed from Bangor bound for Panama on the steamer *Star of the West*, then crossed the Isthmus of Panama and boarded a second steamer, the *Golden Gate*, for the trip up the Pacific coast to San Francisco, where the family settled.[102] Phineas immediately was tapped to superintend construction of the barracks then being built at the Presidio, at Fort Mason, and on Angel Island.[103]

With a growing reputation as a master builder, Phineas was appointed by the federal government as Superintendent of Lighthouse Construction on the West Coast, a position vitally important in California's early development.[104] Under Phineas's direction several lighthouses were erected. They were built in the early 1870s, at Point Angeles on the Strait of Juan de Fuca, in what was then the Washington Territory, and in Puget Sound; Point Reyes, Point Montara, Pigeon Point, and Point Ano Nuevo in California were then added.[105]

1.5 Phineas F. Marston, c. 1883

The Point Reyes location posed danger and challenge.[106] It was the foggiest site on the Pacific Coast and the nation's windiest headland, with wind speed measured at more than 130 miles an hour.[107] The construction complexities involved–materials carried by horse-drawn wagons and men working on precarious 600-foot sheer cliffs–prompted observers to laud the result as "a monumental civil engineering feat."[108] Marston also built a spacious, two-story, keeper's house, but "[a] stiffish gale unroofed [it] soon after its completion."[109] This lighthouse is listed on the National Register of Historic Places.

The Pigeon Point lighthouse in San Mateo County between San Francisco and Santa Cruz is a majestic monument. This Italianate style lighthouse is the most beautiful on the Pacific Coast and the tallest in the Bay Area, with its 115-foot brick tower projecting above a forty foot base of solid rock.[110] "Mr. Phineas F. Marston, lighthouse constructor" was mentioned in newspaper articles as this edifice was being built.[111] Pigeon Point has operated continuously since November of 1872 when it first shined its million candlepower beam eighteen miles out over the Pacific Ocean.[112]

In 1867 Phineas moved his family to Fruitvale near Oakland to embark upon "fruit culture."[113] His oldest son, Franklin Augustine Marston, married there and had two daughters, Abbie and Alice, and a son, Sylvanus Boardman Marston. Even after Frank relocated his family south to Pasadena four months after Sylvanus was born on August 16, 1883, his children saw their grandfather often. During their four-month summer vacations they would often go to their grandparents in Fruitvale.[114]

1.6 Point Reyes Keeper's Quarters, c. 1875, photograph by Eadweard Muybridge

Sylvanus's sister Alice has written extensively about her family's early life.[115] "Fruitvale," she wrote, "...was made up of a number of large estates planted mostly to cherries. In the hills above my grandfather's home lived Joaquin Miller, the poet. We would often meet him as he walked down Fruitvale Avenue, and he would invariably run his hands through my curls and sometimes he would stop and tell us little stories."

Phineas died in 1896, when Sylvanus was thirteen years old. Oakland's Unitarian Church minister rhapsodized at the funeral about his lighthouse-building feats: "They stand to-day shedding their life-saving beams out on the dark and stormy waters and doubtless through those beacon lights many thousand lives have been saved."[116] For Sylvanus, the romance of buildings and design may well have begun in these boyhood years.

A Rural Pasadena Upbringing

...the joy of simple things and a quiet way of living.
- Alice Marston Hastings, *Pasadena Community Book*

For Frank Marston and his family, the relocation to Pasadena in 1883 meant travel by rail from Oakland to Redlands, then by horse and buggy to Pasadena.[117] When the family arrived in December of 1883, Pasadena was still three years from city-hood, which places the Marstons in the group of early residents known as Original Pioneers.[118]

Sylvanus's upbringing in a Pasadena of only 1,000 residents [119] was idyllic. Alice Marston remembered that while the family's house was being built, they lived in a barn that "stood in the midst of waving grain fields in what is now the Oak Knoll district." It was a large, two-story structure with a central area where the carriages were kept. The children loved to play in the hay

1.7 Pigeon Point Lighthouse, San Mateo County

1.8 Rendering of Phineas Marston's Fruitvale residence near Oakland, California, c. 1880.

loft upstairs. At night they would hear the coyotes and other wild animals. "Our poor chickens must have been terrorized at the howling and it is strange that the hens ever laid any eggs, but they did." Sometimes Frank would shoot squirrels for stew. Soon Frank concluded that at one and one-half miles from the center of Pasadena "Oak Knoll was too far out in the woods for his family."[120]

The Marstons moved closer to town, buying twenty acres in two parcels, the largest extending from California Street south nearly to Fillmore Street, flanked by Madison and El Molino.[121] To this day, Pasadena old-timers call the area the Marston Tract.[122] Frank "went through the exciting boom days of 1886 and 1887 and unlike many...did not get caught in the disastrous collapse of property values that followed."[123]

Longing for the old barn, the Marston children would return there and go over the hill to Wilson's Lake and the Old Mill built by the Spanish settlers. Sylvanus and his sisters played tennis and "many of us as soon as school was out would rush for our tennis rackets." The family enjoyed picnicking in the canyons north of Pasadena, especially Eaton and Millard Canyons.[124]

When the Marstons journeyed to Los Angeles, ten miles away by horse and buggy, the trip took all day. Pasadenans could either use the old adobe road that followed the southern edge of the town through Boyle Heights or travel along the Arroyo Seco, the route which the Marstons liked best. Alice has noted: "We had to cross the beautiful little stream which became a torrent in the rainy season."[125]

As a land developer and citrus farmer ("orchardist" as the 1893 phone book put it),[126] Frank Marston planted many kinds of fruit on his twenty acres, particularly orange trees, but also grapes, berries, and melons. A childhood friend of Sylvanus Marston's had this recollection of the Marstons' life then: "The last time that I saw Van Marston...he referred with pride to their two sleek dark bays, Doll and Bell, which were carriage horses and generally pulled the surrey. However, it did not lower their dignity to cultivate the orchard on East California Street."[127]

1.9 Sylvanus Marston, c. 1890

Pasadena was a small and close-knit world back then, and the Neighborhood Church was central to the Marston's lives. Alice recalled coming out of church with all of their friends: "the Clapps, Mungers, Thomases, Nashes, Hamiltons, Hahns, Hendersons, Pages, Prinzes, Traylors, Markhams, Hughes, Allens, and many others."[128]

Upon graduation from Pasadena High School in 1901, Sylvanus attended Pomona College for two years to complete his general education requirements before embarking upon architectural study. It was at Pomona, in 1902, that he met his future wife, Edith Hatfield. Edith later transferred to the University of California at Berkeley, where she received her degree in philosophy in 1906. Her senior year at Cal was unforgettable when, as she put it, she was nearly "shaken out by the earthquake" while living on the third floor of her sorority house.[129] Her other vivid memory is of U.C. President Benjamin Ide Wheeler speaking to her graduation class of 600: "I don't care if you forget everything you've learned here, provided you have learned to think."[130] Both at Pomona and at Cal, Edith Hatfield sought out people "who were serious and earnest in their purpose in life."[131] She found those qualities in Sylvanus who, after Pomona College, went on to study architecture for four years at Cornell University.

The Beaux Arts Tradition at Cornell

For Marston, the choice of Cornell University probably was an easy one. There were few American universities offering four-year architecture degree programs, and none on the West Coast. U.C. Berkeley's School of Architecture had begun in 1903 but had only seven students and two elementary courses, with John Galen Howard the only professor.[132] Cornell's architecture program, which started in 1871, was the second in the United States, following MIT (1868). According to the Cornell University College of Architecture's 125th Anniversary catalog, "it was the first four-year course in architecture in an Ameri-can university.[133] Marston's class would be the first to complete the four-year curriculum.

Architectural education at Cornell was appealing because of the program's high academic ranking and a recent refashioning of the curriculum in line with the French Beaux Arts model. This change was intended above all to "cultivate the esthetic sense,"[134] and to make an architect less an engineer or mere draftsman and more "a man of broad general culture with a thorough-going special knowledge of the evolution of his chosen art and of its relation to certain great historic movements and to civilization as a whole."[135] In Paris, the student "breathes a different atmosphere, aesthetically exhilarating and illuminating."[136] Americans had become mesmerized by the Parisian artistic spirit and "the French point of view."[137]

Design and drawing became all-important. Emphasis in the first two years was on freehand drawing, sketching, and water color painting, and in the junior year clay mod-

1.10 Marston (standing at left) and Cornell tennis team, c. 1907

eling and rendering, followed by a life class (drawing from a live model) in the senior year.[138] Marston's grade card reveals the preeminence of design, indicating that he at first spent twenty-four hours a week in the drafting-room, and that by his senior year it grew to thirty-six hours a week.[139] His highest grades were in the history and elements of architecture, perspective, working drawings, the history of painting and sculpture, and the senior year small seminar.[140]

The French Beaux Arts system that was taking hold in American universities emerged during the reign of Louis XIV. An essential component was its unique method of teaching about design by stressing "Composition...the French academic system's term for what it considered the essential act of architectural design."[141] Its purpose, as one Beaux Arts-trained architect explained, was "a quality of clearness–the science of harmonious results."[142] Students learned to compose well-proportioned elements in a symmetrical and often monumental scheme.

A second emphasis was on a thorough grounding in the classical orders. Students studied the architectural masterpieces of early Greece and Rome and Renaissance Italy. Design problems and the renowned "Grand Prix de Rome" competition in the students' fourth year invariably revolved around one of the classical historical styles.

The virtues and drawbacks of the French model were hotly debated throughout Marston's Cornell education. Its adherents thought it "…necessary at one period of every man's life that he shall believe that the object of architecture is to produce beautiful things."[143] Opponents countered that the approach was impractical and "…no more suited to our modern life than are the stilted forms of classic literature, so pleasing to the undergraduate student of a dead language."[144]

1.11 Marston's photograph in the Cornell class Book, 1907

These were ground-breaking years for Cornell's architectural program. Marston was a member of the Gargoyle Club, Cornell's architectural society. Other members included Andrew D. White, the University President, Charles Babcock, a founder of the Cornell School of Architecture, Clarence Martin, and Jean Hebrard.[145] Martin was probably a mentor of Marston's; a yearbook entry states that Marston "devoted his time, under the direction of 'Pa Martin' to the design of his future California bungalow."[146] Martin deeply influenced Cornell's architecture program. He had begun teaching at it in 1894 and served as Professor in charge of the College (later called Director and then Dean) from 1904-1919.[147] A Fellow of the AIA, Martin was remembered upon his death in 1944 as "a man of vigor and a lovable character [who] made himself very well known in the life of Cornell University and of Ithaca."[148]

Professional credentials derived from such a lofty heritage carried a special aura. Albert C. Martin, Jr., principal in a fourth-generation Los Angeles architectural firm whose family was from the Midwest, believed that there was a "Pasadena type" of architect, with social connections and Ivy-league educations in the Beaux Arts tradition that gave them a special camaraderie.[149]

Marston's days at Cornell were not all spent in the drafting-room. The life of a Cornell architectural student was exceedingly well-rounded.[150] Sylvanus was a member of Masque and the Delta Phi fraternity. An avid tennis player, Marston was on the varsity team all four years. According to a July 2, 1907 *Pasadena Star News* article, "Van Marston Wins the Cup," Marston captured the intercollegiate tennis title for Cornell in July and upon his graduation and return to Pasadena would "bring with him the reward of his prowess with racquet and ball–a handsome championship cup."[151]

1.12 C.C. Thomas house (1907), front elevation; Marston's first commission, in Ithaca, New York

Marston graduated "with high honors," and near the end of his senior year he designed a $7,000 house for a Cornell Professor.[152] The minutes of the California State Board of Architecture reveal that the commission was for the Ithaca house of Cornell Professor C. C. Thomas. Marston, appearing on January 28, 1908 before the licensing panel, explained that he had acted in the capacity of architect in drawing the plans, which were prepared during the latter part of his collegiate course.[153] Marston might have been awarded the design of the Thomas house because of his class stand-ing, or perhaps as a result of his taking Thomas's engineering cours-es, but it is also true that Marston and Thomas were fellow Pasadenans, and Marston's sister, Abbie, was a close friend of Thomas's wife.[154]

C. C. Thomas was an impressive first client for Marston. After Pasadena High School, Thomas attended Stanford University with engineering classmate Herbert Hoover,[155] both in the University's pioneer class of 1895.[156] In 1904, Cornell promoted Thomas to pro-fessor of marine engineering and he wrote the first book on the steam turbine published in the United States.[157] Thomas next accepted an appointment at the University of Wisconsin,[158] and then at Johns Hopkins University where he helped organize its Department of Engineering.[159] Upon his return to Pasadena in the 1920s, Thomas conducted experimental research at Caltech.[160]

The Thomas residence in Ithaca still stands at 216 Dearborn Place, adjacent to the Cornell campus, in an area known as Cornell Heights. It came to be known as the "Browne home"[161] after chem-istry Professor Arthur Wesley Browne, who taught at Cornell for forty-two years and lived in the house the longest. The residence is a fifteen-room shingle over clapboard Colonial-styled dwelling that "looks distinct from other homes in the neighborhood."[162] Remarkably, the seven sheets of drawings prepared and signed by Marston are extant today. They are dated April 2, 1907, and reveal his sure hand and eye for balance and symmetry without being orthodox.

1.13 Sylvanus Marston, c. 1915

With his B. Arch. degree (1907) in hand and two years into his Pasadena practice, Marston married Edith Hatfield. The wedding was announced on February 8, 1910 in Berkeley at an engagement luncheon given for the couple by two of Edith's sorority sisters.[163] The local Pasadena newspaper heralded the event with the headline "Young Architect to be Married" and, in a burst of local pride stated: "Mr. Marston is one of the best known and prominent young architects of Southern California and is rapidly taking front rank among the architects of the coast."[164]

A Winter Colony

I selected Pasadena as the winter home of my family
because I consider it a veritable paradise,
it has no equal in the world.
Pasadena is undoubtedly destined to become...
a most popular American winter residence.
-Adolphus Busch
Tournament of Roses Brochure, 1905

As INSTRUMENTAL AS CORNELL WAS TO SYLVANUS MARSTON'S EVENTUAL PROFESSIONAL SUCCESS, it came second to how fortuitous it was that the nascent architect could claim Pasadena as his home town. Beginning at the turn of the century, Pasadena's allure was unrivaled.

Los Angeles architect Octavius Morgan wrote in 1908 that "when the accumulations of wealth have become dominant, then and there the opportunities for the architect have occurred."[1]

Pasadena's burgeoning resorts at the turn of the century had much to do with the city's rich architectural identity. They created the demand for fine architecture. Sylvanus Marston and other architects flourished as the designers of the great hotels and their cottages, and also later when they created the luxurious houses of the wealthy winter visitors who decided to live permanently in Pasadena.

The earliest resort lodging, including the Hotel Maryland, had been established before Marston graduated from Cornell, yet within two years of opening his practice, that hotel commissioned him to design bungalow dwellings that contributed to the Maryland's renown. During the Huntington Hotel's plushest years, corresponding with its change to year-round operation, Marston was selected to design many important cottages on the hotel grounds. From the Vista del Arroyo, another of the famous resort hotels by the 1920s, Marston received his most extensive hotel commission: the design of the first true hotel structure on the property, its related shops, and half of the dwellings that brought the hotel broad acclaim as "Bungalowland."

With an understanding of the grandeur of the resort era, one can appreciate the importance of Marston's contributions to the elegance, comfort, and sophistication that personified the period.

Pursuing Paradise

By the 1880s Pasadena had become a nationally known winter resort for some of America's wealthiest families.[2] Household names such as Andrew Carnegie, J. P. Morgan, and John D. Rockefeller were turn of the century Pasadena visitors. During this incomparable era the city also welcomed Louis J. Merritt who, with his father and brothers, had discovered and developed the great Mesabi iron range in Minnesota, a venture that became part of the U.S. Steel Corporation; L. V. Harkness of New York City, with massive holdings in Standard Oil Company; Adolphus Busch, the famous beer magnate from St. Louis; Philip D. Armour, who amassed a fortune running Chicago's stockyards; Carroll L. Post, chairman of Postum Cereal Company of Battle Creek; John Milton Durand, Chicago merchant and grocery wholesaler; and James A. Culbertson, scion of a wealthy Pennsylvania lumber family. It was reported that by 1931 there were some 400 millionaires living at least part of the year in Pasadena.[3]

Pasadena's draw related to the stunning first impression it made upon newcomers. Architect Elmer Grey, a peer of Marston's and a transplant from Chicago and Milwaukee who had settled in Pasadena in 1904, wrote the following year in *Architectural Record*[4] of the intensity of his first impression. His reasons for migrating west were the "superb climate, wonderfully beautiful setting....Living here [is] far more enjoyable than in any other place I know....Southern California is growing, prospering and brilliantly promising."[5] Another early Pasadena émigré chose Pasadena "because of the rare combination found here which makes life worth living: matchless climate, scenic beauties, enlightened citizenship, together with peerless churches and schools."[6]

Grey identified a further allure of Southern California: "As a health resort...[it] bids fair to rival the Riviera....The health-seeker is, therefore, an important element of the population."[7] Hundreds of thousands of ill Americans came west during the nineteenth century—the "golden era of invalidism."[8] The backwardness of medical science forced laymen "to place great reliance upon changes of residence or therapeutic travel as the surest means of dissipating a persistent illness."[9] The exodus west, "to nature's sanitarium,"[10] was justified by the region's moistureless air, mild temperature, year-round sun-soaked days, and large expanses of undeveloped and underpopulated land.

These hotels and resorts sought to cater to these newcomers. "The larger developments swiftly became centers of resort for classes, not masses, and many of them became veritable little social and cultural oases for the parvenu and hotel-dwelling rich."[11]

A British physician, F. C. S. Sanders, recorded his impressions of California's "curative properties" in a 1916 book, *California as a Health Resort*.[12] It relates how he escorted a patient throughout the state for a six-week regimen that enabled the patient to return to England with "a new lease on life from the garden spot of the United States."[13] The book's superlatives were reserved for Pasadena. "This fine location and the gravelly formation of the soil furnishes a system of natural drainage which minimizes dampness and makes the spot especially favorable in the winter months to those afflicted with asthma and bronchial affections."[14] Sanders marveled: "There are few houses in Pasadena that are not equipped with sleeping porches, so that it is possible virtually to live in the open air by night as well as by day when the scent of the sweet orange blossoms, and the song of the mocking bird, lulls one into dreamland."[15]

Pasadena's primacy as the great Eden in the West was facilitated by "the magnificence of its hotels...[that] can only be compared to Atlantic City in the East and the Riviera in France;" their luxury, capacity, private grounds and sportsman's offerings of golf links and polo grounds made them "the acme of comfort."[16]

Hundreds of people first made their home in Pasadena for the winter season, from December to May. For years, Pasadena's winter population was three times that for the summer.[17] The *Los Angeles Herald* announced in November of 1904: "Pasadena hotels are ready for annual influx of wealthy tourists."[18] Pasadena's local newspaper even listed the family names of the winter arrivals, their home state, and at which of the grand hotels they were staying for the season.[19]

While the rest of the country suffered through the ills of industrialization, wealthy visitors to Pasadena played golf, tennis, and croquet, rode the railway up to Mt. Lowe where they could dine at the Alpine Tavern, and ambled along the fourteen miles of walkways snaking through the lush sunken Busch

Gardens. A 1905 article notes that "nearly all of the wealthy winter residents" bring "their own horses and equipages from the east" and refers to the "liveried coachmen and footmen, blooded horses stepping high with pride of their silver and gold-mounted trappings...."[20] Guests used horses for riding, playing polo, and hunting. They also visited South Pasadena's Cawston Ostrich Farm, watched the seasonal favorite, the Rose Parade, and scores of them went calling on each other.[21]

There also was club life. The Midwick Country Club, the most elite of its kind when it opened in 1912, boasted four polo fields, tennis courts, a swimming pool, trap shooting, and whippet racing. The club was begun "by a number of influential and very popular sportsmen."[22] Marston was a founding member. Conveying the style of the club, an article in 1925 states: "Add to these sports the brilliant social life in the magnificent clubhouse and one is very apt to say to himself, as many of the Midwick members must at times say, 'What shall I do at the club today?'"[23]

Marston's substantial contributions to three of Pasadena's famous hotels and the sybaritic life they offered began in 1910 and continued to 1935.

The Hotel Maryland

> Across the spread of velvet lawn there is hint of tiled roof and gable,
> and also is caught glimpses of white facades through leafy vista and drooping flowers.
> Walls, massed in purple flowering bougainvillea, and pergolas with rose vine coverings,
> are fitting frame to the distant purple mountains.
> These are the invitations that tempt the winter visitor to come,
> and the casual guest to linger.
> -J.W. Wood, *Pasadena–Historical and Personal*, 1917

This Hotel Maryland was, in its prime, "a rallying point for civic enterprises."[24] Located on Colorado Street between Euclid and Los Robles, it had a splendid eight-acre block of lawn and gardens intermingled with thirty bungalows extending north to Walnut Street. Owner-proprietor Colin Stewart began construction in 1902 and the hotel doors were opened "somewhat informally and with a quiet dinner"[25] on January 29, 1903. Stewart, described as a "high-minded gentleman," named the hotel after his home state, Maryland, "because it was both beautiful and patrician."[26]

Stewart had made his fortune in the livery stable business.[27] Within three months he sold the hotel to D. M. Linnard who had come to Pasadena in 1901.[28] Known for his warm hospitality and lavish hotel entertainment, Linnard would eventually operate hotels in many

2.1 Postcard of The Maryland Hotel, c. 1910

of the nation's largest cities.[29] He distinguished the Hotel Maryland as the first to embrace the bungalow concept and year-round operation. As Pasadena's only large hotel open in the summer, "the Maryland became something of an institution."[30]

By 1910 there already were twenty-six of the eventual thirty bungalows nestled among a profusion of trees, flowers, and climbing vines. Such abundant and wild plant life caused the hotel to be regarded as "a city hotel, with country privileges;" and it was also referred to as "Maryland Bungalowland."[31]

Marston's job records show that in 1910 he designed two Hotel Maryland bungalows located at 96 and 99 N. Euclid Avenue, although one publication reported that Marston "has drawn plans for three bungalows to be erected on Euclid Avenue as an extension of the cottage system of the Hotel Maryland."[32] One bungalow was to have six rooms and two were to contain eight rooms. All were to have plastered exteriors, rustic siding, Malthoid (granulated slate composition) roofs, oak floors, and pine trim.[33]

The two Hotel Maryland bungalows in Marston's job records reveal distinct stylistic approaches. The photograph below by Harold A. Parker depicts one Marston bungalow, in the Mission style —a two-story stucco dwelling with a flat-roof and a projecting visor roof of red tiles. French doors, a ground floor patio, and a second story patio sheltered by a wisteria-covered pergola are features. This matches the description of the Hotel Maryland's bungalows found in a splendid, if gushy, article by Eleanor Gates in a 1911 *Sunset*.[34] There, she warns: "The next time you go to a hotel you will be terribly fussy. You will want French windows opening out upon an adorable clinker-brick terrace to a lawn; or a pergola, or a patio, or an amethyst mountain in the near distance....It is a new kind of living, all green and gay color and fragrance and song."[35]

On the back of the Maryland bungalow photograph shown below is an inscription in Marston's hand that states: "Has never been illustrated in any mag. S. B. Marston Architect, Pasadena, California."[36] This hotel bungalow, surrounded by lawn, park, and gardens, was located adjacent to All Saints Episcopal Church, in the middle of the hotel's extensive property.

Marston's second bungalow for the Maryland is depicted in the *Tournament of Roses Brochure* for 1911 in an article entitled "Pasadena Portico of Paradise."[37] Origi-

2.2 The Maryland's front façade. It featured the second white column pergola in California, and the first to be built in Pasadena.

2.3 Marston's Mission style bungalow (1910) at the Maryland

nally, the hotel's bungalows were shown in a random color scheme, but this "was immediately found to be a mistake. The change resulting from the use of a little white paint was most instructive."[38] A wealth of foliage brought harmony and "made the whole group typically Californian."[39] The article states: "Mr. Marston's little white bungalow...if only it had a tile roof, might well be an advertising brochure illustration of one of those numerous adobe houses in which Ramona was born."[40] Lacking the ubiquitous red tile and stucco, the bungalow appeared more Arts and Crafts in style with its ground floor incorporating clapboard siding and projecting eaves with wooden knee brackets.

The mysterious "third" Marston bungalow noted earlier might be one of several Marston-designed bungalows located near the Hotel Maryland, including one at 91 N. Los Robles Avenue. An announcement in November of 1910 states that plans were drawn by S. B. Marston for a "six-room bungalow to be built in the rear of the Maryland Hotel....It will have cement foundation and porches, plastered exterior...tile roof, three white enamel bathrooms...."[41]

In 1910 Marston also designed the "Maryland Apartments." They were at 95 S. Los Robles Avenue, just one-half block from the Hotel, but not commissioned by it. Still, advertisements depict the apartments as "opposite the Hotel Maryland" and with "home comforts and hotel service,"[42] so there was some hotel con-

2.4 Maryland Hotel Apartments (1910), advertisement

nection. The specifications showed a two-story frame and plastered apartment building of 28 units containing two to five rooms in each suite.[43] The January 1911 *Western Architect*[44] features these Marston designs in an illustration that shows a U-shaped two-storied complex surrounding a narrow central courtyard. The building is an interesting combination of Mission style incorporating modest Beaux Arts classicism.

The year 1911 was a big one for the Hotel Maryland. Not only did Col. William Cody (Buffalo Bill) stay there, but within a two-week period President Howard A. Taft, president-to-be Woodrow Wilson, and ex-president Theodore Roosevelt all gave speeches at the hotel.[45]

The Maryland was also a place of calm. Architect Myron Hunt lived there after the death of his first wife. During World War I many affluent young wives resided there while their officer husbands fought overseas.[46] Still others lived there temporarily while their houses were being built in the area.[47] The place became so highly regarded that the hotel's twenty-first anniversary was celebrated with a special dinner on April 19, 1924, accompanied by a formal several-page printed program whose cover depicts a Harold A. Parker photograph taken in 1911 of the front facade stucco-columned pergola with natural tree branches above, supporting the supple wisteria.

The Huntington Hotel

> The Huntington was built and equipped, is managed
> and maintained, and supplies cuisine, accommodations and service
> exclusively for the class of tourists whose resources and experience
> enable them to demand and appreciate the best.
> -*Huntington Hotel Brochure*, 1915

The Huntington Hotel, like the Maryland, gained its reputation of refined elegance through the attentive hospitality of D. M. Linnard who became its manager. Approximately thirty cottages eventually were designed and built there by some of the region's finest architects, including Myron Hunt, Roland Coate, Wallace Neff, and Marston, Van Pelt & Maybury. The Marston firm designed seven cottages in a cluster of thirteen along Huntington Circle.

The hotel's opening day was February 1, 1907, when it began life as the Wentworth Hotel, named after General M. C. Wentworth, a Civil War veteran from New England.[48] For $84,000 he and several partners had purchased the Oak Knoll site.[49] Unfortunately, the San Francisco earthquake in April of 1906 had diverted funds and man-

2.5 Postcard of The Huntington Hotel

power to the northern part of the state, a development that forced the hotel to close by July 1907.[50]

Railroad tycoon Henry E. Huntington, who owned land to the east and south, purchased the hotel and grounds in 1911, changed its name, and completed construction.[51]

The Huntington Hotel formally opened on January 8, 1914 "with an estimated assemblage of 2,000 drawn from Los Angeles society, Pasadena citizenry, and guests from other cities and hotels."[52] The *Pasadena Star News* coverage, in retrospect, highlights the new automotive era in remarking that the "lineup of automobiles...their glowing lamps, extending for blocks and blocks, presented a brilliant spectacle."[53]

During these first years the hotel was considered "a commanding structure, as it stands amidst its gardens and its orange groves. From afar its appearance is a reminder of a great castle or chateau, and one may easily imagine those walls, facades, battlements and bastions–frowning and impregnable. The view is magnificent from its roof and windows."[54] Back then, when the air was clearer, guests in the south-facing rooms could gaze out on the "sun-kissed waters of the Pacific and Santa Catalina Island."[55]

The hotel's heyday came during the 1920s; it maintained its aura of a "winter retreat;" its operation was not year-round until 1926. Midwestern and Eastern entrepreneurs flocked to the hotel, as did celebrated writers, entertainers, political leaders, royalty, and sports personalities.[56] With the changes wrought by the Great Depression, World War II, and altered demographics, it is no small achievement that the Huntington remains as the only one of the seven luxury resort hotels developed in the Pasadena area at the turn of the century which has remained in continuous hotel use.[57]

Surrounded by a seventy-five acre park, the hotel provided guests with a private golf course near what is now Lacy Park, with historic El Molino Viejo itself as the clubhouse.[58] Other facilities included a minia-
ture golf course, a putting green, tennis courts at the property's south boundary, and horseback riding on nearby bridle trails.[59] Naturally, the hotel promised a full social life, particularly for guests staying through the four-month winter season. There were formal dinners in the colossally sized "great dining room,"[60] ballroom dancing twice a week, church services on Sunday, and a special Easter pageant that attracted as many as 5,000 people.[61]

The hotel's popularity prompted the change in 1926 to year-round operation. A Marston-designed swimming pool was added[62]—the "first pool to feature a white Medusa bottom and the first Olympic-size pool in California."[63] At about this time Linnard introduced to the Huntington the bungalow or cottage concept with which he had such success elsewhere. Most of those twenty-seven structures that surround the hotel today were built during the second half of the 1920s. The dwellings were erected by the hotel with individualized designs and furnishings for guests who sought the extra privacy and space they provided. They often bore a family's name. The families would pay advance rent to the hotel for a predetermined number of years though ownership

2.6 Finleen Cottage (1926)

2.7 Ferncroft Cottage, remodeled by Marston (1926)

2.8 Clovelly Cottage (1926)

remained with the hotel.[64]

A 1926 *California Southland* article has nothing but praise for the Huntington's new cottage plan: "The change which has come over tourist hotels...is in tune with the new note of delight in the discovery of California as an all-the-year state."[65] It continues: "Skillfully these expert hosts of the whole Coast have adapted their hostelries to the longing for home life which comes to the most ardent traveler; wisely have they widened the scope of their hotels."[66]

Cottages at the Huntington

The Huntington Cottages are all listed on the National Register of Historic Places. Marston's firm designed six (and remodeled a seventh) of the elegant enclave of thirteen at 1401 S. Oak Knoll Avenue, along Huntington Circle on the hotel's southwest edge.[67] The houses were put on the market in 1996 as single family residences, and for the first time became independent of any hotel connection.

Finleen Cottage, the first of Marston's cottages at the Huntington, was designed in 1926. Events of national scope took place at this two story, English cottage-style dwelling. Near the end of World War II, Dr. Seely Mudd of Caltech requested a meeting place at the hotel that offered great privacy,[68] and Finleen was recommended. At the time, it was home to the hotel manager, Stephen Royce, and his family.[69] Several prominent scientists gathered on the designated evening. Early the next morning the group flew to Alamogordo, New Mexico to witness the first explosion of the atomic bomb.[70] The group included Dr. Vannevar Bush, General Leslie R. Groves, Dr. J. Robert Oppenheimer of the Manhattan Project, and Dr. Ernest O. Lawrence, U.C. Berkeley physics professor and 1939 recipient of the Nobel Prize.[71]

Clovelly Cottage, with its vaguely English character, was designed in 1926 as a duplex, perhaps because it was to be occupied by Sir Montague Allan and Lady Allan of Montreal and their adult daughter Martha. A 1926

2.9 Designed and built in 1926, Spalding Cottage was the firm's largest structure of this group, with 6,350 square feet. It was built for John Burnham of Chicago, who was a principal in Spalding Sporting Goods.

2.10 Mariner Cottage was designed in 1926 for J. W. Mariner of Milwaukee, and it follows the English style with multiple front gables, bay windows, and some half-timbering at the front entry porch.

2.11 Designed for James Foley in 1927, Chance View Cottage has a dominant forward-facing gable and features distinctive bay windows with diamond shaped panes on the first and second levels.

2.12 Howard Cottage was built in 1927 for Nelson A. Howard, one of the founders of the Santa Anita Race Track.

California Southland article discusses the cottage and provides "a pen and ink sketch made by the firm of Marston, Van Pelt & Maybury especially for this journal."[72]

The firm obviously explored a number of designs for Clovelly Cottage, because the structure that was built bears little resemblance to this sketch, but the rendering is included to display the firm's repertoire of styles under consideration for the Huntington Cottages.[73] The *California Southland* article includes an architect's sketch of the proposed Allan cottage, and makes reference to two other "homey looking houses in the architectural firm's best style. They are fine types of what California can do in adapting the English cottage type to her own climate and landscape."[74] The article's reference to two other designs might have referred to a pair of photographs of English cottages that have been found in the Harold A. Parker Collection, one of which is labeled "Cottage for Hotel Huntington," and both of which are signed "Marston, Van Pelt & Maybury - Architects."

The privilege and luxury these wealthy businessmen secured for themselves in the cottages did not last long. After the stock market crash, "winter reservations dropped to virtually nothing with the closing of the banks...[and] the hotel suffered badly, not recovering until after the Second World War."[75] Another source of trouble came with the 1931 reopening of the Vista del Arroyo Hotel[76] whose spectacular view across the Arroyo was unsurpassed.

The Vista del Arroyo Hotel

> The flowers and grassy spaces; the blossomy
> slope into the misty Arroyo; together with
> the aura of home over the entire menage
> have made the Vista del Arroyo a favored resort.
> -*California Life*, 1922

As with the Maryland and Huntington Hotels, the Vista del Arroyo Hotel had a modest beginning and only reached its stride as a first-class resort hotel when it came under the ownership of D. M. Linnard, who in 1920 commissioned Sylvanus Marston to make important additions to the hotel.

This hotel was one of Pasadena's earliest inns, predating the two *grande dame* hotels already discussed. It was begun in 1882 on a plot of several acres by Mrs. Emma C. Bangs who called it the Arroyo Vista Guest House.[77] Its grandest feature, then and now, is its view of the Arroyo and the "undulating beauty of the San Rafael Hills."[78] Mrs. Bangs died in 1903 and from 1905 to 1918 Henry M. Fowler was owner and manager. Fowler expanded the hotel, purchasing additional acreage and erecting six bungalows, six annexes, and other buildings. The 1913 completion of the Colorado Street Bridge at the northern edge of the property enhanced the hotel's scenic offerings.

The Vista's growing clientele and its attractive physical surroundings did not escape the attention of Daniel Linnard, who purchased it in 1919. Linnard sold the hotel the next year to Stephen Royce, his son-in-law, and to businessman A. J. Bertonneau, but Linnard remained involved with the major additions and is credited with developing the Vista del Arroyo into "an elegant, high-ranking hotel kept open year round."[79] Linnard's influence over the hotel endured for more than twenty years, either through his direct ownership (in 1919 and again in 1936) or his connections with Royce, and with H. O. Comstock, who acquired the hotel in 1926.

Marston & Van Pelt's dramatic renovations begun in 1920 ushered in the hotel's most elegant era. In September 1920 the press reported that proprietors Bertonneau and Royce had commissioned the firm to make major changes: "The remodeled building will have extreme dimensions 120 x 42 ft., and will be two stories with central tower. There will be a new lobby, the dining room will be enlarged and additional sleeping rooms will be provided."[80] It also noted that there would be a plastered exterior, tile roof, ornamental iron balconies and cement terraces.[81] The cost would be $100,000.[82] To accommodate the new structure, owners had purchased an additional 1,000 feet of frontage property along South Grand Avenue which brought their holdings to twelve acres and extended the hotel's property line to Colorado Street.[83]

The plans were ambitious; two hundred guest rooms were added. Also, for the first time, Spanish architecture was introduced to the site, with specifications that included pastel stucco walls, arched windows, tile roofs, a central campanile, and projecting buttresses. While the style has been described as Spanish Colonial Revival,[84] it also borrows from the Mission tradition with its subdued ornamentation, use of buttresses, a projecting visor tiled roof, and bell tower. Sylvanus Marston is credited with primary design responsibility for this commission.[85] The finished hotel was widely photographed, appearing in the *Tournament of Roses Brochure* for 1921 and 1922,[86] *Western Architect*,[87] and *Picturesque Pasadena*.[88]

The main hotel entrance along South Grand featured a projecting vestibule with a hipped roof. The front door was a large arched opening with two formidable wooden doors "glazed in an ornamental clathri pattern with a matching fanlight above."[89] Overhead were paired arched windows supported by flush pila-

2.13 Postcard of Vista del Arroyo Hotel, c. 1921

sters. To the east of the entry was a one-story, tile-covered arcade with six large arched openings separated by piers with projecting buttresses. A similar arcade on the Arroyo side "created a luminous effect on the interior space."[90] The original bell tower south of the front entry, removed in later renovations, featured a red-tiled and hipped roof, with flush plaster pilasters flanking the arched opening on all four sides. The west elevation facing the Arroyo, less photographed, featured a ground floor arcade and a solarium, not called for in the original plans, that extended eighteen feet beyond the main block.

Most of the new building's first floor interior space was utilized as a lounge and dining room, with numerous smaller spaces for patios and terraces. The lobby was described as "a sun lounge decorated in blue and gold with the sunlight subdued to a golden radiance being filtered through side drapes of golden tissue."[91] It featured a high ceiling, side solarium, and eight evenly spaced concrete columns with a travertine finish. "A simulated patio and Spanish flair" described the dining room.[92] The hotel's new ambiance was said to be "friendly, with its artistic appointments and great windows framing the view of

2.14 Pool-side dining at the Vista during Pasadena's resort era, c. 1937

the bridge and the arroyo."[93] As for the Patio Room, it was beautiful "with its romantic red tile roof and soft lacy vines."[94]

Marston's design called for a rustic pergola that extended from South Grand up to the front entrance. This addition of stuccoed Tuscan columns that supported natural tree branches over which grew wisteria is nicely captured in a hotel advertisement in a 1929 edition of *California Life*.[95] Today a reproduction of the original Marston pergola continues to provide an inviting front entrance to the Vista del Arroyo, which is now the Federal Building for the United States Court of Appeals.

During summers in the 1920s the hotel hosted tea dances, cotillions, and many other social events. Most memorable were its evening concerts outside on the lawn, followed by buffet suppers for hundreds of guests "under the light of the golden harvest moon, with the flowery garden spaces and the deep mystery of the Arroyo making magic of the summer night."[96] Lush gardens, riding trails, and a lily pond added to the serene ambiance. With its matchless scenic siting and recent "modernizing" renovations, the Vista eclipsed the older hotels such as the Raymond.

In 1928 Marston's firm again was tapped for new construction, this time by H. O. Comstock and a syndicate of investors who bought the Vista in 1926 from Linnard for more than $1 million.[97] The firm was commissioned "to erect a two-story addition to the Hotel...18 additional rooms with 100% tile baths, hardwood floors, hardwood and pine trim...tile roofing, wrought iron, etc."[98] The firm also was responsible for designing a hotel garage in 1929 and interior shops in 1935.

Further substantial renovations to the hotel made in 1930 by Los Angeles architect George Wiemeyer added the six-storied building and its prominent tile-covered tower.[99] Those changes, along with a fire in 1982, destroyed much of Marston's 1920 hotel, although rebuilding efforts closely tracked the old plans.

The Vista's Bungalows

It was the beguiling bungalows, those "heaven-kissing" dwellings "perched on the brow of this scenic marvel,"[100] that came to make the Vista especially beloved by Pasadenans and visitors. The earliest bungalows appeared in 1920-21, and by 1935 twenty such dwellings dotted the hillside, prompting the Vista (as was the Maryland) to be called "the bungalow hotel"[101] and "Bungalowland."[102] Half of the bungalows were designed by architect Myron Hunt (often with partner H. C. Chambers) and the other half—the most

acclaimed group—by Marston's firm. While six were demolished in 1993,[103] those remaining, along with the main hotel building, are listed on the National Register of Historic Places as a reminder of the Vista's and Pasadena's influential role in Southern California's development.[104]

"Marston's contributions to Vista del Arroyo spanned over twenty years and greatly enhanced the Hotel's image," states a 1980 historic preservation report.[105] While Marston's work may have been a few years shy of the twenty years claimed, Marston's deep influence on this Pasadena landmark is indisputable. The firm's crowning accomplishment, and its best known Vista del Arroyo buildings, are the bungalows it designed for various families between 1925 and 1935.

The bungalows are located along the crest of the Arroyo and along South Grand, and range in size from one and two-story single family dwellings to two, three, and four-story units. Like the main hotel building, they feature subdued Mediterranean ornamentation. They are of wood frame construction with an exterior plaster finish. Those along the Arroyo have "entire facades of open, glazed terraces and balconies to capture the view. The one element that differs between bungalows is the roofing material."[106]

The bungalow feature allowed selected families to pay for the construction of their own dwellings, with free use of them for an agreed time period, usually ten years. When the hotel became the owner it was required to reserve the building for use by the original occupants, who would then pay a rental fee, hotel charges for meals, maid service, and entertainment. The bulk of the bungalows were constructed in the late 1920s through the mid-1930s, with the last of the twenty built in 1937.

"Ironically, the Vista's zenith came as the great age of resort hotels in Pasadena was on the wane."[107] The effects of the Great Depression on other hotels was devastating, with some closing or severely down-sizing their opera-

2.15 B, C, and D Bungalows (1920-1921), c. 1926. Notice the natural wood branches that form the pergola that runs along the Arroyo Seco side of the dwellings. The first three bungalows starting from the left are by Marston & Van Pelt. At the extreme upper right is the main hotel and campanile by the Marston firm.

2.16 The bungalow-dwellers view of the Colorado Street Bridge, the Arroyo, and the mountains beyond, c. 1926. Note the Vista's bungalows in the lower right corner.

2.17 The Vista del Arroyo Hotel (after the 1930 addition by another architect) as viewed through the arch of the Colorado Street Bridge, c. 1935. Hamilton (1926) and Jenks (1928) bungalows are directly below and in front of the tower.

tions.[108] Apparently an asset for the Vista was that it was the grand hotel furthest from the bustle of city life,[109] and was considered modern with all of the latest conveniences.[110] The Santa Anita Race Track in nearby Arcadia, a town with no accommodations, had opened on Christmas Day in 1934, giving the Vista, now the favored hotel, a considerable boost.[111]

The Marston bungalows discussed below are organized according to location: first, those that were built along the Arroyo, followed by those built along South Grand Avenue.

Bungalows B, C, and D

These first bungalows designed by Marston & Van Pelt at the Vista del Arroyo were built in 1920 and 1921 along the edge of the Arroyo and closest to the Colorado Street Bridge. Bungalow C consisted of eleven apartment units and Bungalow D of thirteen.[112] Less is known of Bungalow B. These structures were not built for specific individuals but rented out as rooms in the main hotel would have been, though they offered added privacy and more spectacular views.

The Vista, as with the other grand hotels, provided an easy transition for families contemplating the move west. The hotel's manager observed in 1921: "Apparently quite a few [guests] are coming with the expectation of making Pasadena their permanent residence. Three families who have reservations for the season are shipping their household effects to Pasadena with the intention of picking out permanent homes here during the winter."[113]

Hamilton Bungalow

Built by Marston, Van Pelt & Maybury in 1926, this dwelling located on the Arroyo side had eight apartment units and cost $20,000. Floor plans show a two-story structure with a side-gabled tile roof, a ground floor arcade, rectangular wood frame casement windows; second floor wrought-iron balconies were added in 1934. This bungalow and the Jenks bungalow (below) were later owned by the federal government and are now demolished.[114]

The structure was named for J. E. Hamilton of Two Rivers, Wisconsin. Hamilton was a leading member of the syndicate that financially aided Comstock's purchase of the Vista in 1926,[115] and he was one of the largest manufacturers of steel furniture in the world.[116] He and his family regularly spent six months of the year at the Vista.[117]

Jenks Bungalow

This bungalow, immediately to the north of the Hamilton Bungalow, was designed by Marston & Maybury in 1928 as a "guest house" for the hotel that would consist of ten deluxe apartments. The structure is 7,300 square feet and was built at a cost of $36,000. "Vista Hotel is to Enlarge its Plant," announced the local newspaper in a lengthy front page story.[118] "The present season has been one of the best we have ever had," declared president and general manager Comstock, "and reservations for next season are being received in such numbers that we plan to enlarge our facilities this summer."[119] Comstock happily reported that "for two months the Vista del Arroyo has been filled to capacity....Guests are delighted with their sojourn in Pasadena and are planning to return early next season. Many of them will be accompanied by friends, who are being attracted to our city by the favorable reports sent back by this seasons's guests."[120]

This guest house "immediately overlooking the Arroyo....will be of the Mediterranean type of architecture, to conform with the general theme of the hotel," the newspaper explained.[121] The two-story dwelling had many of the same features as the Hamilton Bungalow, plus iron-barred windows, some vertical wood siding, and projecting buttresses on the north and west elevations like those used on the main hotel building.

The bungalow was named for S. Herbert Jenks, a "retired capitalist,"[122] and substantial investor with Comstock in the Vista. For several years, Mr. and Mrs. Jenks were frequent guests at the Vista before they decided to build their own bungalow.[123]

The four bungalows that extend along South Grand Avenue are more formal. After multi-million dollar renovations in the 1990s allowing for their adaptive reuse as the Western Justice Center Foundation, they rank as classic statements of the Spanish and Mediterranean style which characterized the region's architecture in the 1920s and 1930s and whose imagery suggested the relaxation and romance we associate with our Spanish past.[124]

These structures all feature red-tiled and hipped roofs, stucco exterior, rectangular casement or double-hung windows and French doors on upper and lower floors.

The Stuart Bungalow

This two-story Mediterranean style residence was designed by Marston & Van Pelt in 1925. The smallest of Marston's four South Grand bungalows, it consists of four apartment units. Its front facade faces south toward the main hotel and features a centered Palladian front entry incorporating pilasters and full-length French door side windows.

The house was erected for Holloway Ithamer Stuart, who was born and educated in Indiana and came to Pasadena in 1887 to embark on a banking career.[125] In 1905, he became the president of Union Savings Bank, and in 1921 was elevated to the chairmanship of the board of First National Bank, a position he filled for more than two decades.[126] Stuart was a member of the University and Annandale Clubs, the Presbyterian Church, and also was a 32nd degree Mason.[127]

The Cox Bungalow

Designed by Marston & Maybury in 1935, this bungalow shares with its neighbor the Stuart Bungalow the Mediterranean style and south-facing front entry, but is almost twice as large as the Stuart dwelling. It was built for Amariah G. Cox of Chicago. The most attractive elements are at the rear where windows have Italianate bracketed tops, and there is a brick patio and capacious second floor terrace whose views of the Arroyo must have been arresting in the 1930s before landscaping matured.

2.18 Stuart Bungalow (1925)

2.19 Cox Bungalow (1935)

2.20 Griffith Bungalow (1935) In 1935
Marston and Maybury designed this two-storied
dwelling next to the Cox bungalow as a single-
family residence for W. Cady Griffith. Pictured
is the rear brick patio and second floor terrace.

2.21 Maxwell Bungalow (1929)

Maxwell Bungalow

Most splendid of this row of dwellings is the bungalow Marston designed in the Mediterranean Italianate
style for patent lawyer and noted philanthropist George
H. Maxwell. This majestic "bungalow" is actually nearly
10,000 square feet in size and was built in 1929 for
$58,000. Signaling its preeminence, it is the only bun-
galow of the group along Grand Avenue whose front
entry faces the street.

The recessed front entry, located in a central projecting section, consists of a large arched opening with a
paired front door of leaded glass. The opening is of cast
stone incorporating rosettes and banded columns and is
crowned with an elaborate balcony overhead. That second floor balcony is accessed by paired French doors
with an attractive cast stone surround that is finished
with a triangular pediment. The northeast corner of the
front facade features a second floor balcony and recessed
porch supported by a centered Corinthian column.

The dwelling's rear facade is even more artistically
detailed, with its groupings of two story arched windows
with banded Corinthian column divides. Another second
floor window ensemble consists of a loggia supported by
squared plaster columns that are banded and decorated.
The north elevation features a trio of attractive arched
doors and another loggia. The banded column theme is
repeated on canted ground floor walls on the Arroyo side.

The interior to this day reveals the kind of elegance
that characterized the Vista del Arroyo at its peak. That
decorative details are still visible is unusual, for most of
the other bungalow interiors were later irreversibly altered. The Maxwell Bungalow's plan is organized around
a central, two-storied lounge, obviously designed for
large social gatherings. The ceiling is beamed with heavy
natural timbers and the primary doorways are Tudor with
wooden paneled soffits. Because of this dwelling's splendor, the cost of its renovation alone in 1980s was estimated to be $2.3 million.[128]

George Maxwell was born in upstate New York,
attended Syracuse University (1888), and received his
law degree in Washington, D.C., from what is now
George Washington University (1892).[129] His first legal
job was in the U.S. Patent Office in the shoe and leather division. He later applied that knowledge in opening his own patent law practice in Boston,[130] where he invented a shoe-making machine that earned him a
fortune.[131] Maxwell purchased substantial real estate holdings in Phoenix, Arizona where he and his wife
had relocated for health reasons in 1917.[132] They came further west to Pasadena, which was their winter residence from 1917-28,[133] and they began living there permanently in 1929 when they built this deluxe bungalow. Maxwell was best known as a generous contributor, especially to academic institutions. He gave $1
million to Syracuse University (which named its school of public affairs after him) and $100,000 outright
plus $5,500 a year to Boston University.[134] He also established a lectureship at American University.[135] There
was not much opportunity for Maxwell to enjoy his new house in Pasadena, for he died in 1932.[136]

Restored Grandeur

On February 5, 1943, the U.S. War Department took possession of the entire 15.3 acre Vista del Arroyo property under the War Powers Act of 1943. With very short notice, authorities relocated the 158 guests to other quarters in Pasadena. Linnard responded patriotically: "The important thing is winning the war and we are glad to help in any way possible."[137] Several other leading California hotels were similarly seized, including three in Santa Barbara.[138] All twenty-one Vista buildings were converted to hospital use, transforming the site to a 1050-bed facility called the McCornack Army Hospital. On March 27, 1945, Bob Hope broadcast his radio show from the recreation hall.[139] "Hundreds of wounded arrived from the Pacific campaigns, making the Hotel one of the busiest Army installations in Southern California."[140] The structure was deactivated in June of 1949. Extensive alterations had permanently shifted the Vista's course; it never returned to its grandeur as a hotel. After various uses, the federal government in 1974 declared the hotel surplus property and moved out. The entire site was vacant for several years.

An acrimonious debate ensued over the site's future;[141] in 1978 Richard Chambers, the former Chief Judge of the Ninth Circuit Court of Appeals, began an effort to make the site the location of that circuit court. After a $10.8 million renovation by the federal government in 1983-1985, directed by architect J. Rudy Freeman, the building was completed in 1986. In the same year, Justice Warren E. Burger officiated at a dedication ceremony before an audience of 1,500[142] as this old hotel became the Federal Building for the United States Court of Appeals.[143] In January of 1989 a Presidential Design Award was presented to Freeman and his firm by the National Endowment for the Arts;[144] Page & Turnbull, Inc., also received a Design Achievement Award from the NEA.[145]

In its coverage of the structure's reincarnation as a Federal courthouse, the *Pasadena Star News* paid this tribute to the former grand hotel:

> After the ravages wreaked on her as a hospital during World War II, the Vista del Arroyo Hotel has regained her regal stature and reigns like a queen again on the ridge of the Arroyo Seco at Pasadena's western portal.[146]

2.22 The Crown Prince and Princess of Japan in front of the Vista Del Arroyo in 1925

—— 🌼 **3** 🌼 ——
Embrace of the
Arts & Crafts

SYLVANUS MARSTON'S 1907 CORNELL GRADUATION and the opening of his Pasadena office coincided not only with the early development of the resort hotels but also with the burgeoning California Arts and Crafts Movement, most fervently embraced in Pasadena and Berkeley.

America's turn to the craft ideal was driven partly by the industrial revolution. Its new efficiencies and innovations brought great fortunes to business titans, but often exploited workers and forced upon them a numbing repetition of tasks. These social changes resulted in enormous upheaval. In response, America's Arts and Crafts vanguard called for a return to simpler living and sought to reestablish the importance of the artisan and his handcrafted materials. Gustav Stickley became an influential figure with his *Craftsman* magazine, started in 1901, which by 1909 had amassed 60,000 subscriptions nationwide.[1] It articulated a philosophy for a fulfilling life in modern times: the beauty of simplicity.

Pasadena's Arts and Crafts movement took its own unique form. The area's natural beauty—bucolic and untouched—lured many who would prove easily inclined to appreciate Arts and Crafts values. Railroad and touring company promotionalism had widely proclaimed Pasadena as a paradise of orange groves, possessing a warm climate and offering vigorous outdoor living. Prolific local writers such as Helen Lukens Gaut portrayed the city, in such influential publications as *Craftsman*, as embodying the good life. Citrus was coming to be viewed as inextricably linked to good health,[2] and Pasadena was a major center of U.S. orange production. Tuberculosis was a widespread public health malady, and a sunny, dry climate was believed to be the only sure relief. Ailing people from across the country flocked to Pasadena for its abundant sanitariums in the arid foothills. Pasadena was viewed as the quintessence of healthful living close to nature. For architect Charles Sumner Greene, himself transplanted from the Midwest, California was a place where one can "see the sun set or find a rose in bloom."[3]

It was in this healthful atmosphere that the Arts and Crafts concepts were embraced in the bungalow ideal. The word "bungalow" itself was enticing, carrying connotations of idyllic living. A 1905 *Architectural Record* article claimed that "bungalow" suggested the same kind of charm "as the word Mesopotamia had for a lady in Maine."[4] Many had first associated "bungalow" with American vacation architecture, linking it with leisure, informality, and natural settings. Technically, the word broadly defines dwellings built low to the ground with extended and exposed rafters and roof lines that, as architect Elmer Grey wrote, "are so friendly, gracious, inviting in their suggestion of comfort and shelter that they add the last touch of the feeling of inevitableness that is conveyed by the whole design."[5] Especially in Pasadena, he added, "a house should be planned in relationship to its garden…and with less idea of producing an impressive effect from the street."[6]

This was a rational architecture. "The bungalow was accepted in America as an ideal…from the standpoint of architectural design, family comfort, and structural endurance," wrote architect Charles E. White, Jr., in *The Bungalow Book*.[7] After all, White stressed, a bungalow could be constructed with less expensive materials because "people view bungalows as rather 'rough and ready' and they will tolerate and even admire" this rustic quality.[8] Popular magazines also helped idealize the bungalow. *Ladies' Home Journal*, for instance, featured eight articles in a four-year period highlighting Sylvanus Marston's bungalows.

Marston's Contributions

By the time Marston opened his office in the Chamber of Commerce Building on Colorado Boulevard at Arroyo Parkway, the Greenes, Roehrig, and the few other well-educated Pasadena practitioners had relocated to Los Angeles. Marston, for a time the premiere university-trained architect in Pasadena, possessed an authentic appreciation of the developing Arts and Crafts idiom and an astute sense of public taste and architectural trends. Robert E. Bennett, a second generation Pasadena architect whose father Cyril worked for the Greenes and then for Marston, describes both employers as part of a young, aggressive group determined to do things a new way.[9] The caption next to Marston's photograph in the Cornell yearbook reveals this awareness, stating: "[Marston] has devoted his time, under the direction of 'Pa Martin' [acting dean], to the design of his future California bungalow."[10]

3.1 Barnes bungalow (1909)

Marston designed more than ninety houses in the bungalow style, many of which are still extant in the Pasadena area. Just as the sweep of Marston's career is marked by astonishing versatility, so too are his designs, even within this one style. He prepared plans for Swiss chalet bungalows, those reminiscent of the Prairie and Mission styles, English shingle and Colonial bungalows and, of course, the rustic, dark-shingled Craftsman bungalows that came to beguile Californians because of their harmony with the landscape and their use of natural materials.

Marston made two original and enduring contributions to this genre. In his first year of practice he planned St. Francis Court in Pasadena, recognized as the first bungalow court in the United States.[11] The concept featured a group of free-standing units in a garden setting arranged around a central courtyard. Second, while the Greene brothers brought the bungalow to its highest level of craftsmanship, Marston helped bring it to the middle classes. Marston was "much more of a people's architect," architectural historian Robert Winter has observed.[12] For an architect who spent only a fraction of his career working in the Arts and Crafts idiom and who would be far better known for his period revival styles, Marston's accomplishments as a young architect were bold.

The height of the Arts and Crafts period in Pasadena came between 1910 and the first world war. Even as late as 1920, the first prize in that year's Rose Parade went to Glendale, whose float portrayed a bungalow,[13] so favored had the style become locally. Marston was one of the handful of Pasadena architects who helped make this so.

Marston's First Houses: Bungalows of Every Style

Ella Barnes

The Ella Barnes house at 120 N. Madison Avenue is in the Pasadena Playhouse Historic District and is listed on the National Register of Historic Places. Designed by Marston in 1909, it is a classic bungalow with Colonial style overtones. It is a one and one-half story shingle over stucco dwelling, with a sloping side-gabled roof-line marked by a shed dormer. Clipped gable ends as well as a deeply recessed, full-width porch create a cottage-like effect and render it a good representation of Pasadena bungalow architecture.

L. G. Haase

The L. G. Haase house at 1185 N. Marengo Avenue, designed in 1911 in what is called "Garfield Heights," is a fine example of Marston's Swiss chalet style. The one-story entrance porch is a central feature. It is flanked by tall Roman brick piers with stone caps that support an open wood trellis with tapered rafter ends. The single gable composition and the attic's vertical cut-out wood vents signal the chalet style. For the interior, plans called for "Batchelder tile mantels...oak and pine floors [and] pine and cedar trim."[14] Deemed eligible for listing on the National Register of Historic Places, the residence is considered notable for its fine craftsmanship and architectural integrity.

3.2 Haase house (1911); front porch detail

Sylvanus B. Marston

The Prairie style, originating in the Midwest at the turn of the century, is associated with Frank Lloyd Wright and was developed out of the desire to relate house design to the spreading horizon that dominates the Plains states. The horizontal line is always emphasized, the roof line may appear nearly flat, and other elements such as the chimney or porch are frequently massive, squared forms. More delicate window treatment often is used to soften the bluntness of the overall effect. The Prairie style shares common ground with the bungalow, but its spareness and even severity strongly contrast with the more overtly picturesque bungalow. Marston chose the Prairie style for his own house, built in 1910 at 661 S. El Molino Avenue. He surprised his wife with the new dwelling when they returned from their honeymoon in Hawaii.

3.3 Marston residence (1910)

This stucco over clapboard house is two stories with eight rooms. A pergola with narrow wooden posts lightens the heavier effects of this Prairie style.

In contrast to the typical Prairie structure, front entry is located on the side of the house, under a porte-cochere. Fittingly, one treatise terms this configuration as "a favorite form for smaller, architect-designed Prairie houses and also for those built on narrow urban lots."[15]

3.4 Prairie style house built for H.C. French, Jr. (1910)

3.5 Eason residence (1911)

3.6 Anderson house (1911), shortly after it was built

It is interesting that Marston chose the Prairie style. Its popularity never really took hold in Pasadena. Moreover, this was a somewhat odd choice given that Marston, according to one source, considered Frank Lloyd Wright an "immoral man,"[16] likely referring to Wright's scandalous love affairs.[17] In 1909, newspapers reported that Wright had "lost all morality and religion."[18] Still, the intense press coverage of Wright reminded the country of his eminence. Marston's choice of a style conceived by "the artistic genius," as some termed Wright, may have been an unconscious desire to be associated with architectural fame.

H. C. French, Jr.

The only other Prairie design by Marston was built in 1910 for H. C. French, Jr. and is located at 1011 S. Madison Avenue, just a short walk from Marston's house. French, who had acquired his wealth from U.S. Steel holdings,[19] was the head of a family for which Marston would design six houses in Pasadena. This dwelling's facade is dominated by horizontal rows of casement windows with sharply defined vertical detailing.

Willis M. Eason

The Willis M. Eason residence was built in 1911 and is located at 630 Prospect Boulevard, in the Prospect Park Historic District. A two-story English Arts and Crafts bungalow, its central feature is the porte-cochere with paired columns and brick piers.

Eason arrived in Pasadena in 1894 from Iowa, and eventually came to wield substantial clout in the banking, telephone, real estate, and other industries.[20] Known as a "citrus baron," Eason at one time owned the largest number of acres in the city devoted to orange production.[21] Architects Charles and Henry Greene had designed Eason's earlier home—a modest cottage—in 1895.[22]

Mrs. Robert Anderson

Marston designed an English bungalow in 1911 that favors Tudor design elements. Built for Mrs. Robert Anderson at 695 S. Madison Avenue, the house features distinctive half-timbering on the front oriel and sides.

Maitland L. Bishop

This bungalow was designed in 1911 for Maitland L. Bishop and is located at 422 California Terrace. It incorporates significant architectural detail for so modest a house: clipped gables, half-timbering, and corniced windows. Plans also called for "porch columns" and "screen porches,"[24] details not evident today.

For many years, Bishop was a colorful figure in Pasadena. After graduating from elite eastern schools, he moved to the city in 1909 to recover from tuberculosis.[25] He liked to joke that he came to Pasadena to die.[26] Two years after his arrival, the twenty-two-year-old Bishop commissioned Marston to design his California bungalow. In 1965, at the age of eighty-seven, Bishop was Pasadena's oldest practicing lawyer,[27] and he lived to celebrate his 107th birthday in 1985.[28]

George B. Ellis

Marston prepared drawings in 1911 of a Colonial clapboard bungalow for George B. Ellis, located at 1440 N. Los Robles Avenue. The Colonial style derives from the formality introduced by the intricate arched wooden pergola that extends across the front facade and sweeps around the north side to form a porte-cochere. Paired Tuscan columns flank the front entry and are incorporated in the pergola. Projecting bay windows and arched dormers decorate this large residence, which was known as "Normandie Heights." Such a name evokes an estate rather than a residence—an appropriate image given the huge expanse of land over which the house and its numerous pergolas originally extended.[29]

Rev. Daniel F. Fox

Marston's work can be found in literally every one of Pasadena's earliest developed sections. Orange Heights is one such area, bounded east-west by Los Robles and El Molino streets, and north-south by Washington and Mountain streets. Devoted primarily to citrus groves until the early 1900s, in 1995 the area was listed on the National Register of Historic Places. Scores of mature trees remain—camphor, oak, and windmill palms—giving the area an appealing ambiance. Most of the houses were built between the turn of the century and World War I. The neighborhood association, still active, has stated: "It was a time of unpretentious living, of a return to natural things, and of strong community spirit."[30] The houses are primarily Craftsman-styled bungalows by well-known Pasadena architects, including Marston, who designed a Colonial bungalow in 1910 at 993 N. Madison Avenue for Dr. Daniel F. Fox.

The Fox residence is defined by a full-width front porch (later enclosed) and square bay window in the first story; a shed dormer and sleeping porch distinguish the second floor. A high cobblestone retaining wall harmonizes with the house's cobblestone foundation and porch supports.

Dr. Fox was highly regarded as pastor of Pasadena's First Congregational Church from 1909 forward. In celebration of his ministry, a large group gathered in 1924 for a dinner and evening of tribute. The event made the front page of the *Pasadena Star News*, which called Fox's work a "monument of love."[31]

3.7 Bishop bungalow (1911), side elevation

3.8 Ellis residence (1911) and extensive property with pergolas

3.9 Fox bungalow (1910); wood bracket detail on rear elevation

Jane E. Meeker

Marston also prepared plans for bungalows in the Mission style, one of California's earliest designs which was distinguished, as cultural historian Dr. Harold Kirker wrote, by "shadowy arcades and massive, unbroken wall surfaces."[32] A modest house in this style was built by Marston in 1915 for Jane E. Meeker, at 397 N. Raymond Avenue. The Meeker bungalow, demolished for construction of the 210 Freeway, was featured in a front page article, "California Bungalows," in *Western Architect* in 1918.[33] The author, distinguished Chicago architect Peter Wight, had come to know Pasadena well after retiring there in 1918. He described the Mission style as being one of the earliest forms of bungalow types.

Typically they were of wood construction with rough-cast stucco exteriors and flat roofs, often covered with Mission tiles. He noted that the Meeker house was by Marston & Van Pelt, "well-known architects,"[34] and observed that it typified the Mission style for the "average, middle-class bungalow on a city lot."[35] Wight mentioned with approval that the house dimensions suited the lot size, "for, be it known that a bungalow is not a bungalow if it does not stand alone and have sufficient ground around it for the cultivation of a garden."[36]

3.10 Meeker Mission style bungalow (1915) shortly after construction

For Every Man, A Bungalow

Accepting commissions on speculation from local builders separated Marston from many of his talented peers. Four unassuming bungalows, built between 1909 and 1912 for the early Pasadena developer Kendall-Curtis on the same block of South Mentor, provide a glimpse into Marston's skill at democratizing bungalow construction.

Mentor Avenue Bungalows

Three of the four bungalows were designed in the Colonial style. The first, built in 1910, is located at 623 S. Mentor Avenue. The decorative details are few, but the house's proportions and simple composition brought it great acclaim. It was widely featured in Kendall-Curtis Company advertisements, and in publications as diverse as the *Tournament of Roses Brochure*, the *Year Book of the Los Angeles Architectural Club*,[37] and *Scribner's*.[38] The main decorative elements include a low stucco wall across the front, two Tuscan plaster columns at either end of the facade, and camber windows that mimic the eyebrow eave overhead. Even in this simple dwelling, windows were fitted with attractive leaded glass.

A second house, built in 1911 and located at 636 S. Mentor Avenue, is a modest clapboard bungalow. The cost of the interior details would surely exceed the budget for today's version of a low-cost, "on-spec" house. The dining room has oak built-ins with leaded

3.11 623 Mentor Avenue (1910); Tuscan column porch detail

glass, a plate rail, and a finely crafted wood-beamed ceiling. The substantial fireplace, contained in a recessed area flanked by coved plaster walls, has Batchelder tile facing and is crowned with an oak Craftsman mantel.

The other two houses on Mentor Avenue, located at 599 (1911) and 606 (1912), were featured in

Craftsman in November of 1914 in an article praising their contribution to a "wisely democratic trend" in residential construction.[39] The author, Pasadenan Helen Lukens Gaut, states that Marston was "able to combine the best points of the simple, old-fashioned cottage and the more elaborate and modern bungalow idea" which brought "comfort, pleasure and durability."[40]

The house at 599 Mentor Avenue, now demolished, was a one and one-half story clapboard with an asymmetrical composition that included two eyebrow dormers flanked by two rounded porch columns suggestive of the Colonial style. The roof was covered with moss-green shingles and heavy bargeboard molding.[41] For a house costing the even-then modest sum of $4,000,[42] there is abundant use of built-ins, and a generous pantry-kitchen, as well as substantial space beneath the roof, especially in the back for a sleeping porch. This bungalow was also featured in the *Scribner's* article mentioned above,[43] and in a 1915 edition of *Ladies' Home Journal*.[44]

The other Marston bungalow displayed in *Craftsman*, at 606 Mentor Avenue (1912), while embracing Colonial motifs similar to 599 Mentor, has a completely different plan. Side-gabled, the house has a full-length trellised porch with the central portion accentuated by an arch flanked by paired columns repeated at each end of the trellis. Exterior walls are resawn redwood siding and front windows swing out and are latticed. The front door, heavily cased and with long narrow windows, curves impressively at the top to echo the central arched porch. This house also has upstairs sleeping porches and a dressing room, all built under the rear raised roof.[45]

Clinton P. McAllaster

Other modest houses that adhere to the bungalow ideal and exemplify Marston's development of affordable architecture include two 1909 bungalows—one at 516 S. Oakland Avenue and the other at 658 S. Hudson Avenue—both designed for Clinton P. McAllaster. A new arrival in Pasadena, McAllaster wrote in the 1910 *Tournament of Roses Brochure* of "having left behind him snow and ice and blustering winds."[46] The Oakland Avenue house, built for $3,540,[47] features a bay-shaped dormer.

The Craftsman Bungalow

There are the generic bungalows described above, low-pitched and of various materials and styles, and then there are the distinct Craftsman bungalows, most strongly identified with California. The latter are distinguished by their use of simple forms, natural materials, and rough textures; they embrace most purely the philosophy and artistic ethos of the Arts and Crafts Movement. For many,

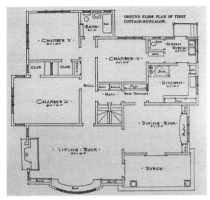

3.13 599 Mentor Avenue plan
3.12 599 Mentor Avenue (1911)

3.14 606 Mentor Avenue (1912)
3.15 606 Mentor Avenue plan

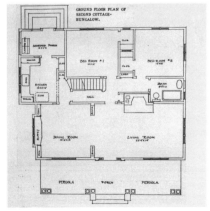

3.16 McAllaster bungalow (1909)

3.17 McAllaster bungalow; interior view

3.18 Swink Craftsman bungalow (1911)

walking into an authentic California Craftsman clothed in bare redwood siding and with its plentiful and unusual interior oak and exotic wood joinery, offers an intermingling of the most appealing ingredients. There are spacious and breezy common areas illuminated by the morning sun piercing the turn-of-the-century bubbled window glass.

This domestic space is designed on a human scale. The pervading feeling is comfort and proximity to cherished things: the family, which dwells in closer quarters with the new emphasis on one-story living; books within comfortable reach in the numerous built-ins; and the outdoor environment deliberately within sight and reach. The three residences discussed below are the purest examples of the Craftsman bungalow among Marston's designs.

Robert A. Swink

The Robert A. Swink house, built in 1911 at 400 N. Los Robles Avenue, now demolished, exemplified the uniquely Pasadena Arts and Crafts style. Its centerpiece was a cobblestone porch railing with brick coping and battered cobblestone supports that extended upward nearly to the eaves.

Henry Roberts Lacey

Built in 1912 at 1115 Woodbury Road on the Altadena and Pasadena border is the house designed for Henry Roberts Lacey. With affluence achieved from Chicago's oil and packing industries, Lacey moved to Pasadena in 1893; he served as vice president of Central Oil of Los Angeles and president of the East Whittier Oil Company. The house most effectively embodies the Craftsman esthetic of design materials harmonizing with natural surroundings. The massive boulder foundation and piers framing the front porch and supporting the porte-cochere to the west, as well as the boldly exposed cobblestone chimney base on the porch, give the impression that the dwelling literally sprang from the earth. A pergola-covered side patio visible through the dining room French doors adds to the sense of being fully surrounded by nature.

Current Marston house owners have commented on the architect's skill in designing residential interiors to be both functional and aesthetically pleasing. This house is one such example. One special feature is the curve of a barrel-vaulted ceiling that the architects repeat in other rooms and in door openings. Yet practicality also prevails: oversized bedrooms keep this residence inherently livable.

The Lacey house had a steep price tag of $9,000.[48] Some of its other features mark it as one of the best of the modestly sized Craftsman houses in Pasadena. Fine woods accent the living room, including Port Orford cedar in the deep baseboards, the plate rail, the window casings, and the ceiling beams. The quarter-sawn oak fireplace surround nicely frames unusual Batchelder tiles that are in scumbled shades of

3.19 Lacey Arts and Crafts bungalow (1912)

sandalwood brushed with blue and display a bird motif.

Joseph E. Hinds

This Swiss chalet-style Craftsman residence is possibly the finest of Marston's larger bungalows. Located at 695 Prospect Boulevard, it was built in 1910 at a cost of $9,500[49] for Marston friend Joseph E. Hinds. Two-storied and redwood shingled, this dwelling has a vast forward-facing gable roof line with tapered eaves supported by exposed roof beams and extended rafter tails. The single extensive gable, with a notched bargeboard, encompasses the entire second story, which has a balcony supported by carved knee brackets that project over the front entryway. The current owners have interpreted the bracket and roof beam ends as "lion heads" and have sought to replicate faithfully this pattern with the handsome pergola recently added to the back of the house. A generous attic at the facade's apex is marked by grouped transom windows

3.21 Lacey bungalow, porch detail

extending along its entire width. A porte-cochere with a second story sun room is located on the north side. Attention is immediately drawn to the pergola, which consists of massive timber beams that are bracketed and supported by a brick porch wall and squared piers on a raised brick foundation.

One is struck by the luminous quality of the residence's interior, a feature distinguishing it from the "dim religious light," experienced in a typical Greene and Greene house.[50] Brightness is achieved in this large house of six bedrooms, three sleeping porches, and a nursery, by a profusion of large camber windows.

The exterior redwood cladding is thirty-inch long hand-hewn shingles, called "barn shingles," typical of the period. Throughout, the dwelling's exposed wooden structural elements show great consistency with Craftsman-derived principle of emphasizing structural forms in lieu of ornament.

The Hinds's backyard contains a garage with a guest house on the second story, apparently built at

3.22 Hinds Swiss chalet residence (1910)

the same time as the house. This was unusual, for Marston generally returned to these early residential commissions a few years later to add garages. The guest house contains a balcony whose railing employs the cut-out forms typically associated with the chalet style.

Joseph Hinds (hence the "H" on the chimney) came to Pasadena from Brooklyn to retire in 1905. In the 1880s he had led the firm of Hinds, Ketcham & Co. which engaged in color printing. He heard rumors of the "Edison fellow" who could create light at night. He met with Edison and presented "every argument he could think of"[51] to persuade him to choose Hinds's commercial plant as the first to use Edison's incandescent lamp lighting system. Hinds's offer to omit pipes for gas illumination in the construction of his new factory prompted Edison to select him for the experiment.

This residence is part of the Prospect Park Tract, located between Orange Grove and Seco, and subdivided and improved in 1906. One of Pasadena's first affluent tracts with restrictive building requirements, the area has been designated a historic district and is now listed on the National Register of Historic Places. "A more elaborate residential park has never been exploited in southern California than Prospect Park...the 'Chester Place' [West Adams section of Los Angeles] of Pasadena," announced advertisements.[52]

Prospect Park Entrance Gate

The nicely crafted stone portals at Orange Grove Avenue and Prospect Boulevard, built with clinker brick and river boulders, further signal the high quality of design in the neighborhood. Those portals have often been attributed to the Greene brothers[53] and certainly give that appearance, but they were designed by Sylvanus Marston. Among Marston's original drawings that have survived is an undated blueprint entitled "Entrance Gates to Prospect Park," nearly identical to the gates that exist on the site today, except that Marston's drawing depicts a wooden sign hanging between the posts stating: "Prospect Park—

3.23 Section of Marston's Arts and Crafts gateposts (1911) in Santa Monica

Private."[54] That part of the original structure disappeared over the years or was never built.

Linda Vista Park Gate, Santa Monica

In 1911, Marston drew plans for another ornamental gateway, this time to the entrance of Linda Vista Park (now Palisades Park) in Santa Monica. The gateway is located on Ocean Avenue and Idaho Street, and plans specified "construction from split granite, and will be ten feet high, with four large pillars, and will carry out the rustic effect of the bluff fence which surrounds the park."[55] The *Pasadena Star News* reported that the contract for the work was awarded to Smith & Stahlhuth in Pasadena.[56] Fred Stahlhuth was the mason "most responsible for interpreting the Greene's designs for boulder and clinker brick masonry work which was rapidly becoming popular among builders who referred to it as 'the peanut brittle style.'"[57] Remarkably, the gateposts are still intact at their original location and were treated with great care during the most recent renovation of Palisades Park. These gateposts and the selection of the stone mason demonstrate Marston's devotion to excellence in craftsmanship.

St. Francis: America's First Bungalow Court

The advertisements were compelling: "A wonderfully artistic arrangement of eleven beautifully furnished bungalows around large private court. Every appointment for comfort and welfare of tenants....Just the thing for winter tourists." The advertisement, in the *Tournament of Roses Brochure* for 1911,[58] sought to promote Marston's St. Francis Court. This residential courtyard concept, which was being planned in September of 1908,[59] is recognized as the first of its kind in the United States. The complex of eleven one-story bungalows was arranged around a central open space. Each dwelling looked out to its own garden. An automobile driveway ending in a turn-around ran along the middle of the grouping of units.

The cottages were designed to have a unified appearance by utilizing gabled roofs of similar pitch as well as dark stained exterior surfaces,[60] yet there were important differences that created interest and individuality. The exterior cladding varied from shingles, weatherboard, or masonry work of brick which sometimes incorporated concrete or stone. All had front porches, and some had two, with the occasional white columns employed to brighten the facade. Some had brick chimneys, others used brick interposed with stone. Five bungalows had six rooms (i.e., three bedrooms), four had five rooms, and two had four rooms.

A consistent theme was the high quality of all the interiors, including many built-ins, generous arched brick fireplaces that were often nestled in an inglenook, beamed ceilings in the living and dining rooms, and vertical decorative stenciling on the buffet and on the side panels flanking the fireplace. The dwellings were intended as rentals and were furnished with such items as Stickley furniture, Oriental rugs, silver, linens, and oil paintings. A few of the bungalows had servants' quarters.[61] There was a narrow passageway along the rear of the complex "for the butcher and the baker,"[62] a further clue to the anticipated affluence of the guests. Such comfort cost $1,000 to $1,500 per year, or $900 to $1,200 for the winter season.[63]

Interestingly, Marston prepared two very different sets of plans for the complex. The first, dated March of 1909, shows that some

3.24 Postcard of St. Francis Court, c. 1915

bungalows were first designed as two-storied houses in the Mission style, featuring stucco cladding, red-tiled roofs with ridge tiles, and chimneys with terra cotta hoods. Others were one-story dwellings whose main exterior features were flared cobblestone chimneys with Spanish-influenced brick cappings. As originally drawn, some of the fireplace facings and surrounds were more elaborate than those eventually built; some revealing intricate geometric brick work, others employing generous use of massive river rock flanked by built-in seats and bookcases. For one stone and brick fireplace, plans called for a tall, narrow leaded window with a metal frame to be set into the fireplace facing. Some interior doors bore the vertical tapering inspired by the Greenes.

The second set of plans which emerged just one month later, while scaled back in certain respects perhaps to economize, contained little artistic compromise and more uniformly reflected Arts and Crafts vocabulary.

The entire court rested on a generous lot on the north side of Colorado Boulevard, between El

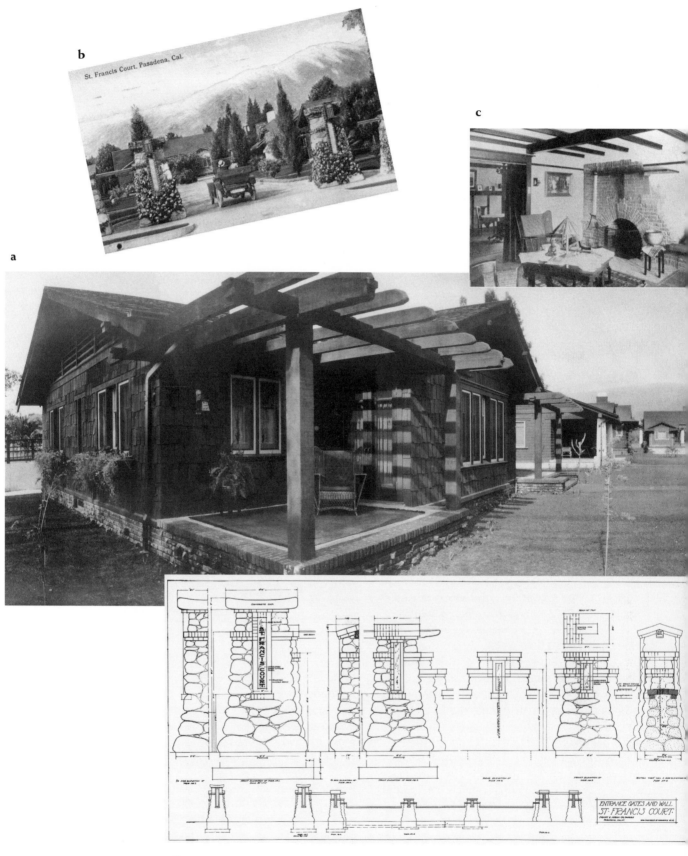

b

St. Francis Court, Pasadena, Cal.

c

a

g

3.25 St. Francis Court (1908), first bungalow court in the U.S.: historic images depicting a variety of architectural details and a style of living for Pasadena's winter visitors

Molino and Hudson streets, with a frontage of 176 feet and a depth of 305 feet. The entrance had low rough stone walls capped with clinker brick with occasional vertical sloping piers. Massive gateway pillars made of large boulders and cobblestones and capped with red brick flanked the main entrance. Each pillar had two lantern-like lighting fixtures, one illuminating the court side, the other the street side. The fountain at the rear of the courtyard, around which residents were fond of congregating in late afternoons,[64] utilized the same attractive stone and brick, with fixed wooden benches on either side of the fountain and an Arts and Crafts style pergola overhead, supported by flared cobblestone piers.

St. Francis Court became a popular seasonal residence for the upper middle classes. The bungalow court was featured in the official *Tournament of Roses Brochure* starting in 1910 and appearing for the next several years, appealing to guests arriving for the winter festivities that made Pasadena famous. It was an especially attractive option for those who wanted to avoid the formality and activity at the leading resort hotels. At the St. Francis, guests could enjoy privacy, quiet, outdoor air, and carefully landscaped semi-tropical gardens, including palm trees—all at arm's reach. In its early years of operation, St. Francis Court was described as being "in the outskirts of Pasadena,"[65] away from more dense development.

The St. Francis received immediate and widespread acclaim. In addition to coverage in two national architectural publications,[66] four articles appeared in *Ladies' Home Journal*,[67] and more locally it was featured in the 1910 *Year Book of the Los Angeles Architectural Club*.[68] In a 1911 *Sunset* magazine article on Pasadena, one writer said that after looking at countless houses in that city "you come to the conclusion that the local architects are—different." In addition to the "distractingly adorable bungalows, they have evolved an even more tempting plan—as unique as it is artistic. It is the court-plan," and the writer cited the St. Francis. "Each bungalow of these courts is prepared, as the spider's web for the trusting fly, to catch the first tourist that comes past."[69]

Sadly, in December of 1925, all of the bungalows were relocated to different parts of the city (five being moved to South Catalina Avenue near the Polytechnic School) to allow for the extension of Oak Knoll Avenue from Colorado Boulevard to Union Street. The newspaper report was wistful: "St. Francis Court has been the home of many notable visitors to this city and was one of the pioneering structures in the history of bungalow courts in the West....The great spaciousness of the court gave the assembled structures the appearance of enjoying the privileges of a private street and the popularity of the homes was evidenced in the fact that they were rarely vacant."[70]

This bungalow court was the only such project that Marston attempted. Since other architects quickly capitalized on the idea, some building several courts, it is more often associated with Pasadena architects other than Marston. The number of such courts in Pasadena reached only eleven in 1919,[71] but climbed to 414 by the early thirties.[72] The style was to become a favorite in Southern California for the first three decades of the 20th century.

The bungalow court holds an important place in Pasadena history. In October, 1914, as Southern California was preparing for an influx of tourists visiting the Panama-California International Exposition in San Diego, the local newspaper heralded the courts as a "leading feature" in available accommodations.[73] "The bungalow court was an important episode in real estate development and the tourist industry—two of the major underpinnings of the growth of Pasadena....The bungalow courts embodied an affordable life style that paid homage to the concept of neighborhood, both in an immediate and in a larger sense."[74] Marston's St. Francis Court must be viewed as one of his most enduring contributions as an architect.

The Hogans: Early Marston Backers

There is an occasional reference to the St. Francis property as having been "designed by Mr. Frank G. Hogan."[75] In fact, Hogan was the St. Francis Court owner, not the designer, and one of the earliest real estate developers in Pasadena. Hogan and his father, Colonel W. J. Hogan, figured prominently and early in Marston's career; he executed at least twelve commissions for them. His jobs for the Hogans included not only St. Francis Court and the nearby "Hogan bungalows" replete with stables for the Colonel, but also the Maryland Apartments and two bungalows for that prominent hotel. Marston also did considerable work at the Hogan-owned Hollywood Cemetery. The business relationship lasted at least twenty years. While the Hogans worked with other noted Pasadena architects, such as the

Heineman brothers[76] and later, Wallace Neff,[77] they most often chose Marston.

William J. Hogan or "Colonel W. J." as he was known, was born in Louisville, Kentucky in 1845, and was "well known as a lover of fine horses and in financial circles."[78] Upon his retirement in 1907, he and his wife relocated to Pasadena with their only child, Francis (Frank) Griffiths Hogan. The Colonel, who perhaps acquired the title during government (albeit civilian) service at the time of the Civil War, was an early board member of the Tournament of Roses, and a member of the Annandale, Overland, and Midwick Clubs.[79]

Son Frank, more Marston's contemporary, formed the Hogan Real Estate Company, and by 1915 was considered one of the area's leading real estate developers.[80] He was an Overland Club member and assisted in the sale of subscriptions to build the Rose Bowl. In 1911 he became president of the Tournament of Roses and served as grand marshal of the parade.[81] Around 1913 Frank Hogan's company owned and developed a subdivision in Altadena, the "Altadena Country Club Park Tract." Hogan used the talents of Marston's firm for the project. This tract can be seen in a photograph in the *Tournament of Roses Brochure* in 1913.[82]

Arts and Crafts Eclectic

During Pasadena's Arts and Crafts period the Marston firm designed three distinctive residences within three years of each other, each larger than the previous one. These houses show a mixture of influences. Verticality, steep-pitched roofs, the use of stucco cladding instead of only wood, subtle half-tim-

bering, and more formal gardens, are borrowed from the English Arts and Crafts Movement. The interior wood forms and materials were loyal mainly to the American Craftsman ideal, but details such as Tudor arched doorways and windows were also characteristic of English design. The firm's conceptual originality—the turret of the Thomas house for example—is evident in these structures. These residences remain to this day among the best illustrations of the Marston firm's dedication to quality craftsmanship, creativity, and timeless design.

3.26 Roscoe Thomas residence (1911)

G. Roscoe Thomas

The first of the three residences, designed in 1911, was an eight-room dwelling for retired Pasadena dentist G. Roscoe Thomas, at 574 Bellefontaine Place.

This design incorporates theoretically inconsistent stylistic themes. There are Swiss chalet elements in two overlapping forward-facing roof gables and in the cut-outs of the front wooden porch and side balcony enclosure; on the other hand, there is half-timbering against stuccoed wall surfaces as well as suppressed Tudor arches in a number of doorways and windows. The overall composition of the house as viewed from the backyard is enhanced by a generous squared chimney alongside an octagonal-shaped post-medieval English stair tower with a steep, pointed roof.

The facade is one-storied, preparing the eye for an unassuming structure. But the site drops sharply to the west (toward the Arroyo), revealing an extensive second, lower level. Since the stair tower is invisible from the front, the magnificence of the house seems to unfold the deeper one goes into the property.

A gabled wing extending northward, visible from the front and the rear, has as an outdoor cantilevered porch on the upper or street level, the one concession to the casualness of the bungalow style as compared to the structure's overall formal tone. The back entrance features a pointed arch doorway. These elements add to the uniqueness of the overall design.

Perhaps because of the Gothic interior elements, the dwelling conveys an ecclesiastical aura, beautiful and ethereal. There is extensive use of natural quarter-sawn white oak on the tower's stairway and the interior doors and window moldings. Wallpaper borrows heavily from William Morris designs. Pointed arch casement windows with deep reveals and a ribbed-vault ceiling proliferate.

Roscoe Thomas came to Pasadena in 1885, nearly contemporaneous with the arrival of the Marstons.

3.27 Roscoe Thomas holding the American flag, celebrating the arrival of the first horse-drawn street cars in Pasadena in 1886

Born and educated in New York, Thomas practiced dentistry in Detroit for eighteen years before his poor health brought him and his family to Pasadena. He became involved with banking and real estate and by 1907 had purchased "much valuable property,"[83] including early sections of Elevado Drive, Terrace Drive, Logan Street, Mentor Avenue, Mentoria Court, and Bellefontaine Street.[84] It was he who named the streets: the Mentor name was in honor of his wife, Caroline C. Clapp, who was born in Mentor, Ohio.[85]

It was Thomas's second-born child, Carl C. Thomas, the Cornell professor mentioned earlier, who in 1907 had commissioned Marston to design his Ithaca, New York house. The son apparently recommended architect Marston to the father for the job on Bellefontaine. Roscoe Thomas, who died in 1918, was a member of Pasadena's first Board of Trustees, and a leader in Pasadena's early development.[86] A well-known Pasadena photograph taken in 1886 depicts a crowd gathered in front of the old Grand Hotel celebrating opening day for the Pasadena Street Railroad Company and the arrival of the first horse drawn street cars in Pasadena. The man standing on top of one of the street cars waving a huge American flag is Roscoe Thomas.[87]

William Hespeler

The second "eclectic" Marston residence is also a two-story English stucco dwelling. It was designed in 1912 for William Hespeler at 239 N. Orange Grove Avenue. This nine-room house with its multi-gabled front has an unusual diagonal placement on the property. A focal point is the house's forward-facing gable with the classic English cottage features of a clipped gable and a "thatched shingle roof."[88] The exterior cladding is ochre-painted stucco with vertical half-timbering. Three grouped casement windows each with fifteen small, equal sized lights per window further the cottage look. The dark brick balustrade across the front entry coordinates well with the nearby Greene and Greene houses built for Mary Ranney and David Gamble.

The Hespeler house attracted considerable attention in architectural circles. It was featured in the 1913 *Year Book of the Los Angeles Architectural Club*.[89] Additionally, *Architect and Engineer* noted it in its 1913 and 1914 publications, which contained exhortations on the importance of better country house design through emphasis on structural integrity, simplicity, attractive form, and proportion. The articles addressed the need to reduce pretension but retain grace and beauty. In words that could apply to the Hespeler residence, the 1914 article contends:

> The architecture is...developed mainly from what might be called the cottage craftsmanship of the plain people, as distinguished from the degenerate elegancies and the diluted and grandiloquence of styles invented long ago and far away for the palaces of sovereigns.[90]

The dwelling's interior remains virtually unaltered, revealing extensive use of fine woods: a Dutch-styled oak carved front door whose top one-third swings open; beamed ceilings even in the entryway; extensive built-ins with leaded glass in the dining room; crown moldings and a quarter-sawn oak stairway with flat-sawn balusters. Most of the original Steuben Glass lighting fixtures are still extant and display Arts and Crafts floral motifs.

Henry Newby

The third house in this triumvirate was built in 1913 and located at 1015 Prospect Boulevard.[91] While known as the Newby house because its first resident was Henry Newby, technically it was designed on speculation as the model residence for the Arroyo Park Corporation,

3.28 Hespeler residence (1912); architects' watercolor

which created the new Arroyo Park Tract subdivision in 1910. This sixty-lot subdivision was located immediately above the affluent Prospect Park Tract, developed in 1906; it adopted that tract's same restrictive building requirements. A promotional brochure boasted that the area was a "West Side Residence Subdivision, Exclusive — Restricted" and that it commanded "an unsurpassed view of the mountains, the Arroyo Seco, and San Rafael Hills."[92]

The Newby house is a twelve room, 8,000 square foot, rambling structure with nine bathrooms, built for the then-lavish sum of $14,000. Sitting impressively on a double corner lot at the southern entrance to the Tract, it is across from the Chandler School and within striking distance of the Rose Bowl.

Stylistically, it is a Tudor Revival with overtones of the English Arts and Crafts Movement. It is discussed here because it was built during, and evokes, Pasadena's Arts and Crafts period, and because the modifications over time have diminished the Tudor influence.

This residence has a moderately pitched hipped roof. A gable roof line at either end of the main facade falls at a forty-five degree angle so that the wings become one story. Each of the end gables has a flat dormer with a whisper of half-timbering and with fenestration matching the main facade. Originally, these wings were open arched porches, but the owners soon decided to enclose them, giving the residence a more imposing appear-

3.29 Newby residence (1913) today

ance. The front entrance, facing directly south, is covered by a jerkinhead gabled portico with almost imperceptible half-timbering. Rather stolid-looking when built on its barren lot, the appearance of this dwelling has been softened by the maturation of the landscaping. Deodars, pines, California oaks, and a large cork oak surround the house. With two huge pine trees in front practically dwarfing it, the Newby residence now appears as a baronial country residence nestled deep in the woods.

The interior is something to behold, both for Marston's design and the present owners' enhancements. There are two Batchelder tile hearths, handsomely scored to resemble stonework, which support carved wooden pilasters and mantels. The living room is accented by an unusual ceramic ceiling border with a rosette pattern. There is generous use of cedar, mahogany, and oak in the woodwork and hardwood floors, with beamed ceilings and crown molding in the living and dining rooms, fine craftsmanship in the door and window moldings, the stairway balusters, and in the generous handcrafted built-ins. The kitchen is clad in plaster and scored to resemble turn-of-the-century tiles. The plan allows for an easy, ambling flow through common areas such as the kitchen, pantry, breakfast room, and dining room. Suggestive of this dwelling's lavish origins, there are five rooms devoted to servants' quarters, two sleeping porches, and an internal buzzer system wired for sixteen locations for the owner's convenience in summoning servants.

3.30 Newby residence shortly after construction

There is a formal rose garden on the west side with a lily pond and fountain. At one end is a sitting area with the original stone benches surrounded by a short stucco wall featuring Batchelder tile and protected overhead by the original pergola. The garden and distant Arroyo can be seen from the dwelling's second floor.

This residence is listed on the National Register of Historic Places and has been featured in such publications as *The American Architect*[93] and the 1915 *Tournament of Roses Brochure*.[94] In 1913, it was Marston's largest and most expensive residential commission.

It made sense that a man such as Henry Newby would reside in this Pasadena landmark. Given that he and his wife had only one child, their choice of this capacious design was not born of necessity, but desire. Coming to Pasadena in 1887 at the age of nineteen, Newby entered banking as a clerk. By 1900, he had purchased control of a recently consolidated bank and remained its president for the next sixteen years. Upon retirement, Newby joined with D. M. Linnard to acquire several California resort hotels. Newby "was one of the most popular men who ever walked down Colorado Street."[95] "Actively identified with the business and social life and civic progress of Pasadena," he was a member of the Overland and Annandale Clubs, and the Elks and the Masons among others. On top of it all, Newby was a "crack amateur baseball player" and "one of the most enthusiastic golfers" at Annandale.[96]

3.31 Newby plan

Revival Architecture

D URING SYLVANUS MARSTON'S FIRST SEVEN YEARS IN PRACTICE, which coincided with the Arts and Crafts movement, his designs were largely for middle-class patrons who were taken with the notion of plain living then in vogue. But from about 1917 through the 1920s came a widespread thirst for period revival architecture. Residential design now required of architects greater artistry and design fluidity. Houses were built in a profusion of styles, and neighborhoods featured a kaleidoscope of historical images.

Unable or unwilling to adapt, distinguished architects such as Greene and Greene faded from public view. In contrast, Marston hit his stride, even as his clients' demands intensified. These new patrons were wealthy, more cosmopolitan, and well-informed; many had had the experience of building houses else-where. A large number were acutely attentive to style, making choices based on a real or at times an imagined architectural heritage. Marston was adept at meeting these expectations; his ear for appre-hending clients' wishes is especially apparent during these years.

Some critics attribute the public's turn toward revival styles to the influence of the motion pictures whose stage sets featured distant exotic lands,[1] others to America's exposure to European culture con-veyed by Americans who fought abroad during the First World War. Revival architecture flourished because many of the upwardly mobile aspired to mirror European aristocratic tradition, and because Beaux Arts architects such as Marston were steeped in the scholarship of historical styles.

Marston's period revival estates were prominent among those abounding in affluent Southern California during the first third of the twentieth century. No one epoch better exemplifies the mastery of styles which defines Marston as an architect.

Colonial Revival

Francis H. D. Banks

In 1916, Marston & Van Pelt designed a twenty-seven room Georgian mansion in South Pasadena for Mr. and Mrs. Francis H. D. Banks. This style dominated in the English colonies. It is characterized by a formal arrangement of parts and employs a symmetrical composition enriched with robust classical ele-ments. Georgian residential design is typified by a two story, five-bay box, predominantly brick clad with a hipped or gabled roof, and a central door crowned by a pediment. Special features of the Banks residence are arched and pedimented dormer windows, eaves detailed as classical cornices, chimney stacks connected by a parapet, and an elliptical fanlight above the front entry. The portico has freestanding Tuscan columns.

Francis Banks made his fortune in Midwest factories and stockyards and retired to Pasadena in the early part of the twentieth century. There he married Lillian Dobbins, formerly of Philadelphia, whose entrepreneur father was responsible for Philadelphia's great Centennial Exposition of 1876.[2]

The story of how—and where—Francis and Lillian Banks settled in Pasadena is an interesting one. On a winter visit from the East in 1890, Lillian and her mother stayed at the fashionable Raymond Hotel. While relaxing on its veranda, the mother spotted in the distance a lush oak-shaded pasture that was part of the historic Rancho San Pasqual. She decided to purchase twenty-six acres there and eventually developed them into the moneyed neighborhood of Ellerslie Park. She deeded a portion to Lillian and Francis, who commissioned Marston to design a house on that property. They chose a Georgian Colonial style, reminiscent of the eighteenth century architecture of Lillian Dobbins' Philadelphia roots.

4.1 Banks residence (1916)

The Banks house rests on an acre of land at 1210 Chelten Way, a street whose lanes are divided by a solid row of the original oak trees.

This residence of 8,500 square feet includes eight bedrooms, five baths and an open porch with Tuscan columns. The interior reveals a structure built for gracious entertaining. A grand formal entry leads to an authentically replicated Georgian stair hall with hand-carved spiral balusters, leaded-glass windows, and an antique brass chandelier. Upstairs are two spacious master bedrooms, each with a glassed-in "retreat," or sun porch with picturesque exposures.

Throughout the years, the house has been a favorite of Hollywood filmmakers. *Pollyanna*, starring Mary Pickford, was filmed there in the 1920s; in more recent years, Mel Gibson and other well-known actors have been featured in films shot there. The late

4.2 Thomas residence (1923) in Hancock Park

columnist Jack Smith wrote that houses like this "have reminded us that we have an honorable architectural tradition here, despite the notion, so cherished by Eastern journalists, that Los Angeles, including Pasadena, is the capital of kitsch."[3] In fact, this is one of several Marston residences selected to receive the prestigious annual Pasadena Showcase of Design Award by the Pasadena Junior Philharmonic.[4]

Dr. Roy Thomas

Marston & Van Pelt designed another stately Georgian residence, this one for Dr. Roy Thomas. It is located at 523 S. Muirfield Road, in the Hancock Park district of Los Angeles. Built in 1923, it is distinguished from the Banks's design by having four evenly-spaced pilasters across the facade and an elaborate front door entablature crowned with a broken ogee pediment. Keystone lintels accent the windows.

Thomas E. Hicks

A striking and well-proportioned English Colonial Revival residence was designed by Marston in 1913 for Thomas E. Hicks.[1] Located at 255 Madeline Avenue in Pasadena, it was demolished in the 1920s for construction of the Westridge School. A 1917 *Architectural Record* article[6] features this commission and its focal point is the entry porch supported by Tuscan columns with a second story turned-spindle balustrade. Design details include elliptical windows on the second story and an eave cornice with modillions.

This residence had a curious beginning. T. E. Hicks's brother-in-law was James A. Culbertson, scion of a Pennsylvania lumber magnate who had become an established client of the Greene brothers (235 N. Grand Avenue, 1902), as were three of his unmarried sisters (Cordelia, Kate, and Margaret) who also hired the Greenes to design their house (1188 Hillcrest Avenue, 1911). Despite the Culbertson

4.3 Hicks Colonial Revival house (1913) shortly after built; Mrs. Hicks on the left

family's exclusive use of the Greenes, in 1913 these Culbertson relations hired Sylvanus Marston to be their architect, with the building permit listing J. A. Culbertson's name[7] followed by that of T. E. Hicks.[8] Three days after Marston acquired the building permit, James Culbertson wrote a letter addressed to Marston in which he sought his assistance to supervise the painting of Culbertson's Greene and Greene house.

September 11th, 1913.

Dear Sir:

I want the pass pantry of my Pasadena house painted white during my absence this fall and I think the sooner it is done the better. Can I get you to superintend the work and have it done?

I think what you call an egg gloss in the specifications of Mrs. Hicks' house is what I want. If I remember rightly this in not rubbed down with pumice stone but has a smooth gloss surface. I want a good job and a surface that will wash clean. I want the cupboards painted inside and out, in fact every thing wooden except the floor which is covered with linoleum and must be protected and kept free from paint spots. The ceiling also is to be painted. Also the pantry side of the two doors.

I think I am wrong about the sink board. It should not be painted, but the opposite shelf under the cupboards is to be white....

Yours truly,

James Culbertson
(signed)[9]

It seems apparent that James Culbertson had appreciated the specifications Marston prepared for the Hicks house, and thus sought Marston's help concerning the painting of his own residence. Edward R. Bosley, Director of the Gamble House, suspects that Culbertson may first have asked the Greenes to handle the painting job and they refused: painting wood that they had carefully selected for its beauty would have been anathema to them.[10] If true, this anecdote not only highlights the prominence of Marston as an architect in Pasadena during this early period but exemplifies the importance he placed on the wide-ranging wishes of clients.

4.4 Nelson Eddy house (1939) in Brentwood

4.5 Nelson Eddy (left) and Edgar Maybury in a Virginia hotel, reviewing the St. George Tucker house plans which influenced the Eddy house design, circa 1939

Nelson Eddy

As late as 1939, Colonial Revival architecture was the dream of some Californians, especially if they were from the East. Above Sunset Boulevard at 485 Halvern Drive in Brentwood is the residence Marston & Maybury designed that year for the popular actor and baritone, Nelson Eddy.

Sylvanus Marston's son, Keith, and the current owner, actress June Haver (the widow of Fred MacMurray) have both recalled this dwelling's genesis. When Nelson Eddy decided to build a house, he informed Marston & Maybury that he wanted it to look "just like the St. George Tucker house in Williamsburg, Virginia." Eddy was from the East and apparently had seen the house and vowed to build one like it for himself.[11] Tucker, a Revolutionary War hero, was not the original owner of the house, yet because of his reputation his name is associated with the Virginia dwelling. This is one of the finest houses in the Williamsburg historic district.[12] Edgar Maybury traveled to Virginia where he met Eddy in order to review the plans for Nelson Eddy's house.[13]

The Eddy residence is generous and ambling, situated on a very private two-and-a-half acre lot. The treatment of the front facade is spirited, with its gabled porch and door with transom lights and sidelights. Other attractive features include corniced molding with dentil and five-ranked windows that have black louvered shutters with functional iron tie-backs. The interior includes numerous keystone arched doorways, and the carved spindle balusters of the stairway match the spindle work of the fence that surrounds the house.

This foray into entertainment world clientele was short-lived, for by inclination, that was not Marston's metier. Maybury's daughter recalls that Marston & Maybury, along with a handful of other prominent architectural firms, was asked to submit a full set of plans to compete for the commission to design a house for Bing Crosby. Marston declined to enter the competition, having little enthusiasm for bearing the expense of producing complete plans, nor for business dealings with motion picture celebrities.[14] Marston was more comfortable with the businessmen and industrialists who defined Pasadena.

Frances and Helen Hamilton

Pasadena's Prospect Park Historic District is distinguished for the beauty and variety of its period architecture; one Colonial Revival residence designed in the "Adam" style is a conspicuous case in point. Designed in 1924 for elderly sisters Frances and Helen Hamilton,[15] the dwelling sits with great dignity on its sweeping corner lot at 445 Prospect Square, near the District's southern entrance. The Adam style, named after the late-eighteenth century British architect Robert Adam, follows Georgian architecture's strict symmetry, though it has fewer elaborations and is marked by lightness and delicacy. The Adam period reached its zenith in the prosperous New England port cities in the early part of the nineteenth century as a style favored by wealthy merchants.[16]

This two-and-one-half story side-gabled house is distinguished by high-style refinements: an elaborate roof-line balustrade or "widow's walk," paired, double-end brick chimneys, brick side walls, and a front gabled portico. The entry features an elliptical fanlight and is flanked by slender side lights. All windows are double-hung eight-over-eight, have flat lintels and prominent sills, and are flanked by dark green shutters against yellow stucco. Gabled dormer windows in the Palladian style further distinguish this design.

4.6 Hamilton residence (1924) in the Adam style

W. DeWitt Lacey

In 1917, Marston & Van Pelt constructed a French Colonial residence for W. DeWitt Lacey at 1105 Arden Road. The high hipped roof, reminiscent of a pavilion, is the most telling stylistic element. The centered chimney, wide clapboard cladding, and open and flared eaves are also consistent with this idiom. Hip knobs originally finished the roof corners. The lengthy eyebrow at the roof line and the segmental pediment above the front entry have, in contrast, a distinctly English pedigree. The climbing vines on either side of the front entry conceal uncommon trellis work over the first floor windows. This is a novel design even for architecturally sophisticated Pasadena.

Lacey was a well-known Pasadena banker at First Trust and Savings Bank and a member of the Midwick Club. According to his daughter, Marian Lacey Bassett, who grew up in the house, her father knew many local businessmen through his investment work at the bank, though he probably knew Marston from Midwick. She recalls that so great was her father's fondness for the club that when investors threatened to purchase and demolish it, he joined with a group that sought to buy it first. Upon his return home, having lost out on the bid, he was, Bassett recalls, ashen-faced.[17]

4.7 Lacey house (1917) shortly after construction

4.8 Bain house, Palms (1924)

Neoclassical

Ferdinand R. Bain

Throughout his career, Marston's architectural style closely reflected prevailing architectural trends. In 1924, his firm drew plans for an estate for Marston's friend, Ferdinand R. Bain, located in the Palms area of West Los Angeles. The following year the project was featured in both *American Architect*[18] and *Architectural Digest*.[19] The firm returned numerous times for additions–a lattice pavilion, cow barns, and a wind screen–so it must have been an extensive property. The residence was Neoclassical in style, a popular genre in the United States from the turn of the century through the 1950s, fusing elements of the earlier Colonial Revival and Greek Revival traditions.[20] The style is distinguished by full-height porches with classical columns as supports and front facades that are symmetrical and monumental in scale.

The column work—slender and void of elaborate capitals or fluted surfaces—reflected a development that emerged after 1925 across the United States.[21] By incorporating these subtle stylistic changes in this 1924 commission, one can see how alert Marston was to architectural developments.

The Bain design with its corniced porch, side-gabled roof, and squared columns borrows from the Greek Revival period. The front entry stresses the structure's Colonial heritage, with a keystone elliptical fanlight over a corniced front door and an elaborate door surround with elongated sidelights. Urn finials extend upward from either side of the entry entablature.

Bain was an important figure in Marston's practice. As the president of Southern Counties Gas Company, he commissioned Marston to design five of his company's offices located in Ventura, Santa Barbara, Tustin, Orange, and Santa Ana. Marston also drew up plans for the family ranch house in Stockton.

Tudor Revival

Samuel S. Hinds

Marston's firm designed more than a dozen residences in the Tudor style, some reminiscent of large country estates. The most exquisite was the first that Marston built, in 1915, predating revival architecture's popularity in Southern California. Built for Samuel Southey Hinds, the dwelling was featured in

4.9 S. S. Hinds Tudor residence (1915)

4.10 Samuel Southey Hinds in a playful pose on his brick terrace, circa 1920

Architectural Record articles in 1916 and 1922.[22] Hinds was a son of Joseph Hinds, whose Arts and Crafts bungalow was discussed earlier, and the great-grandson of English poet Robert Southey. Quite possibly it was that English past Hinds honored with this stylistic choice.

Built at 880 La Loma Road, the residence is situated across La Loma Bridge, on the Arroyo's San Rafael side. The site occupies more than three acres, appropriate for the 9,000 square foot dwelling. This Tudor design is primarily side-gabled and follows a graceful plan that includes a semi-circular conservatory on the south end and a gabled end porch on the north. The stately front entryway, facing the garden and the Arroyo beyond, has a segmental pediment with a cartouche. Rustic brick and half-timbering with stucco infill, massive fireplaces, and second story overhangs with wooden brackets featuring expressive gargoyles decorate this house.

His was a lavish residence when built, costing $25,000. *Architectural Record* in 1922 highlights the richness of detail:

> The house for Mr. S. S. Hinds is one of the best things done by the firm…the craftsmanship, especially that of the wood work, is deserving of the highest praise. The construction is honest throughout and the half-timber more than mere ornamentation. There are bits of delightful wood-carving, particularly on the corbels, which often take the forms of grotesques.[23]

A 1920 *Architect and Engineer* article features the results of a design competition sponsored by the Southern California Chapter of the AIA. The Hinds residence won in part because, according to the article, "the house and garden seem literally to be growths each of the other and the resultant effect produces that quality of unity and fitness which is the ultimate aim of all good design."[24]

Hinds and Marston were contemporaries and close personal friends.[25] Hinds was born in Brooklyn in 1875. Following his Phillips Academy Andover and Harvard education,[26] he arrived in Pasadena with his family in 1905 and became a distinguished Pasadena attorney with Waldo, Hinds and Lawrence. Friend and fraternity brother Ward Ritchie, a leader of the fine press movement in Los Angeles, jokingly wrote that Hinds's reluctance as a young man to join the legal profession "was tempered with the pleasant amenities of life as lived in California's conserva-

4.11 Whimsical gargoyles decorate the garden elevation of the Hinds residence

tive, socialite Pasadena."[27] Hinds was deeply involved in Pasadena social life as a nine-year director of the Annandale Club and five-year director of the Overland Club.[28] He also was a pivotal figure in the creation of the Pasadena Playhouse, and was one of its accomplished actors.

Hinds spoke the first words on stage during the Playhouse's very first play[29] and acted in some forty-six different productions. When the depression hit in 1929, Hinds said: "I found myself so broke, so absolutely flat, that I was eating at drug store fountains to save the twenty-five cents that a meal in a restaurant would have cost me. And the worst of it was that I owed $50,000 I didn't have and could see no way of getting."[30] He lost his magnificent house.[31]

After a slow start at finding work after 1929, Paramount hired Hinds to speak exactly nineteen words in *If I Had a Million*, starring Gary Cooper and W.C. Fields. There was a touch of irony since Hinds played the part of a millionaire.[32]

Hinds's *New York Times* obituary (1948) referred to him as "dignified, suave and handsome" and as "one of Hollywood's busiest character actors."[33]

There have been only four owners of this estate. The current owner—from a family which first came to Pasadena in 1903 and has remained in the city for six generations—has lived on the estate for more than forty years.

Mark R. Bacon

Marston designed a handsome stucco over brick Tudor residence for a close personal friend, Mark Reeves Bacon. The dwelling, built in 1923 at 60 S. San Rafael Avenue, has fourteen rooms and cost $65,000. The dominant facade element is a forward-facing gable with half-timbering on the second story overhang. Originally the roof was built with dark shingled material intended to resemble a thatched roof. Gothic windows abound and at the rear is a Romanesque round tower with a conical roof. The stacked chimneys have multiple shafts; one curiously bears a fleurs-de-lis.

4.12 Bacon residence (1923) circa 1920s

Mark Bacon was born in Illinois, admitted to the bar there in 1876,[34] and then married Mary B. Ford, daughter of Edward Ford and granddaughter of Captain John Baptiste Ford, who founded the Michigan Alkali Company and is known as the father of the American plate glass industry.[35] Edward Ford inherited the business, and after consolidation it became the Libbey-Owens-Ford Glass Company.[36]

Marston designed for the Bacon family for decades, including a residence at 65 S. San Rafael for son John B. F. Bacon (directly across from father Mark's house) and various improvements for John Bacon's second residence in Montecito. Photographs below depict the neighboring Marston-designed houses of Mark Bacon and William Peters (discussed in chapter five) under construction simultaneously.

4.13 Bacon and neighboring Peters (see chapter five) residence under construction simultaneously on South San Rafael in 1923

Herbert M. Vanzwoll

Marston & Maybury designed an ornate Tudor Revival in 1928 for Herbert M. Vanzwoll at 4230 Chevy Chase Drive in Flintridge. Vanzwoll had immigrated to the United States from Austria, a fact that is relevant in aspects of the dwelling's design. Apparently Vanzwoll brought with him a highly skilled craftsman who was responsible for the exquisite woodwork throughout.

This gated residence rests on one-and-a-half acres and contains 7,000 square feet of living space.Its asymmetrical front facade features a large forward-facing gable with a highly decorated bargeboard borrowed from the Gothic and half-timbering with either plaster or patterned brick infill. The striking slate roof is of recent origin, but closely resembles the original terra cotta roof tiles by Gladding McBean. There are five elaborated chimneys soaring above the roof line—all octagonal brick with cast stone quoins and multiple shafts.

4.14 Bacon residence under construction in 1923.

4.15 Architects' 1928 rendering of Vanzwoll Tudor residence in Flintridge

This is a high-style house. A two-story foyer and majestic stairway with carved oak balusters contribute to the opulent interior. The living room is cross-beamed and partially wood-paneled, has a cast stone fireplace, and contains bay windows with cast stone quoins. Repeated throughout the house is the suppressed Tudor arch over doorways, windows, and fireplace surrounds.

The dining room is refined with its beveled oak paneled walls decorated with oak leaf and grape and vine motifs. The original molded plaster ceiling in unusually fine condition contains floret designs interspersed with heraldic devices, relating possibly to the European origins of the original owner.

Final signs of the residence's splendor at the rear elevation include a four-bay brick window with a parapet and several copper drain spouts decorated with crowns. The well-landscaped backyard, depicted in a 1930 *Architectural Digest* article on this commission,[37] is replete with a rose garden with 120 varieties, a lap pool, guest house, and chapel.

Italian Renaissance

"Orange Grove Boulevard and Grand Avenue, with their tributary streets comprise the fashionable West Side—the Fifth Avenue district of Pasadena and here is congregated more wealth than most towns of the same size can show in their entire population," the local newspaper declared in 1905.[38]

Most of Marston's residences embodying Italian architectural precedents were located on these two streets. The preference of many of his clients for Italian Renaissance architecture is understandable. They were among the richest industrialists and businessmen in the country, coming from the East and Midwest, where architecture embraced the classical tradition for its grandeur and aristocratic bearing. Authoritative but less picturesque than some historical styles, Italian Renaissance Revival usually called for stuccoed or masonry walls, and incorporated classical details such as pedimented windows, elaborated shields or cartouches, pilasters, and monumental paired columns. These embellishments occasionally achieved Beaux Arts grandiosity. Domestic models tended to be a central block with projecting wings, with hipped and tiled roofs and often with raised terraces and a balustrade. There is wide variation in this style's decorative exuberance.

Joseph E. Tilt

The Joseph E. Tilt residence, designed by Marston & Van Pelt in 1920, is in the style of an Italian villa. It has a low-pitched and tiled roof, asymmetrical composition, cast stone balustrade, and loggia. It stands on 2.3 acres and originally cost $134,536.[39] Located at 707 S. Orange Grove Avenue (now 455 Bradford Street), this house of 14,000 square feet contains seventeen rooms and eight bathrooms. Ornamental stonework, wrought-iron, and imported marble and tile proliferate. Entry is through a one-story porte-cochere with an overhead balustrade alongside a spacious loggia whose columns feature composite capitals. A belt course and distinct window treatment differentiate each story, with full-length arched windows on the first and rectangular casements on the second story.

Lavish in a manner more European than American, the interior begins with a palatial sixty-two-foot long hall with alternating black and white marble square tile flooring and a paneled wood ceiling with exaggerated beams and decorative brackets. The living room features lunettes and a marble inlaid Second Empire fireplace. Yet, local references were not forgotten: Batchelder tiles pave the breakfast room floor.

In 1926, the Marston firm made an important addition to the house—a sizable library and marquee. Described as "cavernous,"[40] the room has a vaulted ceiling and arched doorways with stained-glass transoms. Such elaborations were arguably appropriate for a man such as Tilt who reputedly had one of the most impressive private libraries in the West.[41]

In its day this residence did not go unnoticed by leading design authorities. A 1922 *Architectural Record* article on Marston & Van Pelt notes that this residence's location and bearing give it "a certain repose and impressiveness."[42]

That the inordinately wealthy lived in the Orange Grove district is not to imply that they all were the idle rich who never saw a day's work. Tilt founded the Joseph Tilt Shoe Company in Chicago and was said to be "a man who knew shoes from last to uppers," and a genius for organization and "sales acumen."[43] The residence was selected as the 1984 Pasadena Showcase House.

Thomas W. Warner

The Tilt commission, facilitated by a generous budget, proved a useful prelude for Marston, Van Pelt & Maybury as it prepared in 1924 to design a $175,000[44] tile-roofed Mediterranean mansion for Toledo automobile magnate Thomas W. Warner.[45] This was the most expensive residential commission of Marston's career. Located at 891 S. Orange Grove Avenue and demolished in

4.16 Italian villa designed in 1920 for Joseph E. Tilt

4.17 Courtyard garden of Tilt residence

RESIDENCE for MR. T.W. WARNER
MARSTON·VAN PELT & MAYBURY ARCHITECTS
PASADENA CALIFORNIA   DECEMBER 1924

4.18 Architects' 1924 rendering of Warner residence - Marston's most expensive residential commission

1974, it was a stucco over brick, twenty room dwelling which "promis[es] to be one of the finest residences ever built in Pasadena."[46]

The dwelling would have "all the general characteristics of the picturesque Italian type of architecture," including "a tower with a western outlook enhancing the style."[47] The structure's main block had a tiled roof and wide, exposed eaves with decorative bracketing. First floor windows were grouped and arched, and those on the second floor were grouped rectangular casements with louvered shutters. There was extensive exterior use of cast stone for the trim, the base course, and the wide balustrade.

According to a 1927 issue of *Architectural Digest*, the interior featured walnut paneling and trim, massive cast stone fireplaces, custom woven Oriental rugs, a wrought-iron balustrade on the stairway, pocket screens, and earthenware Gladding McBean tiles decorated with Italian opaque glaze.[48]

Warner was "largely a self-made man, and built his career on a technical education obtained through a correspondence school."[49] Deeply involved in the early automobile industry, he founded Borg-Warner and other well-known companies. Marston and Warner both belonged to the Annandale Country Club and were 32nd degree Masons.

Seman L. Bird

"The last of the Magnificent Mansions" is how the residence built in 1920 for Seman L. Bird, located at 251 S. Orange Grove Avenue, was described when it was on the market in 1981.[50] Like so many of its neighboring properties, this house has been demolished. Conceived in the Italian Renaissance genre, the design received great fanfare: "A residence which gives promise of being one of the show places of the city...for S. L. Bird, a winter visitor....Plans have been prepared by Marston & Van Pelt...who have designed many of the most distinctive homes in Pasadena and other Southern California cities."[51]

The living room, measuring 36 by 25 feet, was intended for use as a ballroom with its beamed ceilings,

4.19 Bird residence (1920) on Millionaire's Row

huge marble fireplace and three hand-carved window seats. French doors opened to a large covered terrace. Italian hand-carved moldings and paneled ceilings were used throughout the house. The sweeping staircase was exquisite: there were stained glass windows at the landing and a motorized chair which operated on the stair handrail. The dwelling's 5,826 square feet included a billiard room, kitchen, butler's pantry, breakfast room, library (with fountain), dining room, four tiled bathrooms, and six bedrooms, including a master bedroom with one of three fireplaces.

Beyond the ground floor terrace were extensive gardens, entered through a 9 by 30 foot pergola with art stone columns supporting sawn rafters.[52] At the end of the pergola were the fish pond, fountains, and swimming pool.

Bird was a highly successful Detroit businessman and merchandising executive who founded his own clothing company, S. L. Bird & Sons. After spending many winters in Pasadena, he and his wife retired there, and he became involved in the cultural and business life of the city.[53]

William K. Jewett

The William K. Jewett residence, the most formal and monumental of these mansions, was designed by Marston & Van Pelt in 1915. Located at 1201 Arden Road (later 1145), the construction cost of this vibrant Palladian villa was a then-lavish $50,000. Total square footage is 20,000, which includes seventeen rooms, nine of them bedrooms; a billiard room; two pantries; a studio; and three servants' rooms.

This is a seven-ranked, two-and-a-half-storied dwelling with projecting eaves and terra cotta peaked ridge tiles. The grace and openness of a loggia with paired columns at either end soften the overall robust exterior appearance. There are two gabled dormers, each decorated with a plaster cartouche. The shape of the one-story entry porch echoes that of a Palladian window and incorporates Beaux Arts-inspired paired columns, with a balustraded balcony above. Quoins are used at the structure's corners, and to enhance the French doors on the second story.

The monumental dignity of the residence was further reinforced by paired double interior chimneys and a striking solarium in the back, as captured in a 1924 edition of *Architectural Digest*.[54]

One commentator in a 1922 *Architectural Record* article summarizes the design this way: "As an *ensemble* it is hardly open to criticism, the simplicity of the mass and the satisfactory relation of its elements atoning for a few bits of perhaps questionable detail."[55] (The terra cotta window frames were thought too heavy.)

The original estate was nine acres and, as with his more opulent residences, Marston's commission also included the design of gardens, seven, on this property. Although the estate was subdivided in

4.20 Palladian villa designed in 1915 for William K. Jewett

4.21 Jewett residence, side elevation on this nine acre estate

1948, the dwelling still lies on a generous plot of more than two-and-a-half acres and it retains its majestic iron-gated entry and deep set-back. When the property was subdivided the "garage" which housed a ball-room and "five chauffeur's apartments," was demolished.

The vast gardens required the attention of six full-time gardeners. The landscape plan was praised by regional house and garden writers who were mesmerized by the beauty of the pergolas, fountains, and mass of Cecile Brunner roses.[56]

The Jewett estate has long been a magnet for the motion picture industry. The house was seen in the Marx Brothers' *Duck Soup*, Paramount Pictures' *Terms of Endearment*, and numerous television programs. It is best known for the long-running TV series *Dynasty*. Viewers of that show may recall the spat between Joan Collins and Linda Evans which ended with everyone in the reflecting pool; this was filmed on the Jewett estate.[57] As far back as 1927, regional literature named this estate as a favorite Hollywood site.[58] It was the Pasadena Showcase House for 1998.

William K. Jewett was born in Youngstown, Ohio, where he got a promising start as an heir to a rail-road fortune.[59] He made a second fortune himself as president and general manager of the London Mines Company in Colorado, one of that state's largest gold mines.[60] He was a well-known philanthropist, sportsman, and musician.[61]

Josephine Everett

The Italian villa that Marston & Maybury designed at 171 S. Grand Avenue exemplifies the firm's attentiveness to client style of living. Built in 1928, the residence was intended to accommodate Mrs. H. A. Everett's extensive art collection and provide a suitable setting for the notable musical performances she sponsored.

The exterior handsomely incorporates the essential elements of its Italian origins: a low-pitched and tiled roof, broadly projecting eaves supported by carved wooden brackets, a piazza complete with a fountain and balustrade, and an upstairs loggia.

The plain stucco wall facade, sparsely enhanced by squared windows with wide, flat stone frames, is a striking contrast to the heavily embellished front entry set in a Classical motif. The entrance is an ornamental cast stone arch with an overhead broken triangular pediment holding a plaster cartouche. Ionic pilasters flank the entry.

The 9,000 square foot interior is grand in scale. The owner contemplated large gatherings, and the architects responded accordingly: the ballroom/music room is 40 by 30 feet, a formal living room is 32 by 23 feet, the kitchen is 30 by 16 feet, and the foyer is 18 by 17 feet. Mrs. Everett's art collection exceeded ninety pieces, and at times it was made available for public viewing.[62] The art work was strictly American. Upon her death in 1937, the local paper explained her viewpoint: "America must carve its own future as a world cultural center." Mrs. Everett hosted debut performances for many outstanding musicians.[63]

Mrs. Everett was a generous contributor to Pasadena's Civic Orchestra and Community Playhouse, and the Hollywood Bowl claims her as one of its founders. According to the local newspaper:

"[The Bowl] was in the dream stage when Mrs. Everett's check for a substantial sum, followed by another check from her sister, made the realization of a dream possible."[64]

4.22 Everett residence (1928)

THIS CULTURED CLIENT AND HER SISTER FROM NEW YORK (who visited Pasadena frequently) were "very after your dad," Keith Marston was told by a member of an old Pasadena family. Apparently the women admired Marston's handsome and dignified bearing. This is further evidence of Marston's personal rapport with clients, and in particular with his not inconsiderable female clientele.[65]

The Everetts were from Cleveland, Ohio. Henry A. Everett "became one of the leading electric street railway experts in the country and directed the transforming of the Toronto and Montreal systems from horse cars to trolleys. He became the president of the Northern Ohio Traction and Light Company."[66] The Everetts began vacationing in Pasadena in 1912; Henry Everett died in 1917.[67]

As with the neighboring Vista del Arroyo Hotel, the Everett house was occupied by the federal government during World War II.[68] From 1972 to the present the Shakespeare Club has used this structure as its headquarters. The club was founded in 1888 as Pasadena's first women's club organized for the purpose of "social, cultural and intellectual improvement," a mission it still fulfills today. Membership rolls hit their peak in 1926, with 1400 members,[69] including Marston's sister, Annie Palmer Marston.

William D. Petersen

An elegant flat-roofed example of Italian Renaissance design is located in the Altadena foothills. Built by Marston for William D. Petersen in 1912 and located at 1095 Rubio Street, "the house will be

4.23 Petersen residence (1912) in the Altadena foothills

one of the finest and most beautiful even in beautiful Altadena," claimed the *Pasadena Star News* on May 10, 1912. "It will be in the Italian renaissance style, with plastered exterior over hollow tile or metal lath, artificial stone exterior finish, reinforced concrete foundation and porches.[70] This residence, consisting of fourteen rooms plus three servant's quarters and a two-story garage, cost $27,845.[71] The design incorporates two tile loggias and two sleeping porches.

4.24 Bidwell house (1913)

The front facade features a one-story entry porch with alternating columns and square supports, and a balustraded balcony overhead. The second story balcony's centered doorway is pedimented. The principal rooms are finished in mahogany and quarter-sawn oak, and there is ornamental iron work and wood carving throughout the house.[72] A raised terrace with a stone balustrade underscores the dignity of this well-proportioned dwelling.

From the start, the one acre gated Petersen property was called Villa Sarah, so proclaimed on an iron plate fixed to the imposing plaster gateposts. *Architect and Engineer* featured this residence in 1913 and 1914.[73] The 1913 article urges higher standards for domestic architecture in words that could apply to the Petersen residence:[74]

> The design of a proper dwelling is based upon structural integrity and honesty of expression; on right proportion and simplicity of outline....It pretends to be nothing but what it is, and it therefore contains no qualities which detract from simple dignity.

The Country House

> Congenial groups of architects are actually gaining courage to think and build for themselves, as though they were Twentieth century Americans and not Fifteenth century Italians or Englishmen of the reign of Anne. They are making the past their servant instead of their master. Their work is seldom of purely English, French or Italian derivation but more often of mixed origin adapted to its modern purposes. —*Architectural Record*, 1926

IF THE NATION AT LARGE WAS DRAWN to country living in the first two decades of the twentieth century with country house construction having tripled since 1918, Pasadena's appetite was all the greater, given its balmy climate, taste for the outdoor sporting life, and enviable amount of open space. Marston's country house designs were many and, while they can be classified stylistically, they also reflect the eclecticism suggested by this *Architectural Record* article.

English Country

H. E. Bidwell

Marston designed an English country house for H. E. Bidwell in 1913 at 1047 S. Madison Avenue, which was featured in the 1922 *Tournament of Roses Brochure*[75] and in a 1917 *Architectural Record* article entitled "The American Country House," written by A. D. F. Hamlin who was the former chairman of Columbia University's architecture department.[76] This charming English stucco dwelling, asymmetrical and side-gabled, is distinguished by three eyebrows at the roof line and small-paned windows grouped in threes and fours.

The interior has extensive built-ins including the "quaint, high-backed English bench that settles for an ingle nook"[77] in the spacious 18 by 29-foot living room. That central room also has crown molding and white cedar paneling "which feels like soft brown satin to the touch." A handsome mahogany and white cedar stairway is visible upon entry. The fireplace is a central feature, made of "soft brown tiling...which is a Batchelder masterpiece." Carved into the fireplace mantle is "Entre es su Casa, Amigo," an intriguing phrase in this distinctly English dwelling.

The backyard is decorated with extensive trellis work which was originally intended as a triumphal entry for two of Bidwell's friends who were coming to California to honeymoon in 1914, but which now creates the flavor of living outdoors.

Bidwell, originally from Pittsburgh, was in business with his father, a co-founder of the Bidwell-DuPont Powder Company.[78] The son visited Pasadena for many winters and finally decided in 1913 to build his own California house while still maintaining a Pittsburgh residence. Active in Pasadena life, he was a founder of the Playhouse and a generous supporter of the Civic Orchestra.[79] A descendant of California's famous '49er, General John Bidwell, his love for California perhaps came easily. General Bidwell, originally from New York, wrote *Echoes of the Past About California*[80] in which he chronicled his California explorations, especially during the Gold Rush. H. E. Bidwell himself traveled extensively throughout California for twenty-five years, to such an extent that "friends say he 'knew every foot of the state.'"[81]

John N. Van Patten

Exemplifying Marston & Van Pelt's eclectic country house design is the essentially English manor residence designed for John N. Van Patten in 1922, located at 282 S. San Rafael Avenue. This structure is at

4.25 Van Patten residence (1922); rear elevation detail

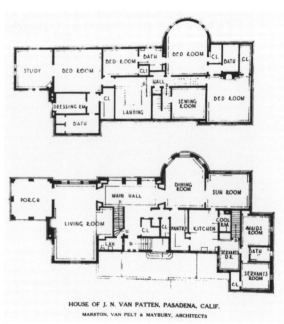

4.26 Van Patten property viewed from across the Arroyo Seco, circa 1925

HOUSE OF J. N. VAN PATTEN, PASADENA, CALIF.
MARSTON, VAN PELT & MAYBURY, ARCHITECTS

4.27 Van Patten plans

once Postmedieval English, Gothic, and Tudor. It is two and one-half storied, has a sparsely decorated facade, and stands on the crest of a hill–an imposing sight. Its wall cladding today shows only concrete, though that originally was covered with a stucco layer. Characteristic of English design, all gables are steeply pitched with minimal eave overhang. The recessed front entry is decorated with a compound pointed arch bearing acanthus crockets, the facade's singular nod to the Gothic.

The back of the house features greater architectural detail: a row of Gothic arches defines the first floor, while five cross gables animate the roof line. Occasional half-timbering is the strongest suggestion of Tudor influence. A Romanesque round tower creates a medieval castle feeling.

The Van Patten residence was featured in *American Architect* in 1925,[82] complete with plans and photographs of the interior and the rear elevation. The house has fifteen rooms including five bedrooms.

Douglas Morris

If the Van Patten residence displays Marston's virtuoso ability to successfully integrate architectural styles, the 1928 Douglas Morris house at 725 Holladay Road is a further demonstration, but on a more diminutive scale. This design draws its influence primarily from the manor houses found throughout the English countryside, with elements of the Tudor, English medieval, and the folk cottage. The walls are stucco clad, punctuated by grouped, leaded casement windows with small lights and a handsome bay window on the south side. The steep roof, with its low and varied eave line, is dominated by an impressive double-shafted chimney. The ox-eye window far above the front entry reveals the generous thickness of the walls.

4.28 Morris house (1928)

The wrought-iron front door is the original and is flanked by a cast stone door surround which includes quoins and, surprisingly, fleurs-de-lis ornamentation–a subtle, late Gothic accent. The dwelling's interior is rich, with a beamed ceiling entryway and glass-paned pocket doors between living and dining rooms. The living room's cathedral ceiling features beams and trusses. In that room is located one of the structure's three cast concrete fireplaces, complete with a grape and acanthus leaf cartouche.

4.29 Haldeman house (1928) in Beverly Hills, shortly after construction

Harry F. Haldeman

Marston designed estates in Beverly Hills and Bel Air. One such dwelling, at 711 North Maple Drive in Beverly Hills, was built in 1928 for Harry F. Haldeman. It is an elegant English manor house. A 1929 *Architectural Record* article discusses the house, focusing on the sharply-pitched roof and massive brick-clad end chimney.[83] The journal notes that the brick wall cladding is "painted with white paint to resemble white-wash, some of the paint being rubbed down to the brick to give effect of a weathered wall."[84] Simons Brick Company made the bricks and promoted this treatment by featuring the residence in its advertisements.[85] This commission was also featured in a 1928 edition of *Pacific Coast Architect*.[86]

Harry F. Haldeman, who inherited his father's prosperous plumbing, heating, and air conditioning supply business and supported Republican causes,[87] was sandwiched between two generations of Haldemans who came under the scrutiny of the criminal courts. His son was H. R. Haldeman, who served eighteen months in prison for his role in Watergate,[88] and his father was Harry M. Haldeman (the "M" stands for Marston coincidentally), who lead the conservative Better America Foundation, and became engulfed in the C. C. Julian oil and stock scandal of the Roaring Twenties.

Julian conned the public into purchasing shares in Santa Fe Springs wells through heavily propagandized "oil rush" advertising. Harry M. Haldeman, along with other influential public figures such as Louis B. Mayer and Cecil B. deMille,[89] invested in the venture. Within only a few months, Haldeman got back his initial investment of $20,000, plus $15,000 in profit and quit the scheme before disaster struck: the stock was watered and for most investors, their holdings became worthless. Haldeman was indicted three times but never convicted. According to Jules Tygiel, who wrote *The Great Los Angeles Swindle: Oil, Stocks, and Scandal During the Roaring Twenties*,[90] Haldeman fell from public favor because many believed that his participation in this shady business deal to make a quick buck ran counter to his life-long "law and order" proclamations.[91]

4.30 Paddock residence (1932)

Charles Paddock

After the Haldeman project, Marston & Maybury designed another acclaimed white-washed brick residence, this one in Pasadena. The elegant English house was built in 1932 at 985 Linda Vista Avenue for Charlie Paddock, famed USC and Olympic sprinter (1924, 1928), who was depicted in the film *Chariots of Fire*. Renowned for legs "which he lunges out piston-like,"[92] Paddock dominated the local sports pages throughout the late teens and early 1920s. He grew up in Pasadena, attending its public schools, and later settled there. He married the daughter of the publisher of the *Pasadena Star News* and the *Long Beach Press-Telegram* and became a sports writer and executive at both papers.[93]

The property includes nearly four acres of land that accommodate a tennis court and hill in back, and a huge front lawn for Paddock's dog kennels and putting green. One of the few residential sites in the neighborhood with its original acreage, it has maintained the aura of the commodious English country dwelling.

A compilation of regional designs published in 1939 by the Southern California Chapter of the American Institute of Architecture[94] features the Paddock residence,

4.31 Ogden country house (1930)

and states that "a feeling of balance and repose pervades this house despite the unsymmetrical character of the main block. The entrance has an interesting treatment of rusticated brick work."[95] The understated facade is accented by a cut-out vent on the second story, brick dentil, and an elaborate wrought-iron lantern over the front entry. A 1933 issue of *Architectural Record* features the residence and its plans.[96]

Harold V. Ogden

In 1930, after Van Pelt had left the firm, Marston & Maybury received a Southern California Chapter AIA honor award for the design of an English country house for former Chicago businessman Harold V. Ogden. The structure is located at 1125 Armada Drive, adjacent to the Arroyo and part of the Prospect Park Historic District. The architectural prize, awarded by leading architects across the nation, sought to honor designs that were "in harmony with the history, climate and habits of this locality."[97] The local trade press noted that "the jury was disposed to discourage the award of steep-roofed houses and was unanimous in the opinion that California has a distinct tradition and type to adhere to."[98]

The Ogden house has English cottage features which had become vogue in the region: rough stucco walls with heavy timber trim, small casement windows with barn shutters, and low eaves with minimal overhang. The dwelling's courtyard layout was deemed particularly well-adapted to Southern California living, and the house was featured in *Architectural Digest*,[99] *California Arts & Architecture*,[100] and *House Beautiful*.[101] The latter journal describes the design as "carefully planned to take advantage of the view at the rear."[102]

French Country

The Chateau style—embracing massive masonry construction, steeply-pitched roofs, arched dormers, or commanding towers—became more universally popular in the U.S. by Americans who served in France during World War I.[103] As will be discussed in greater detail in the final chapter, Sylvanus Marston spent nine months in France during the Great War as a civilian aide attached to the French Army. The experience deepened his appreciation for and interest in French design.

William R. Staats

The grand French manor house designed by Marston, Van Pelt & Maybury in 1924 for William R. Staats at 293 S. Grand Avenue is so striking that, for the architecturally attuned of Pasadena, it needs no introduction. Legend has it that it received such acclaim when built that a Wallace Neff client instructed Neff to visit the Staats house and build him a house just like it. Neff did build a French classical residence at 1771 Virginia Road in 1929, called the Richter House, and the design is very similar to that of the Staats house.[104]

The three-storied Staats residence has a steep, hipped and variegated slate roof over brick walls which still wear a coat of decades-old antiqued beige paint. The front facade is characteristically slightly asymmetrical. Entry is through a vestibule protected by an exquisite wrought-iron grille beyond which is a walnut paneled front door, carved by Pasadena furniture designer George S. Hunt.[105] Over the entry is a bracketed cornice with a small elliptical window in the second story.

The seventeen room, 10,000 square foot dwelling has five bedrooms, six wood-burning fireplaces, ten bathrooms and a maid's quarters of two rooms and a bath, plus a back stairway.[106] There is also an elevator. The original cost was $72,500, and the house was built on approximately one acre. Upon entrance, one is greeted by a 60-foot long formal entry hall, which has a vaulted ceiling, original wrought-iron sconces, and alternating black diamond and white square marble flooring along with a black marble base board.

4.32 French manor house designed in 1924 for William R. Staats

Custom-made bronze French doors with eighteen lights and steel encasements are used throughout the ground floor. The formal living room is a palatial space, virtually unchanged since the 1920s. It is entirely wood-paneled, with seven sets of French doors that open onto the terraced backyard which overlooks the Arroyo. At the end of the main hallway is a romantic two-story and staired tower. The stairway balustrade is composed of decorative wrought-iron in a pattern that is repeated throughout the house.

The terraced gardens, which spill down into the Arroyo and contribute to the dwelling's regal nature, were also the work of Marston's firm. The gardens presently include a sizable lawn and a pond on the lowest terrace, and on the terrace above that a swimming pool and formal rose garden surrounded by a stone balustrade, and the original trellised potting shed.

4.33 Formal entry hall of Staats house

4.34 Erkenbrecher house (1931)

4.35 Harwood residence (1926)

As a pioneering real estate developer and banker, William R. Staats was a major force in early Pasadena business and civic life. Staats's influence extended beyond Pasadena to Los Angeles, where he opened an office in 1905. Born in Connecticut, Staats came by steamship to California in search of better health, arriving in Pasadena in 1886 at the age of nineteen.[107] Pasadena was undergoing a historic land boom, and Staats's first job was in real estate. He soon founded his own real estate business, and he also became a broker in stocks and bonds as well as a mortgage loan banker.[108] An intimate friend of Henry E. Huntington, Staats joined forces with him in 1905 to become the exclusive agent for subdividing and developing for sale the Oak Knoll district of Pasadena.

According to one account: "Three of the greatest business institutions in Southern California might be said to have been born in the Staats offices. They are the Southern California Edison company, the Union Oil company, and the banking organization which has become the Pacific Southwest Trust and Savings bank."[109]

Staats was a celebrated Pasadena gentleman,[110] involved in cultural, educational, and recreational aspects of Pasadena life. He and others successfully persuaded the Carnegie Scientific Foundation to select Mt. Wilson as the location for its observatory. Upon his death in 1928, Staats left a $25,000 gift to Caltech."[111] Staats and Marston had many club memberships in common, including the Annandale and Midwick Clubs. Before this residential commission, Staats had Marston design his bank and office building on East Colorado Boulevard, which has since been demolished.

Attribution of the Staats's design, considered one of the firm's best, has been contested by representatives of Marston and Van Pelt. Architects who acted as references for Van Pelt in his 1963 AIA Fellows nomination believed that he had sole design responsibility for the Staats house.[112] Others are convinced that the design emanated from Marston,[113] given his friendship with Staats and his extensive travels in France.[114]

Reference to the commission's plans is not helpful, showing only the initials of the draftsmen responsible for the drawings, "BTS" and "HHB," persons whose full names are unknown to the author. As draftsmen they were most likely not responsible for the overall concept. Given the evidence, it is possible that both Marston and Van Pelt made significant contributions to this design.

4.36 French chateau residence designed in 1929 for J. J. McCarthy

Joseph B. Erkenbrecher

In 1931, Marston & Maybury designed a residence at 750 Chester Avenue in San Marino for Joseph B. Erkenbrecher. Its asymmetrical front facade was featured in an article in the local newspaper which stated: "The style of the house is French provincial and some exceptionally fine effects have been achieved in the plans."[115] Those effects included stucco-over-brick cladding, keystone arch windows with dripstone molding that break the eave line, a steep roof with hipped dormers, and two massive chimneys. While not as large as the Staats house, the Erkenbrecher residence is stately in form, proportion, and composition.

Edward C. Harwood

In 1926, Marston's firm designed the Edward C. Harwood residence, with Chateau style roof ornaments and decorative iron balconets, located at 905 Orlando Road in San Marino. It was featured in *Architectural Digest* in 1929.[116]

J. J. McCarthy – Herbert E. Bell

Marston & Maybury secured commissions in 1929 to design two French chateau style residences located on the west side of the Arroyo and above what is now the 134 Freeway. These residences, one at 1199 Chateau Road for J. J. McCarthy, the other at 243 N. San Rafael Avenue for Herbert E. Bell, are adjacent to each other and are similar in style.

The Allure of the Small House

If Marston differed from some of his distinguished peers in designing houses for developers who built affordable housing for the middle classes, he certainly approached the task with the same high standards and workmanship that marked his larger commissions. The compromises were in scale, amenities, ornamentation, but not in architectural character or integrity. Much later, in 1932, an "Architects Small

House Bureau" was organized in Pasadena[117] to stress the importance of improving small house architecture. Important local architects such as Myron Hunt, Reginald D. Johnson, Robert H. Ainsworth, and Roland E. Coate participated.[118] Marston's early willingness to design for a wide variety of clients brought architectural character to Pasadena's modest neighborhoods.

An area centered on three streets—San Pasqual, San Marino, and Berkeley—is a case in point. Between 1926 and 1928, Marston was commissioned by the early Pasadena developers Thomas and Stephenson to design eight houses in close proximity to each other. They were featured in *House Beautiful* (1930),[119] and *Architectural Digest* (1927).[120] Three of these are considered below.

4.37 Sturgis cottage (1926)

4.38 Diggs house (1926)

4.39 Crawford house (1926)

Catherine G. Sturgis

The Catherine G. Sturgis dwelling, at 2015 San Pasqual Street, designed in 1926, is today owned by a practicing architect whose training and inclination have aided him in restoring the original purity of the house and gardens. The two-story stucco-clad residence derives its charm from its large and steeply pitched roof and overscaled stucco end chimney. Vertical plank wooden window and front door shutters further the English country flavor. Typical of Marston and to great effect, the arch of the front windows is continued on doorways and hallways in the interior. The house has eleven rooms including a maid's room and a breakfast room, plus a ground level porch. For a small house built on speculation, all of its attributes seem generous and individualized: the charming exterior architectural character; the high quality interior wood work on the crown moldings and door and window frames; the occasional decorative curved plaster walls; and the award-winning professional landscaping.

The original garden was laid out by Florence Yoch and Lucile Council, well-known Southern California landscape architects. Plans and photographs appear in *Landscaping the American Dream,*[121] *California Gardens,*[122] and on the cover of *California Arts & Architecture* in 1931.[123] The Sturgis garden is described as an "informal formal garden," that includes a round central pool which is a "mirror setting for Verocchio's famous fountain figure, a reproduction which is itself almost an antique."[124] Further descriptions are enticing: "There are some piquant color combinations, where wooden gates, painted a blue-green, pierce a whitewashed brick wall, and are overhung by clusters of oranges, or by pink roses and purple wisteria."[125] Yoch's designs created the illusion of "natural vigor and whimsy."[126] She worked with many of the best architects and on some of Southern California's finest residences.

Diggs House

The other two residences are just a few doors from each other on South San Marino Avenue. House number 395, whose first occupant was a Mr. Diggs, is distinctive for its two overlapping and forward-facing, steeply-pitched gables. The thick and roughly surfaced stucco, painted white, is so satisfying that little further decoration is needed, save the hearty wooden lintels painted brown over the front door and windows. The stucco flanking the front door curves inward, and underscores the material's appealing texture. This house of 2,000 square feet has four bedrooms and three baths. It came on the market in 1934, and the local newspaper stated that it was "considered unique in the field of English cottage architecture."[127] More recently it has been listed for sale for more than half a million dollars.[128]

E. S. Crawford

The other house, at 423 S. San Marino Avenue, whose first occupant was E. S. Crawford, is stylistically similar to 395 except that there is more activity at the roof line with two overlapping side-facing gables, a stout central chimney, and a gabled dormer.

George S. Hunt

Marston, Van Pelt & Maybury designed a residence that we may not consider small by today's standards, yet in 1925 it was "awarded first prize for the best small house built within the past three years" west of the Mississippi.[129] *House Beautiful* gave the award to Marston's firm based on the following competition criteria: "Excellence of design, adaptability to lot and surroundings and convenience or economy of plan."[130] Planned in 1924 for George S. Hunt, Pasadena's premiere custom furniture maker, the residence could not have been better situated. It was built at 1280 Park View (later 1415) in Linda Vista, and thus had a breath-taking view of the mountains and the Arroyo Seco.

This design received widespread acclaim. The Southern California Chapter of the AIA awarded Marston's firm a Certificate of Honor for the structure at its April 1924 meeting. The jury consisted of John Galen Howard and Ernest Coxhead of San Francisco and William E. Parsons of Chicago.[131] A local newspaper, reporting on the award, commented that the house "is typical of the rural style of home to

4.40 Award-winning Hunt house as it looked in 1924

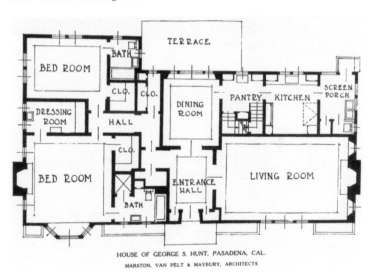

HOUSE OF GEORGE S. HUNT, PASADENA, CAL.
MARSTON, VAN PELT & MAYBURY, ARCHITECTS

4.41 Hunt house plan

be met with in the British Isles, particularly Scotland and Ireland, occupying a situation near a roadside, the style portrays that of the average peasant cottage…in those countries and forms one of the most distinctive buildings to be seen in this locality."[132]

The news story about the AIA award reveals Edgar W. Maybury's insight into the collaboration involved in the project: "The owner cooperated with the architects in every respect. Mr. Hunt had many fine ideas on home building and his views frankly expressed to us always found us able to coordinate our plans to his ideas. The result has proved happy to all concerned."[133]

A 1925 *House and Garden* article[134] highlights the residence's distinctive features: "The low lines of this house…coupled with the spirited pitch of the roof, give it an unusual distinction which is increased by the surface texture of the white walls. The latter are built of stone, but are so completely parged with cement that there is only a suggestion of the actual material underneath."[135] The article adds: "The chimneys, parged and whitewashed to match the walls and set with terra cotta chimney pots, are nicely placed at each end of the house to serve as accents in the architectural scheme and add to the clean-cut appearance of the building."[136]

House Beautiful in 1925 stresses the artistry of the front door: "The deep reveal of the entrance doorway produces a deep shadow which in turn gives the necessary accent to this important feature of the house; a simple plaster molding and the deep, rich coloring of the paneled door make the only attempt at decoration."[137] The living room, with its "pervading air of quiet simplicity," features a "coved ceiling with simply carved beams," as well as built-in bookcases flanking the fireplace.[138]

American Architect features the house in a 1925 article, and includes several photographs and the plan. It refers to the result as: "A good example of a house that fits its site. The general treatment is one of fine artistic perception and a clever use of materials."[139] In the same year *Architectural Digest* also features this commission.[140]

The plans showed nine rooms of living space on the ground floor, and upstairs a large work room for Hunt as well as a maid's room and bath.[141] As with other Marston residences, this one "has obviously been designed for very definite individual requirements."[142]

The New Regional
Idiom

Spanish Colonial Revival architecture gave rise to Marston's best-known designs. The style emerged during the revival period of the 1920s and 1930s, but its genesis had roots in early California, which may well account for its continuing hold on the region's imagination.

As early as 1909, AIA President Cass Gilbert implored California's architects to develop a style that embodied the region's history: "Forget the Georgian architecture of New England; forget the Elizabethan style of England; forget it and adopt the precedent of the Southern Latin countries like Spain and Italy."[1] California design had started by imitating the European, but by the 1920s it had reached a place where it was venturing to be original, local, and native.

Perhaps not coincidentally, the Spanish domestic architecture that flourished in Southern California had much the same appeal as the bungalow architecture that preceded it: informality, livability, and harmony with the outdoors. An architectural critic has noted that the Arts and Crafts consciousness was "usurped by the Spanish Colonial Churrigueresque introduced at the Pan-Pacific Exposition of 1915 in San Diego."[2]

That year-long Exposition was held to celebrate the opening of the Panama Canal, whose closest American port would be San Diego. Acclaimed New York architect Bertram G. Goodhue was selected to supervise design. He first considered the California missions as models, but concluded that the style was too limited. The Spanish Colonial, on the other hand, he decided, not only had historical significance in California, but also had "the gaiety and color so necessary for a fair."[3]

Goodhue's decision was well-informed, for he had traveled extensively through Mexico in 1900 preparing plans for Sylvester Baxter's landmark book, *Spanish-Colonial Architecture in Mexico*,[4] which examined Mexico's architecture during Spanish rule from the sixteenth through the eighteenth centuries. It was an era of great wealth and a time of "a very high level of architectural skill."[5] Outstanding, if isolated, examples of the style already existed in California, but clearly the Fair's impact "was to make this mode popular and fashionable," wrote architectural historian David Gebhard.[6] "By the end of the 1920s the Spanish Colonial Revival had become *the* architecture of Southern California,"[7] although some critics scoffed that the style evoked an "imagined" Hispanic past.[8]

The popularity of Spanish Colonial was understandable. California's Beaux Arts-trained architects sought a more sophisticated medium than the "rudimentary work of the Padres"[9] and also "quite naturally sought their source in specific historical examples, not in loose adaptations" of the Mission style.[10] Southern California in the second decade of the twentieth century experienced rising affluence. It needed a "vigorous architecture that best expressed the energy, hopefulness, and surging cultural confidence of the young city of Los Angeles."[11] The rustic, earthy, and even primitive bungalow and Mission styles, so popular a few years earlier, "could not fulfill the desire felt by client and architect for increased opulence and display."[12]

Hollywood celebrities' growing preference for the Spanish also began to transform the public's architectural taste.[13] Rudolph Valentino's "Falcon Lair" estate above Benedict Canyon "was a tile-roofed extravagance with Italian gardens."[14] Harold Lloyd's majestic forty-room, twenty-six-bath Spanish Colonial Revival estate made headlines with its 800-foot lake for canoeing, golf course, and tennis and handball courts.[15] Other movie greats such as Charlie Chaplin and Bette Davis[16] built Spanish mansions that gave them the "airs of instant grandees."[17]

Spanish architecture enjoyed stylistic adaptability. Essential ingredients were thick stucco walls and terra-cotta roof tiles, but beyond that a wide variety of treatments defined the genre. The roof line might be side-gabled, shed, or hipped. Door and window treatments might be focal points for Italian or Moorish decoration, and especially Churrigueresque detailing: the concentration of intricate, often ecclesiastical, ornamenture amidst great expanses of blank wall. Named for the seventeenth century Spanish architect Jose de Churriguera, the style was richly in evidence at the San Diego Exposition. For all these reasons, *Architectural Record* maintained in 1926 that:

> In developing an architecture of stucco...architects...have combine[d] with their native
> sources such borrowed elements as the Moorish, the Mexican, the Andalusian, and the
> South Italian. They may speak Spanish, but it is with an accent all their own.[18]

That assessment describes Marston's approach to Spanish design.

Marston's Imprint

The July 1922 issue of *Architectural Record* declares that Marston and Van Pelt houses in the Spanish tradition "merit first place...[and] are especially pleasing."[19] Marston's firm solidified its reputation for excellence during the 1920s in large part because of its Spanish Revival designs. The firm's approximately fifty residential commissions in this new idiom were fewer in number than its bungalow designs, but the projects generally were more magnificent and luxurious, and constituted the firm's most lucrative work. With offices by then both in Pasadena and Los Angeles and more than a decade of achievement behind it, the firm attracted a greater number of clients who could afford extravagance: large residences on greater acreage with more opulent interiors.

The Spanish Colonial idiom was a favorite of Van Pelt's, who lectured[20] and wrote[21] on Spanish architecture. His book, *Old Architecture Of Southern Mexico*,[22] recounts his trips deep into southern Mexico, "a land to tempt the brush of an artist and to intoxicate an architect in search of the picturesque."[23]

Marston, Van Pelt & Maybury's prominence as Spanish Colonial revivalists in California has been acknowledged in the professional literature, including Marcus Whiffen's survey of American architecture.[24] In addition, the firm's distinction in Mediterranean design in general–the architecture of Spain, Italy, and Mexico–is evident by the considerable attention devoted to it in architect and professor Rexford Newcomb's 1928 hallmark review, *Mediterranean Domestic Architecture in the United States*,[25] a book Alson Clark has called "a magnum opus of the California regional school."[26] Six of Marston's residences are featured. The firm responded to the desires of clients who sought a connection with a romantic Spanish past, "close to the dreams that had brought them to Los Angeles:" a warm and beautiful environment, freedom from convention, semi-rural open space, and leisure.[27]

Marston's impact upon the development of Mediterranean design in Southern California was formidable. His firm was the first to employ color on exterior stucco walls, which "found instant favor in the popular mind, with the result that now many of the small and audacious houses which spring up almost over night about Los Angeles, display a veritable riot of the palette."[28] The firm excelled at developing a residential plan that exploited the advantages of site, such as the A. L. Garford house on the crest of a hill in Oak Knoll,[29] and the W. T. Jefferson residence on the edge of the Arroyo Seco.[30] It was said that the firm's

Spanish and Italian residences exhibited "generous diversity and originality....There is no conscious striving after effect, notwithstanding the fact that their work has a decidedly picturesque quality."[31]

Marston, Van Pelt & Maybury was one of a small group of fine architectural firms in Southern California that achieved renown for Spanish-derived design. George Washington Smith, the acclaimed Santa Barbara architect, specialized in that genre, and is known for his grand, white-washed Spanish manor houses. Wallace Neff, who opened his office in Pasadena in 1922[32] more than a decade after Marston, produced admirable French country, Italian, and other designs,[33] but concentrated on Spanish themes. Mediterranean precedent also predominated in the work of Johnson, Kaufman & Coate.[34] Marston, Van Pelt & Maybury achieved comparable prominence in the Mediterranean genre, while also mastering an array of other architectural styles. Such wide-ranging expertise demonstrates the firm's adroitness.

As with Marston's other design motifs, there is marked variation within its Spanish interpretations. Smith and Neff designs were often recognized by signature effects. This is less true with Marston's designs, which begin from a starting point of attentiveness to mass, form, outline, and proportion, but become widely divergent in style and overall composition.

Marston's clients who sought a Mediterranean design relished adaptation to site, individualized the plan, and often decorated the interiors in an exceedingly rich manner. Architect Charles Moore spoke for them when he described the Spanish revival style as "a Southland archetype...the image of our transformed semi-desert, climatically Mediterranean landscape, the architecture of our innocence. It is our primal idea of home."[35]

Mediterranean Eclectic

Arthur Lovett Garford

A challenge for American architects captivated by Spanish Colonial Revival was to adapt the style, which originated in the great cathedrals and public monuments of Spain and Mexico and was later featured on massive buildings at the San Diego Exposition, to the proper scale and proportion for domestic enjoyment.

That is why Marston & Van Pelt's first Spanish residence, designed for Arthur Lovett Garford in 1916 just following the Exposition, at 1126 Hillcrest Avenue in Oak Knoll, is especially noteworthy. A 1919 *Architectural Record* article devoted to this commission observes

5.1 Garford residence (1916) in San Marino; Marston's first Spanish Colonial Revival domestic design

that its "exterior presents an adapted use of Spanish baroque detail, sparingly used...."[36] A comparison of this house with the Marston-designed 1910 Mission School in New Mexico—flat-roofed, roughly textured, with projecting *vigas*—underscores the sea-change in Spanish architecture caused by the Exposition.

Geography influenced the Garford design. Oak Knoll was still largely undeveloped and quite hilly. The two-acre site that Garford and his architects selected was chosen because "its terraced slopes afford [a] wonderful chance for a cascade garden on the hillside and because the view can never be cut off since the canyon runs at its rear."[37] These factors introduced irregularity into the plan, and the architects responded with a design where "its main axis gives a clear vista over the tree tops to the sunny country beyond them, and the terraces, porches, and belvedere all concentrate on this aspect."[38]

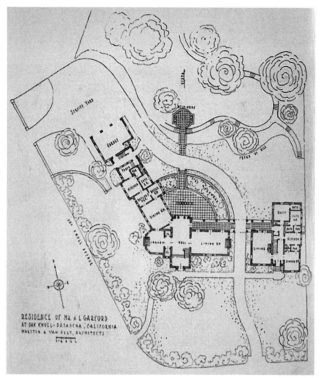

5.2 Garford plan

Garford posed a challenge to the architects: he sought two separate residences that would somehow be connected. Marston and Van Pelt responded with a principle structure at 1126 Hillcrest Avenue which was built simultaneously with its neighbor, at 1132 Hillcrest, and the two residences were joined through a second story galleria which no longer exists. This artifice enabled separate living but close proximity to Garford's daughter Louise and her family.

The principle residence incorporates some of the decorative techniques introduced at the Exposition: variegated "Granada" roof tile and broad expanses of plain wall surfaces punctuated by occasional cast stone decoration. A Renaissance-inspired front entry is the focal point. The second story balcony overhead is crowned with a broken pediment.

The residence's 7,000 square feet consist of five bedrooms, a breakfast room, study, library, kitchen, living and dining rooms, a butler's pantry, and servants' quarters. There is extensive use of fine woods throughout the house, including mahogany, African walnut, and oak, utilized in flooring, exposed beam ceilings, moldings, and cabinetry. At the back of the house, French doors open to a large covered terrace and garden and reveal the San Gabriel mountains beyond.

The house at 1132 complements its neighbor, though it is more modestly scaled. Its recessed front entry with a gated portal crowned with low-relief ornamentation is remarkably similar to the Exposition's California Quadrangle north garden entrance, with its Churrigueresque volutes and shouldered arch.

Not only was this commission one of the first in the Oak Knoll district to utilize the Spanish Colonial themes, it was "one of the first 'pink' houses built in this style in Pasadena," reports *California Southland*.[39] A Southern California architectural jury charged with designating "notable examples of architecture" within a twenty-mile radius of the Los Angeles City Hall found the Garford house "of such high order as to merit special honorable mention."[40] The local newspaper reported it as "one of the Southland's prettiest" houses, "one of the large and very handsome places in the state" that is "famous as a show place."[41]

The Garford commission, concludes *Architectural Record*, "presents a truly gratifying success in the treatment of its plan, which is clever and unusual...and, in addition, furnishes a most individual interpretation of a house for two families, united yet each distinct."[42]

Upon Garford's purchase of the property the local newspaper proclaimed: "Pasadena has added a third national manufacturer of automobiles in its notable and growing list of permanent residents."[43] Garford was an inventor and industrialist from Elyria, Ohio. He founded his own automobile parts business, the Garford Company,[44] which by 1905 was the sole supplier of chassis parts to Studebaker.[45] Studebaker's 1910 models with a Garford chassis were even advertised as "Studebaker-Garfords" in factory sales literature.[46] The "Garford Six" was a luxurious six-cylinder touring car priced at $2,750 in 1912; it was advertised as a real treasure in *The Saturday Evening Post* in 1912 and 1913.[47]

Garford had great political enthusiasms. He was a life-long Republican in the progressive tradition of Theodore Roosevelt, whom he knew personally.[48] Nominated for Governor of Ohio by the Progressive Republicans at their 1912 party convention, Garford lost on the fourth ballot.[49] He and his wife then left for a tour of Europe, but were called home by cables from Teddy Roosevelt, seeking Garford's help in his race for President under the banner of the newly-formed Bull Moose party.[50] The two men campaigned together throughout Ohio in 1912, often using a Garford touring car.[51]

F. A. Hardy

Marston, Van Pelt & Maybury designed "Villa Verde" located at 800 S. San Rafael Avenue for F. A. Hardy, retired chairman of B. F. Goodrich. Primarily Spanish Colonial Revival in style, this 1927 design was influenced by Italian themes: a low roof line, overhanging eaves with exposed decorative brackets, and repeating arcades with Ionic columns.

Listed on the National Register of Historic Places, this twenty-two-room residence appears all the more impressive given its position atop a knoll overlooking the Arroyo Seco. The facade "bears the dignified simplicity found in high quality Mediterranean style structures."[52] The front entry features an arched and raised paneled double front door with a rusticated cast stone surround.

5.3 Hardy hillside residence (1927)

A striking contrast is achieved between the light stucco cladding of the exterior walls and the darker-toned cast stone columns, trim, coping, and beltcourse. The dwelling's several porticos with their vaulted ceilings and overhead patios connect the interior with the outdoors. Interior detail is underscored in a 1929 *Architectural Digest* article.[53]

The property retains its approximately two acres, and still features Hardy's formal gardens which draw upon Europe for inspiration with the ordered composition, the fountains, and the long avenues of trees. The current owner's summary of the gardens begins: "Picturesque and asymmetrical, it is a landscape that might have been designed by a contemporary of Keats or Shelley."[54] The front and side yards include acacia and orchid trees, a Montezuma cypress reportedly 100 years old, fruit trees, and conifers.[55]

Hardy was born in Seaforth, England, in 1851, of American parents from Boston who were traveling abroad on business. He attended Boston Latin School until his father experienced business failure.[56] Hardy took a series of jobs in optical goods before he eventually founded his own firm in Chicago, where apparently every eye doctor had an F. A. Hardy eye chart on his office wall.[57] But Hardy's most successful business enterprise came after his brother Walter approached him in 1900 for financial backing for his ailing Ohio rubber company. Hardy obliged, became part-owner, and, after its merger with Goodrich Rubber, ran the company that became B. F. Goodrich.[58]

The current owner is an investment adviser and author, and former actor who had roles in such celebrated films as *Mrs. Miniver* with Greer Garson, whom he married.

5.4 Pratt residence (1924)

R. A. Pratt

In 1924, Marston designed a distinctive residence for Coca-Cola's West Coast director, R. A. Pratt, located on five acres at 363 Sturtevant Drive in the Sierra Madre hills.[59] With this commission, Marston again broke away from the purely Spanish revival and produced an even more overtly Italian design, with such elements as a deep shadowed second floor loggia supported by plaster corbels and wooden Tuscan columns. The facade's focal point is the arched front entry with a floral patterned archivolt. Above is a cast stone low-relief medallion. Other decorative features of the facade include paired arched windows and small windows with iron grilles. The rear elevation best dis-

5.5 Pratt residence, east elevation

5.6 "Villa Alegre" designed in 1920 for John Henry Meyer

5.7 Meyer estate: rear elevation and extensive gardens
(Paul G. Thiene, consulting landscape architect)

plays this 8,000 square foot residence. It features grouped and arched French doors that open out to a raised terrace, and well-spaced and elaborated windows—some crowned with a triangular pediment, and others supported by bracketed shelves.

John Henry Meyer

Marston & Van Pelt's use of pink stucco on the Garford commission was only the beginning of the firm's exploration of exterior color. The array of colors it chose to augment the Mediterranean residence designed in 1920 for John Henry Meyer brought the firm further national attention. *Architectural Record's* July 1922 issue describes the Meyer house at 1021 Oak Grove Avenue in San Marino as:

> One of the first to employ color to any extent upon the exterior walls.... They may be described as pink, though through variation it becomes at times an ochre and Naples yellow... found instant favor in the popular mind.... As one of the first to revive external color, Messrs. Marston and Van Pelt are to be complimented. Color was the one thing most needed in the architecture of Southern California.[60]

"Villa Alegre," as the residence is called, is 8,300 square feet and had a contract price of about $125,000.[61] This design incorporates many of the classic elements of the Mediterranean style. The plain surfaces of the massive facade are relieved by the concentration of Plateresque ornamentation. Such decorative motifs originated a century before Churrigueresque; they are said to resemble the fine work of Spanish silversmiths. A 1922 issue of *California Southland* refers to the house as "a beautiful example of the Spanish-California style," and emphasizes its "imposing entrance."[62] An *Architectural Record* issue of the same year elaborates on this feature: "Attention is justly drawn to the entrance by virtue of its being the one spot of ornamentation, in itself a study of elimination in favor of conscious refinement."[63]

The rear elevation, seen in articles in the 1922 *Architectural Record*[64] and a 1925 *California Life*[65] is even more alluring. The garden entry, on the same axis as the front entry, is a spectacular ensemble; it includes a plaster surround incorporating a scalloped door head flanked by engaged columns. Windows with bracketed tops draw inspiration from the Italianate style. Paul G. Thiene was the consulting landscape architect, and his plan appears in the *Architectural Record* article.[66]

The interior is quite grand. The entry hallway is resplendent with its exposed beamed ceiling showing cross beams with scrolled bracket supports, a black and white marble floor, and a marble stairway with a black marble Corinthian column at its foot as a post support. The primary spaces for living and entertaining feature high ceilings and hardwood or marble floors. The seven bedrooms "are richly finished,"[67] some with barrel ceilings and French doors, and all are designed to have a view of the backyard garden and pool. Arched door and window openings abound, many with scalloped heads and all with a deep reveals. The commission is featured in Rexford Newcomb's 1928 *Mediterranean Domestic Architecture in the United States*,[68] and in a 1923 *Western Architect* article exploring California's developing architecture.[69] In 1998 the house was listed for sale for more than three million dollars.[70]

Meyer was born in Germany and emigrated to the U.S. in 1882; at the age of 16, he moved to California.[71] He became a substantial landowner in Orange County, raising primarily oranges and walnuts.[72] Marston had a number of commissions in the Orange County vicinity starting in 1917. Meyer likely met Marston there and later contacted him when he bought land in San Marino and needed an architect.

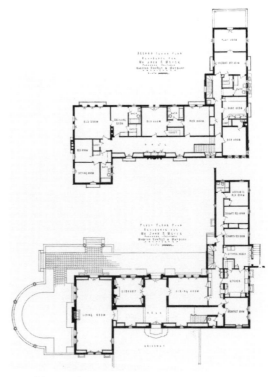

5.8 Meyer plans

Hannah Nevin Shaw

Hannah Nevin Shaw and her husband Major Roy A. Shaw selected Marston in 1924 to design their house, located at 335 Wigmore Drive adjacent to South Orange Grove. The residence resembles the block configuration of the Meyer residence but is executed on a smaller scale which gives the design its intimate and friendly character. A central focus is the front entry with its Renaissance-inspired cast stone surround with an ornamental entablature overhead. A corner balcony is supported by decorative wooden brackets and a cast stone pilaster.

Roy Shaw, a St. Louis, Missouri native, served in the Army during World War I. His career in business primarily was spent at Union Carbide Sales Company, a firm to which he was elected vice-president and director in 1914 at the age of thirty-one.[73]

5.9 Shaw residence (1924)

He moved permanently to Pasadena in 1920, and became active in the Annandale Golf Club and the Valley Hunt Club; he was a member of the Pasadena Presbyterian Church.[74]

W. T. Jefferson

"Elsewhere, buildings may arise from unconsidered surroundings, but not in California. Ramps, terraces, balustrades, and fountains are integral parts of its gay, sylvan existence."[75] This statement, appearing in a 1922 *House Beautiful* article exploring California's burgeoning Spanish architecture, applies aptly to the residence Marston & Van Pelt designed for W. T. Jefferson at 35 N. Grand Avenue in Pasadena. Now demolished, it was constructed in 1921 on the edge of the Arroyo Seco, in a manner which sought

5.10 W. T. Jefferson residence (1921)

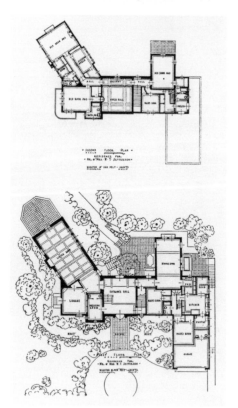

5.11 W. T. Jefferson plans

the most intimate connection with the outdoors. A moat with a foot bridge over it stood at the front entrance. At the rear were terraces, balconies, and sleeping porches designed to maximize views of the Arroyo. A 1922 *Architectural Record* article entitled "Some Recent Works of Marston & Van Pelt" describes the stunning setting:

> The premises lie along a shady and somewhat narrow street about which still lingers much of the old [Spanish] tradition....To the rear...the land falls away rather abruptly in a series of natural terraces which are overgrown with a dense tropical verdure, while below it widens out into an extensive and wooded valley. The setting is incomparable even in this land of extraordinary beauty.[76]

The Jefferson residence was an imposing side-gabled and red-tiled dwelling with a strikingly plain front facade, punctuated with asymmetrical and varied small window openings. The heavily texturized stucco and the front entrance's restrained, classical detailing and richly carved and paneled wooden door evoked the architecture of the sixteenth century Spanish countryside.

Architectural Record's article devotes considerable attention to the Jefferson design and declares that it "marks a high point in the work of the firm and, as an example of style, is one of the best arguments in favor of Spanish adaptation in Southern California."[77] "The ordonnance of the plan was determined by the irregularities of the land, giving an arrangement both interesting and ingenious in its workings."[78] It notes the importance of the full-height entrance hall that sets off the living room. A 1922 *California Southland* article describes the effect: "The view up the canyon through a great window in the baronial living room is a joy which few houses possess."[79]

The only known published interior illustrations are in *Architectural Record*, and in Newcomb's *Mediterranean Domestic Architecture in the United States*.[80] They show handsome tile floors, heavy wood-paneled doors, arched doorways, abundant wrought-iron sconces, balconies, grille work, paneled ceilings, massive projecting cast stone fireplace mantels, and barrel ceilings, as well as dark-stained, finely carved Spanish furniture. *Architectural Record* says of this interior: "The architectural and decorative treatment is handled throughout in a subdued way, in keeping with...the canvases of old Spanish masters."[81]

Picturesque Pasadena,[82] the *Pasadena Star News*,[83] and *Western Architect*[84] also concentrated on this particular commission. Judging from the widespread and detailed attention, it seems accurate to say that this Spanish residence was considered one of Marston's most important. The *Architectural Record* article describes its significance: "As a whole, the [Jefferson] house is a distinct contribution to the architecture of Southern California and to the residential work of this country."[85]

According to the *Pasadena City Directory*,[86] Jefferson and his wife lived at this location until 1934. In 1933 he started working in real estate at 16 S. Oakland Avenue in the Singer Building. In 1935, the Jefferson house was vacant and the owners are listed as living in an apartment at 80 N. Euclid.[87] After 1938 there is no residential or business listing. The couple likely lost their fortune in the Great Depression and had passed away by 1938.

5.12 James Scripps Booth residence and art studio (1922)

James Scripps Booth

In the early 1920s, the Arroyo Seco was home to artists and their studios. Acclaimed California painter Alson S. Clark and his wife Medora lived on the east bank. In 1923 Mrs. Clark told of the neighborhood's allure in a *California Southland* article:

> The Arroyo Seco...seems to have been preserved for painters. They have begun to cling to its precipitous banks, and to spread out with a feeling of hopeful serenity. They perch on its edge....They arrive, they see, they want to stay, they buy and begin to build.[88]

Mrs. Clark then noted that the studio Marston built for James Scripps Booth on the west bank was surrounded by "a mass of native chaparral and the open Arroyo bed gives a sense of space and freedom."[89]

James Scripps Booth commissioned Marston & Van Pelt in 1922 to design a Spanish house and studio. Booth, originally from Detroit and Grosse Pointe,[90] began his career as an automobile designer, creating the Scripps Booth car in 1913. Booth studied art in Europe[91] and in 1919 began living part of the year in Pasadena,[92] devoting himself to painting and sculpture.

Booth's father, George, was the publisher of the *Detroit News* for forty years.[93] In 1887, he had married Ellen Warren Scripps, daughter of James E. Scripps, the founder of the paper, and at the suggestion of Mr. Scripps, sold his prospering iron foundry business to enter journalism.[94] In 1904, he and his wife bought a 225-acre estate in Bloomfield Hills and named it Cranbrook, after his ancestral home in Cranbrook, England.[95] In the 1920s, he found-

5.13 Side elevation of Booth residence

ed on his estate the now flourishing Cranbrook School and, in 1942, the Cranbrook Academy of Art.[96]

The original address for Booth's studio was at 1771 Linda Vista Avenue; the site extended from Linda Vista Avenue to the Arroyo's edge. The property has since been subdivided, with new development on all sides. The address now is 1660 Charles Street.

The Booth design is distinct from Marston's other Spanish residential plans in its departure from the imposing central block configuration and in its incorporation of Andalusian influences. This composition and scale, and the prominence of natural timber beams, lend an intimacy to the design in spite of the dwelling's 6,000 square feet of space.

Originally the residence was approached from Linda Vista by way of a long drive that led to a circular motor court with a fountain (now a swimming pool). The front entrance is distinguished by a wood-paneled door and a thick lintel beam. To its left is a ground floor loggia; its square stucco columns, heavy beams, and arresting iron window grilles strongly signal Andalusian influence. To the right of the entry is a heavy-timbered, cantilevered balcony which received special attention in a 1923 *Architect and Engineer* article announcing that Marston & Van Pelt had won an award for this commission.[97] Such detail "is a relic of Indian or Arabian ideals which was continued by the Moors. No Spanish home is complete without its balconies and window grilles."[98]

A *Pacific Coast Architect* article[99] depicts Booth's studio, with its below-grade elevation, formidable corner fireplace, barrel ceiling, and thick stucco walls that ensure quiet. It is truly an artist's lair.

5.14 Entry gates to the Booth estate. Originally the property extended from Linda Vista Avenue to the Arroyo's edge

This commission gained considerable critical attention. A 1923 issue of *Architectural Record* cites this residence among others to show that "American country house architecture has a flavor of its own...and [is] distinct from any other."[100] *Western Architect*[101] includes the dwelling in a survey of California's changing architecture, and it also is highlighted in Newcomb's *Mediterranean Domestic Architecture in the United States* with several illustrations and the plans.[102]

The Booth residence also has received contemporary attention. In 1983, Robert Judson Clark cited it in his analysis of Southern California architectural development. Out of the large number of Spanish-styled houses in the region, Clark chose the Booth design as emblematic of the Spanish Colonial Revival style favored in the Los Angeles area, distinguishing it from Irving Gill's stark "bald surfaces," yet finding it "comparatively conservative" in contrast to the "more operatic" styles Smith and Neff produced for some of their "extremely lavish" commissions.[103]

Ellis Bishop

The Ellis Bishop Spanish Colonial Revival residence in Rancho Santa Fe, designed in 1928, merits considerable attention. It was Marston's second most expensive residential commission, and it was designed for a particularly impressive site. It also illustrates the firm's residential work beyond San Gabriel Valley. Its second owner leased the estate to the U.S. Navy during World War II for use as a convalescent hospital. That patriotic involvement was a factor in the structure's inclusion on the National Register of Historic Places.[104]

Rancho Santa Fe is located about one hundred miles south of Los Angeles and thirty miles above San Diego. The name first stood for the development company, a subsidiary of the Santa Fe Railway. An ambitious subdivision project began in 1922, and from the start there was a conscious attempt to build a Spanish-styled community and to keep it exclusive. It was to be a "highly restricted community...with assured income."[105] Not surprisingly, in time, quite a colony of Pasadena people built or bought country houses there.[106]

"Atop a knoll, with both sea and mountains in view [the Bishop home] is rich with the atmosphere of early California days." So states a 1941 issue of *Arts & Decoration*[107] in describing the Bishop residence. The dwelling is located on the development's highest point, at 4802 El Arco Iris Avenue. The initial estimated cost was $107,000 in October 1928, when Marston submitted early drawings to the Rancho Santa Fe art jury for approval.[108] The Bishop estate, on seventy-three acres, was constructed between October 1928 and March 1930[109] and included stables, gate lodge, tennis court, swimming pool, gardens and green house, a storage building and pump house. The contract price grew to $137, 243.[110]

The plans included a house of 9,000 square feet with twenty rooms, plus a private chapel.[111] While not the first house to be built in Rancho Santa Fe, it was among the earliest and grandest.[112] Although a local publication praises it as "quite the most imposing home yet built at Rancho Santa Fe," it notes that it is "without attempt at staginess or pretentiousness."[113] Its splendor partly relates to its prominent mountain top location which, according to *California Arts & Architecture*, provides a view of "oak-trimmed canyons full of orchards that open down to breezes from Pacific waters."[114] The local publication quotes the "designing architect," believed to be Marston, as stating:

> There will be a warmth and hospitality in the exterior effect to stamp it unmistakably
> as a gentleman's home rather than as a peasant's. It will…possesses many more elements
> of true Spanish architecture than the deep reveals and mass effects which are too often
> considered sufficient to mark a home as Spanish.[115]

IN 1933, THE RESIDENCE WAS HONORED by the San Diego Chapter of the AIA as representing "exceptional architectural merit."[116] The Bishop commission would be one of a group of four residences upon which the AIA based its decision to elevate Sylvanus Marston to Fellow in 1942.[117]

The Bishop house is a U-shaped stucco dwelling with a "Cuban Junipero roof of tile."[118] The roof is primarily side-gabled and low-pitched with attractive multi-level roof lines. There are also eight chimneys composed of decorative tile, stucco, or cobblestone, some of which are capped with small tile roofs. The garage, which accommodates eight cars, has a shed roof with two dormer windows. Stucco and tile decorative vents punctuate the exterior walls and add to the Spanish ambiance.

The house was originally approached from a circular drive at its south elevation. High stucco walls bracket the delicate tracery of the wrought-iron entry gate. Beyond the gate is a formal garden that leads

5.15 Bishop estate in Rancho Santa Fe as depicted in an architects' rendering drawn in 1928

to a 50 by 65 foot interior courtyard paved with flagstone and cobblestone,[119] with a centered sunken fountain. Arcades "define nobly the sides of the spacious patio."[120] Hand-carved Spanish benches and paneled doors with classical embellishments adorn the courtyard.

The living room, which *California Arts & Architecture* describes as being "of lordly proportions,"[121] is distinctive with its wood-paneled high ceiling, textured plaster walls, and Spanish fireplace "paneled in mellowed oak" that rises nearly to the ceiling.[122] In the living room stands a "richly carved oak refectory table,"[123] an heirloom left by Ellis Bishop.

5.16 Courtyard view of Bishop residence, circa 1930

Past the living room's oversized north-facing window lie a large terrace, then lawn with a balustade along the perimeter, which provide an expansive view of Rancho Santa Fe's hills beyond. The estate's partially subterranean chapel built for Bishop, who was a retired Episcopal priest, is now used as a wine cellar–still offering "spiritual sustenance."[124]

Ellis Bishop, the original owner, was born and educated in New England. For twenty years he served as an Episcopal priest, with his final assignment as rector of St. Stephen's Church in Boston.[125]

Bishop came to Pasadena with his wife and family in 1914 for health reasons.[126] In 1919, he established himself in real estate[127] with his own business, Ellis Bishop & Co., focusing on "high-grade" properties.[128] He became a substantial land owner in Pasadena.[129] By 1926, he was Pasadena's exclusive sales representative for the Santa Fe Land Improvement Co., and a few years later became Vice President of the Rancho Santa Fe Corporation.[130] For perspective on how lavish the Bishop house (costing $137,243) was, an advertisement in a 1926 *California Southland* article mentions that "24 houses were already built in Rancho Santa Fe, some of them at a cost of from 20 to 40 thousand dollars."[131]

5.17 Rendering of north elevation of Bishop residence as it appeared during World War II when it was converted into a U.S. Naval Hospital

When Bishop died in 1933, one obituary explained the source of his great wealth and the timing of the commission with Marston: "The former eastern clergyman was prominent in Pasadena real estate and business circles ...In 1928 he inherited a large sum of money from a New York relative."[132] Bishop was a member of Marston's favorite association, the Overland Club.

John Burnham, the second owner, lived in the house from 1936 until the early 1960s, and the place became known locally as the Burnham house.[133] Burnham was from Pasadena, a client of Marston's, and a friend of Bishop's and honorary pallbearer at his funeral.[134] At the turn of the century, he founded John Burnham & Company of Chicago, the nationally prominent investment banking firm.[135] He was the son of Daniel Burnham, the Chicago architect who designed many buildings for the World's Columbian Exposition of 1893.[136]

It was John Burnham who, from January 1943 through November 1946,[137] urged the Navy to operate the estate as an annex of the U.S. Naval Hospital, using it for forty-five ambulatory Naval officers wounded in the war.[138] The estate was a sailor's heaven. There was a 9-hole pitch-and-putt golf course, shuffleboard courts, a tennis court, stables for riding, and a large swimming pool.

The current owner is Marianne McDonald, a Classics Professor at U. C. San Diego, and the daughter of E. F. McDonald, Jr., who began as an electrician in New York and ended up in Chicago as founder and chairman of the Zenith Radio Corporation.[139]

E. S. Skillen

The E. S. Skillen residence, built in 1925 at 1905 Lombardy in Pasadena, is notable for its exuberant Churrigueresque entrance decoration, similar to the transept window detail of Goodhue's California Building at the San Diego Exposition. The Skillen design incorporates lions, urns, acanthus leaves, and scallop shells, among other elements. Such Churrigueresque vigor reminds one of the story told of architect Henry Hobson Richardson when he observed Spanish architect Churriguera's facade of the Santiago Cathedral. Apparently Richardson remarked:

5.18 Churrigueresque entry, Skillen residence (1925)

"This is not the sort of thing to do, but if you want to do that sort of thing that is just the way to do it."[140] Wood window grilles and other wooden posts and beams provide further decorative detail.

The design is significant in Marston's repertoire because its interior displays the often flamboyant Moorish influences prevalent in the high-style Spanish residences of the 1920s. Such architectural influences favored the contrast of unadorned walls with lavishly decorated doorways and other openings.[141] Crossing the threshold of the Skillen house, one stands in a double-height entry hall where the enclosed stairway, rising to the second floor, can be seen through a Moorish window opening. Throughout the ground floor there are arched doorways with rope moldings and elaborated cast stone frames. The house has an interior courtyard framed on two sides by an arcade incorporating molded corbels supported by engaged Corinthian columns.

Monterey Colonial

The Monterey Colonial style was favored by those who thought that "romantically designed Mediterranean houses necessitated too great a break with the background and traditions familiar to most Americans."[142] Starting in about 1925, architects seeking respite from the exuberant Churrigueresque became interested in this little known early residential architecture that was native to California, circa 1815 to 1855.[143]

Helen D. Chandler

A particularly attractive Monterey Colonial residence, depicted in a 1932 publication *Altadena: The Community of the Deodars*,[144] was referred to as a residence that "reflected unpretentious dignity." It was designed by Marston & Maybury in September of 1929 for Helen D. Chandler at 2424 (now 2124) Midlothian Drive in Altadena. The original drawings show that this 6,400 square foot house was built to the family's unique needs: one room was designated as "Mother's Bedroom," implying that Helen Chandler's mother lived there; another room facing the mountains on the second floor was called "Studio," strategically located for its northern light where, according to the current owner, Mrs. Chandler kept her easel for painting.[145] A daughter and son each had their own room.

Mrs. Chandler was the widow of I. D. Chandler before she moved to the residence in 1930.[146] The Chandler family lived on Midlothian for a very short time, because by 1934 they had relocated to a modest house on the border of San Marino and Alhambra.[147] Immediately before their move, Mrs. Chandler ran an advertisement in the local newspaper that announced "AUCTION! Antique Arts — Exhibition Today — Sale Tomorrow."[148] Apparently she sold her own furniture and belongings that consisted of "over one thousand priceless antiques."[149] It is likely that Mrs. Chandler lost her savings in the Great Depression and had to cede her newly-built home and possessions.

5.19 Chandler Monterey Colonial residence (1929) shortly after built

5.20 Mrs. Francis E. Stevens residence (1927)

The front elevation demonstrates the classic traits of the Monterey style: a side-gabled and low-pitched roof with a second story covered balcony supported by wood posts; double-hung eight-over-eight windows with workable shutters and occasional plaster grilles for decoration. Moreover, in this residential example, the gracious entrance includes woodwork reminiscent of that made by the Colonial craftsmen of New England: a wood carved fan above the door, molded trim, transom lights, and shutters.

The interior is defined by simplicity and spaciousness, with hardwood floors, a striking beamed ceiling in the living room, and deep reveals at window openings. The house is built on a modest slope, allowing for a two-level ground floor. The building permit describes the house as a "part basement residence."[150] The entry opens into the below-grade dining and living rooms, but one must climb three wide tile steps to enter the rest of the ground floor rooms as well as the backyard. The extensive grounds were a gardener's paradise and home to a pony and to chicken coops.

The third owners were David and Nina Bushnell, creators of the Bushnell Company, once the nation's largest seller of quality sport optics.[151]

Mrs. Francis E. Stevens

Marston & Maybury built another Monterey style residence, for Mrs. Frances E. Stevens, at 807 Las Palmas Road. Built in 1927, this house is depicted in *Mediterranean to Modern: Residential Architecture in Southern California*.[152] Since demolished for construction of the 210 Freeway, this house was notable for its "use of strong horizontal lines,"[153] its then-rural setting "among the orange trees, olives, palms and native oak"[154] and its "pergola of logs [that] screens the cobblestone retaining wall."[155] A 1929 issue of *Architectural Digest* also contains a photograph of the structure, and notes that leaded and stained glass were used, as well as roof tiles by Gladding, McBean.[156]

Mediterranean Eclectic

Wiley W. Stephens

Marston, Van Pelt & Maybury won the contract in 1925 to design an unusual Mediterranean residence for Wiley W. Stephens at 484 S. San Rafael Avenue.[157] The signature design feature of the front elevation is a full-width corbel table between the first and second levels that provides a strong horizontal line. The dwelling lies on the western edge of the Arroyo on a lot with a frontage of 160 feet and a depth of 320 feet.

The architects exploited the sensational site: the Arroyo elevation features a first floor loggia connecting the dining and living rooms and two second floor porches that open off sizable bedrooms. The plan focuses on the outward view, but it also provides a centralized interior courtyard that is 24 by 32 feet and which has its own small pool. This cloistered area outdoors provides cool, shadowy depths and succeeds at seeming to bring the garden within the house itself. As one writer noted of the virtues of California's Spanish lifestyle: "The glories of a generous nature were woven into the domestic fabric...like a thread of gold."[158]

The interior of this residence includes wood-paneled ceilings, a loggia supported by Corinthian columns, and imposing fireplaces. These features and the structure's plans are seen in a 1926 article in *Architectural Record*[159] that point out the "fresh and unique conceptions" of the plan.[160]

W. W. Stephens was an Illinois-born businessman who in 1901 organized his own manufacturing firm which grew to yield an annual revenue of ten million dollars.[161] In 1927, he moved permanently to Pasadena, a city he had been visiting during the winters since 1915.[162]

5.21 W. W. Stephens residence (1925)

Bertha Holt Clark

When Marston & Van Pelt were designing James Scripps Booth's sprawling Andalusian residence on Linda Vista Avenue in 1922, they were also drawing up plans for "a handsome home of Italian architecture"[163] across the street from Caltech's Athenaeum for Bertha Holt Clark, wife of Rufus Clark, the inventor of the Bon Ami cleanser formula.[164] The Clark residence, at 587 S. Hill Avenue, was called "Casa Contenta," as its original stucco portals at the California Boulevard entrance still declare.

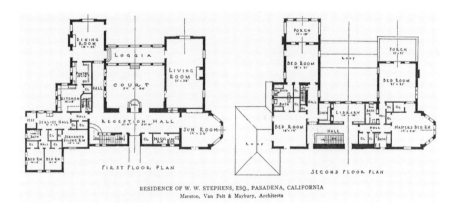

RESIDENCE OF W. W. STEPHENS, ESQ., PASADENA, CALIFORNIA
Marston, Van Pelt & Maybury, Architects

5.22 W. W. Stephens plans

Casa Contenta is located on one acre of land at the southwest corner of Hill and California. This 6,800 square foot residence is well-proportioned for its 160 by 265 foot lot. The front elevation is a side-gabled central block with cross-gable end wings. The Italian influence is evident in the stone trim about the entrance, the corbel table flush to the wall and just under the eave line, the simple roof line, and the louvered shutters. The recessed front entry is rich in detail, with a three-inch-thick raised panel front door with a hidden opening to enable the owner to surreptitiously ascertain arriving visitors. The original, elaborate wrought-iron grille gate stands in front of the door.

Casa Contenta is featured with photographs and plans in Newcomb's *Mediterranean Domestic Architecture in the United States*.[165] The interior of the house is distinguished by its grand, tile-covered entrance hall with a richly paneled ceiling and arched openings at either end. This great hall, plus the cloak room and dressing room that flank the front entrance, suggest that the structure was built to accommodate a considerable social life. The ground floor includes a solarium with an earth-toned Batchelder tile floor and French doors that open onto the backyard terrace and garden.

The grounds were beautifully landscaped, as seen in Newcomb's illustrations. There was a Spanish gazebo and a reinforced concrete lily pond and fountain featuring various exotic plants. Some of these details can still seen on the property. A swimming pool was added in 1949.

In 1941, Phil J. Regan purchased the residence. A former New York City policeman who broke into show business as "the singing cop," Regan became a popular performer in the 1940s and friend to many politicians and Hollywood stars.[166] According to the deed history, Regan lived there until 1974, although from 1960 to 1974 the legal owner was the "Kennedy Foundation," which possibly provided Regan with financial backing.[167]

5.23 "Casa Contenta" built in 1922 for

5.24 Garden view at Casa Contenta

Regan's daughter recalls that her father used to laugh at the dwelling's name, "Casa Contenta," given the family's "wild Irish ways."[168] During the Regan occupancy, Perle Mesta, social doyenne of the Truman years, gave parties at Casa Contenta. New Year's Eve became the annual gala, when the Regans filled the house with friends and family and entertained them with a three-piece band. The solarium was turned into "the bamboo room" and there guests could quench their thirst or appetite. At midnight the family threw open the shutters, and Phil sang while guests danced in the huge front hallway.

Casa Contenta was host on several occasions to Harry Truman. Regan's daughter recalls that her mother, Jo, asked Truman "if he wanted another Bourbon," to which Truman counseled "never ask if someone wants *another*." Apparently it is also true that Truman slipped and fell in the pool during one of his visits.[169] Hollywood greats were frequent guests, including James Cagney, Pat O'Brien, and Jimmy Durante. Big-city Mayors Richard Daley, Sam Yorty, and William O'Dwyer also visited.[170]

In the early 1970s, Regan lived mostly in Montecito, where his politicking got him into legal trouble. He was convicted in 1973 of attempting to bribe a county supervisor concerning a controversial land deal. Regan maintained his innocence but served one year in prison.[171] A decade later, Regan was pardoned by Governor Jerry Brown.[172]

William Henry Peters

Marston, Van Pelt & Maybury's most eclectic Mediterranean residential design was prepared for William Henry Peters and is located at 70 S. San Rafael Avenue. In 1923 the firm began drawing up the plans which called for a nineteen-room, frame dwelling with a tile roof, stucco exterior, hardwood floors and trim, and tile baths, to be built on a foundation 88 by 152 feet, with the total cost estimated at $50,000.[173]

The structure's footprint is unusual. The nearly 9,500 square feet are concentrated in a central block configuration whose center holds the front entry and entry hall. A diagonal wing with canted walls angles toward the Arroyo and forms the south elevation where

5.25 William Henry Peters Mediterranean residence (1923)

the grand living room and loggia (on the first level) and the master bedroom and deck (on the second level) are located. The opposite side of the central block has another section of rooms that project both beyond the front facade and also into the backyard.

This Mediterranean dwelling resembles a majestic castle as it stands atop a hill along the Arroyo. The carved front doorway is three inches thick. Its cast stone surround is a defining feature that has been widely applauded in both scholarly and popular design publications: *Architectural Record*,[174] *Architect & Engineer*,[175] *Arts & Decoration*,[176] *Mediterranean Domestic Architecture in the United States*,[177] and *Picturesque Pasadena*. [178] *Arts & Decoration* said in 1926 that the front entry contains "elaborate detail [that] indicates the influence of the Baroque period in Spain."[179] The flamboyant ornamentation incorporates pineapple, symbolizing hospitality; acanthus leaves; pilasters and engaged fluted columns crowned with obelisks. Barely detectable are delightful, whimsical face profiles above the column and pilaster on either side of the surround.

The facade is set off by original hardscape designed by Marston's firm: a stucco fountain and front wall ensemble incorporating two formal stair approaches and a circular turn-around with a crenellated balustrade at the base of which is a garden and fish pond decorated with Baroque ornamentation. The wrought-iron front gates provide a finishing touch: reportedly they were dipped in the Grand Canal in Venice to ensure proper aging.[180]

Entering the residence one stands in a grand, full-height entry hall in which the dominant element is a "finely proportioned balcony in which the carved details are characteristic of Spain."[181] A 1927 *Architect & Engineer* article emphasizes this detail.[182] The ceiling is vaulted and partly illuminated by scalloped windows with deep interior and exterior reveals over the balcony.

Separating the entry hall from the dining room is a doorway decorated in a twelfth-century carved and gilded frame in a classical motif that Peters obtained from a monastery in Granada, Spain. This is one of the many antiques that the owner acquired during his travels in

5.26 Peters residence, rear elevation and extensive property that borders the Arroyo Seco

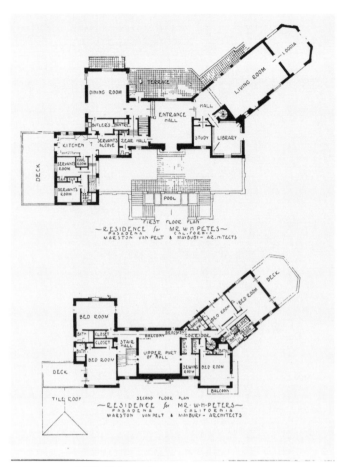

5.27 Peters plans

Europe both during and after the residence was built.[183] The entry floor tiles also date from the twelfth century and were also part of the family's European acquisitions.

Plaster walls throughout the dwelling reveal an unusual vertical texture achieved by applying the plaster in a "candle wax" pattern.[184] Throughout the house are the original wrought-iron sconces, carefully scaled to the rooms.

The living room features cedar plank floors, a hand-carved ceiling with decorative cross-beams, and French doors opening to the rear terrace. In that room still stands the grand piano which Peters purchased in Europe, sent to Venice to be hand-painted, and then had shipped to Pasadena. Reportedly it is one of the rare grand pianos that is also a player-piano.[185]

The loggia on the southern elevation also utilizes twelfth century floor tiles. A small stream runs along the eastern wall that helps cool the room on the hottest Pasadena summer days, although the house's three-foot-thick exterior walls usually ensure a pleasant temperature.

The house was the setting for many film productions, including *White Man's Burden, Eighty-three Hours Till Dawn,* and *Running Mates* with Tom Selleck, as well as a mini-series on Elizabeth Taylor and a documentary on Frank Sinatra.[186] It also has some secrets. Interior rain gutters designed to feed water into the front pool are hidden; so too is a passageway to servant's quarters. A spiral stairway that leads to the master bedroom is entered through a secret panel in the library.[187]

From the second floor one looks across the gardens to the Arroyo Seco, the Vista del Arroyo Hotel, and the mountains beyond. The original backyard ended in an abrupt 200-foot drop to the bottom of the Arroyo. During construction of the 210 Freeway the owner bought a huge quantity of solid fill from Caltrans and extended the backyard to include a duck pond and extensive plantings.[188]

William H. Peters and his wife lived in the house until the early 1950s. Local historians believe Peters belonged to the family that owned a firm variously called Peters Ammunition Company or Peters Cartridge Company, a business that got its start in Cincinnati in the 1880s.[189] The firm had great success until the depression. "In 1934 the Dupont/Remington Arms amalgamation acquired The Peters Cartridge Company."[190]

Will Peters, as his neighbors called him, was deeply affected by the depression.[191] Next-door neighbor John Bacon would occasionally see Peters on a balcony holding a gun.[192] During that period Peters was heard exclaiming that "Roosevelt is a Bolshevik!"[193] Peters died on December 12, 1951,[194] reportedly while he was in the kitchen yelling at the cook.[195]

The Nicholson House:
China in Pasadena

IN 1924, WHEN PASADENA ART DEALER GRACE NICHOLSON sought an architect to design her dream of a Chinese palace, there were a dozen or so accomplished firms in Southern California she might have considered. At the time, California was smitten with Spanish Colonial Revival architecture. Drawings of arcades, corbelled balconies, and red tiled roofs filled the drafting rooms of architectural offices. Chinese design was foreign and "different," requiring the talents of an architect appreciative of historically derived design and tempted by the challenge to master an exotic genre.

Marston, Van Pelt & Maybury embodied the strengths Nicholson sought, and she selected the firm to design the "Grace Nicholson Treasure House of Oriental Art."[1] This two-story, rectangular building with an inner courtyard is located at 46 N. Los Robles Avenue in Pasadena. It has 32,570 square feet of building space, measures 100 by 170 feet, has four chimneys, six fireplaces, and a roof of green bamboo-patterned tiles.

These statistics, however, hardly convey the structure's grandeur.[2] "It is far and away the most interesting and beautiful commercial building Pasadena can boast. No skyscraper, no ordinary office building can compare with it," declared *California Southland* in 1925.[3] "It is a remarkable piece of architecture... one of the finest and most colorful buildings in Pasadena," maintained architectural historian Robert Winter.[4] "It is one of the first truly genuine reproductions of such architecture in the U.S.," wrote Jeanne Perkins, who has studied Nicholson and her building for decades.[5] The *Los Angeles*

6.1 Grace Nicholson Treasure House (1924); now the Pacific Asia Museum

News explained that "inside is the only authentic Chinese court garden in America."[6] Nicholson's building was uniquely designed for the dual purpose of private residence and art gallery. Her Treasure House was modeled after buildings in Peking's Forbidden City, so it is fitting that it now houses the Pacific Asia Museum.

6.2 Grace Nicholson on a collecting expedition in a Northern California Indian village in 1905

Grace Nicholson

Grace Nicholson must have been one of Marston's most challenging clients. She was an independent woman of large enthusiasms, intellectually curious, well-informed; ahead of her time. She was born in Philadelphia in 1877 and orphaned at the age of 15.[7] On Christmas Day in 1901, with a modest inheritance from her grandparents, Nicholson came by train to Los Angeles for her health.[8] "I had a little office in L.A. and took to typewriting."[9] She began her secretarial business at 314 W. 4th Street.[10] In 1902, she moved to 41-43 S. Raymond Avenue in Pasadena.[11] Among her first clients for secretarial services were Mrs. P. G. Gates and G. Wharton James. Mrs. Gates "was doing some special investigating for the Pueblo Indians," as Nicholson recorded in her dairy,[12] while James, a Pasadena resident for more than thirty years until his death in 1923, was a recognized authority on the American Indian in the Southwest.[13] These clients ignited Nicholson's interest in American Indians, and she soon changed careers to begin selling Indian artifacts.[14] In 1903 she moved to larger quarters at 46 N. Los Robles, adjacent to the Maryland Hotel; this was the site where she would eventually build her Chinese palace.[15] Nicholson would often sit at the Pasadena train station, selling Indian baskets to arriving visitors.[16]

Nicholson pursued her new enterprise with the help of C. S. Hartman, a family friend from the East, who was her confidant and buyer until his death in 1933.[17] She would embark upon collecting expeditions to remote Indian villages in Northern California and as far away as Vancouver Island. She took copious notes, rich with the details of how she rode horseback to distant tribes, "canoed down Trinity and Klamath rivers to Weitchpec...[took] horses to Saltzman's...walked 20 miles to Somes Bar-Hotel kept by Sam Frame..."[18] In 1912 she traveled for four months by automobile and train to Indian centers in California, Nevada, Arizona, New Mexico, and Colorado. On the trip she observed the corn and medicine dances at Taos, the flute dance at Walpi, and antelope and snake dances.[19] According to her diary, in 1909 she and "Mr. H," as she called Hartman, "left on sailing trip to the East Coast, with trunks filled with embroidered novelties and jewelry, etc."[20] (Hartman concluded his letters to her "As ever, Friday," an acknowledgement of his subordinate role.[21])

Although Nicholson became a highly successful commercial art dealer, her interest in esthetic values and culture transcended the profit motive. She dis-

6.3 Nicholson near her retail store (with her favorite cat) before Treasure House was built on the same property, circa 1910

cussed with the Indians the meaning behind the crafts, how they were made, and the rituals surrounding their use. Hartman described her rapport: "They welcomed her as a person of great occult power, one who understood their secrets, and was therefore entitled to any and all of their charms, feathers, obsidians, and even the sacred pipes."[22]

Nicholson's clientele soon included the President of New York's Hotel Astor, the New Zealand Dominion Museum, and John Muir. By 1925 she "supplied 60 per cent of the museums of the world with art treasures and has placed at least 30,000 specimens in the museums of the United States."[23] Institutions who bought from her included the Field Museum of Chicago, the Philadelphia Museum of Art, the Smithsonian, the Carnegie Institute, and Harvard's Peabody Museum.[24] Recognition came to her early. In 1904, the American Anthropological Association elected her to its membership.[25] Five years later she was honored for her exhibit at the Alaska-Yukon Pacific Exposition in Seattle.[26]

6.4 Nicholson stationary, circa 1913

Nicholson soon expanded her collecting and trading to include Asian crafts. This evolution occurred after F. Suie On, owner of the long-established Chinese antiques store in Pasadena which still exists, took over Nicholson's lease on Raymond in 1903.[27] Additionally in that same year, according to Nicholson's diary: "Mr. H. was hired by F. Suie On as auctioneer."[28] By 1913, Nicholson announced her business as: "Grace Nicholson Oriental Art, Antiques, Indian Baskets," and soon had purchasing agents in China and Japan. In 1929, she and Hartman embarked upon a spectacular tour of the Orient. Soon collectors and dealers throughout Asia were sending her regular shipments. The coming of World War II severed these ties, but Nicholson's collection by then was immense. Clients for her Asian antiques included J. P. Morgan, Phoebe Apperson Hearst, Avery Brundage, H. J. Heinz, and the Kraft family.[29] Nicholson's personal wealth became substantial.

The Building

David Kamansky, Director of the Pacific Asia Museum, states with admiration that Nicholson constructed the Chinese palace "with $200,000 in cash—earning every nickel of it herself."[30] Nicholson thus could afford to build something extraordinary. According to Marston, Van Pelt & Maybury's architectural drawings, the building would contain galleries, retail shops, an exhibition space available for rental, a 100-seat lecture hall/auditorium, a library, and studios. Nicholson would make the west side of the second level her personal residence. One room, called the "basket room," was specifically designed for her American Indian collection.[31] Decorated with a Pueblo-style stucco fireplace and hundreds of American Indian baskets, this was where Nicholson "held soirees"[32] for her many cultured friends from around the world.

Nicholson devoted years of study to the traditions and architectural precedents that would define her building. She had dozens of photographs of Chinese temples taken at her direction by others in China, which would prove invaluable as models for the architects.[33] These photographs are part of her collection which is preserved at the Huntington Library. Nicholson made careful notes on the origins of certain details:

> 1.- The carved stone arch, at entrance to 46 was taken from the Buddhist's Hall entrance in the Shao-hsi-tien ground....
>
> 2.- Gate arch and also arch opening to Art Gallery from those of the Temple of Agriculture.
>
> 3.- My carved stone balustrades copied from the five bridges spanning the small winding stream...
>
> 5.- Copper dragons over the entrance to the Gold Room is from the Tsuni Gate...[34]

Other notes reveal the philosophy her building would embrace:
Characteristic spirit - religious...
Chinese-unity of man and nature...
Monotony in Chinese architecture;
General plan one of symmetry;
General mode of building is t'ing...
Roofs decorated by glazed tiles;
imperial foundation;
Always used the arch, curved lines...
Gates - Chinese architecture feature...[35]

Grace Nicholson's daring and knowledge were recognized at the time: "To gather together her ideas in tangible form and present them to the chosen architects was the great task of the originator...performed with striking force and originality," said one observer in 1926.[36] But that was only a start. The architects had to capture this dream, fully appreciate every detail of arrangement and design, and develop their plans within an altogether unfamiliar architectural vocabulary. This posed special challenges. Obviously it meant that Marston's team and Nicholson would spend significant time together, to study Chinese symbols and history and to understand the meaning and placement of Nicholson's authentic Chinese ornaments—sculptures, tiles, and wooden grilles—that she wanted incorporated into the building. The architects incorporated Nicholson's detailed concepts, but did so in a manner that reflected their own vision. Historian Robert Winter has observed that "while the details were authentic, the arrangement of them was freely interpreted....the effect is arresting and certainly unique."[37]

Nicholson's banker balked at the whole idea. "He expressed his fear that she was making a great mistake, and advised a cheap, one story, structure, which would rent for low prices."[38] His trepidation was unjustified. *Western Architect* announced the successful result in 1929:

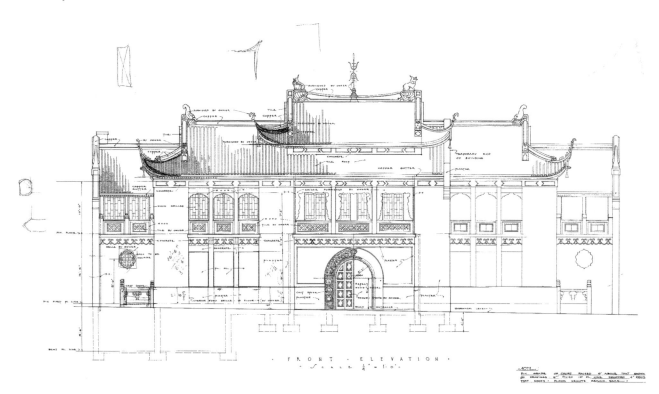

6.5 Architects' plans for Treasure House, front elevation

The architects, Marston, Van Pelt and Maybury deserve much credit for the sympathetic manner in which they have caught the spirit of the thing and incorporated the owner's purpose.[39]

ONLY BY EXAMINING THE BUILDING UP CLOSE, can one appreciate how well-placed Nicholson's confidence was in Marston.

Entrance. "The main-entrance arch is an example of the painstaking adaptation" which epitomized the design.[40] It is a picturesque opening with a substantial cast stone door surround of individual panels depicting Chinese themes. The lower panels contain Buddhist iconography, including elephants and urns. Above them, panels reveal a composition of arabesque and Chou hooks from ancient Chinese bronzes. At the center of the arch is a garuda man-monster figure.[41] An elaborate wrought-iron gate-grille "with a spirited motif of writhing dragons"[42] stands in front of the opening. Ming Dynasty Fu dogs from Peking originally flanked the main entrance and functioned as temple guardians. All of the building's hardware–latches, locks, pulls, and escutcheons–utilize Chinese symbols and were made by West and Company in Pasadena.

Roof. The roof is perhaps the most exquisite and the most conspicuously grand element of the whole design. "The roof is, with the Chinese, the chief thing," explained Pasadena author M. Urmy Sears, in writing about Nicholson's building.[43] Viewing the building from the street, the sloped roof runs nearly the full width, with a smaller, identical sloped roof raised and centered over the main entry. More than 3,300 green glazed pantiles that resemble bamboo were used in the multilevel roof. Contrary to reports claiming they were from China, they are authentic reproductions made by the Los Angeles Pressed Brick Company.

Intriguing roof details include projecting eaves with exposed rafter tails in the Chinese tradition. All roof corners are turned up, a motif said to derive from the flaps of Mongol tents,[44] and are finished with elaborate copper finials made by Ohrmund Brothers of Pasadena. Copper, now aged green, was also used in the roof ridges, the gutters, downspouts, and for the sweeping talons at either end of the front facade.

Grotesques also accent the flamboyant roof, including six painted ceramic dogs, located at the ridges and corners; a dolphin sculpture at each end of the main ridge pole; and copper dragon heads crowning the downspouts. Centered on the smaller ridge pole is a flaming pearl. The dogs, fish, and pearl date from the late Ch'ing Dynasty (late nineteenth century) and came from Nicholson's collection.[45] M. Urmy Sears, who must have interviewed Grace Nicholson, wrote in a 1926 article: "Miss Nicholson tells us [that the Chinese] made their grotesques originally to frighten away evil spirits and if they succeed in making them uglier than that which they fear they are satisfied."[46]

Courtyard. In China, courtyards and their decorative ele-

6.6 Treasure House roof detail: copper finial and bamboo-patterned tiles

6.7 Courtyard detail; stone balusters in a cloud pattern with lotus blossom finials

ments are rich in symbolic meaning. In discussing Nicholson's building, *California Southland* explained that architecture of the Orient "was conceived in a different spirit from our own ....A building was regarded...as a fusion of man's handiwork into Nature, the whole surroundings of the scene making part, and perhaps the chief part, of the architect's conception."[47] Courtyards are so revered in China that building value is calculated by their quantity.[48]

The design of the four stairways located in the courtyard's corners embodies important symbolism. Stone balusters and lotus blossom finials were cast by the William Smith Architectural Stone Company in Pasadena. The balusters are decorated in a cloud pattern that represents an upward journey. At the foot of the stairway is a carved stone bracket that depicts a circle with five smaller circles inside. This symbolizes the sixth sense that is created when all five senses function in unison.

Nicholson took great pleasure in her garden. Writing to a friend, she said that her garden "complements my Chinese building....A court garden open to the sky is called by the Chinese 'Heaven's Well'...[There is a variety] of openings into the garden. The moon gate and often a vase-like shape or some symbolical form are used. To the Chinese, their garden is an intimate spot to be used for reflection and contemplation. It is an embodiment of a philosophy of life."[49] Originally, plants were placed along the stone balustrade. Ginkgo trees, Nicholson's favorite, used to predominate in the garden. A friend's last memory of Nicholson was watching her being carried out on a stretcher to an ambulance, and Nicholson asking the men to stop so that she could get a last glimpse of a ginkgo tree.[50]

Today, this building is well-utilized, locally cherished, and nationally recognized. A staff of twenty-six is needed to oversee its many programs, which include classes in Taiko drumming, the Chinese language, Japanese flower arranging, and Tai Chi martial arts. An Asian art display on tour internationally is usually featured in the gallery space. The auditorium has been used for films, lectures, and musical groups. In 1997, the building was renovated at a cost of one million dollars.[51] It is listed on the National Register of Historic Places and is a California State Historic Landmark.

6.8 View of the courtyard

Grace Nicholson, a stunning platinum blonde in her younger years, never married. She was often seen driving around Pasadena in her "beautiful new" Chandler Royal Eight sedan.[52] Nicholson was part of an active women's social circle in Pasadena,[53] which is how she developed a friendship with Mrs. Sylvanus Marston. That friendship apparently influenced Nicholson's selection of Sylvanus Marston's architectural firm.[54] The Treasure House was Grace Nicholson's vision. But her dream was made real by the talents of her architects, who incorporated their high level of architectural skill with a sympathetic appreciation of Nicholson's desires and needs. In that era, a highly independent woman client acting alone, over a project propelled by her own resources and well-informed opinions, could be an impressive challenge.

---— ◢ 7 ◣ ——---

Designing
Community

MARSTON, VAN PELT & MAYBURY, unlike some of its distinguished competitors,[1] won awards not only for its magnificent houses, but also for its extensive portfolio of public and commercial buildings that enriched centers of commerce, learning, worship, and social life. The firm left an indelible imprint on Pasadena's downtown area and brought marked beauty and distinction to other communities in Southern California. Today, many of these buildings have achieved landmark stature.

Pasadena Central Business District

The 1920s was a golden decade of building in Pasadena, as the Central Public Library, City Hall, Caltech's Athenaeum, and other notable structures were erected.[2] Pasadena's (and the region's) population boom prompted the extension of the business district eastward on Colorado Street. Marston's business colleague Frank Hogan liked to say that "Colorado street is the main road between Alaska and Mexico,"[3] and hotelier Daniel Linnard predicted that Colorado Street would become a "second Rue de la Paix."[4] At the suggestion of businessman (and Marston client) W. T. Jefferson, in 1927 the city of Pasadena changed the name of its "most luminous bisecting artery" from "Colorado Street" to "Colorado Boulevard."[5]

"Pasadena is a uniquely self-centered city that self-consciously planned and built a setting that would reflect the importance given to itself," wrote Pasadena architect William W. Ellinger, III.[6] Many of the region's best known architects, including Myron Hunt, H. C. Chambers, Julia Morgan, Carleton M. Winslow, Cyril Bennett, Fitch Haskell, John Bakewell, Edwin Bergstrom, and Frederick L. Roehrig designed buildings in the central business district, which accounts for its uniformly high level of architectural expression. Marston, Van Pelt & Maybury contributed a greater number of

7.1 Art Deco Warner Building on Colorado Boulevard (1927)

7.2 Warner Building glazed tile detail; Vromans Book Store was a tenant at this location for many years

structures in a broader range of architectural idioms than any other architects. So wide-ranging were their stylistic themes that few observers would guess that their public and commercial buildings emanated from a single firm.

The Warner Building

Marston & Maybury designed the Warner Building for established client Thomas W. Warner. Built in 1927, it is located at 469-483 East Colorado Boulevard. The building was intended to house a row of deluxe retail shops catering especially to guests at the nearby Maryland Hotel. Eventual tenants included Pasadena's oldest bookstore, Vroman's, the Harold A. Parker Photographic Studio, Le Trianon, and John C. Bentz Oriental Antiques. "This building," observed Ann Scheid Lund, a local architectural historian, "expresses the exuberance of Art Deco decoration better than any other…in Pasadena."[7]

The jade green decorative tile facade is the chief design feature. The tiles were made by Gladding, McBean & Company, California's premier terra cotta company in the 1920s. These glazed tiles take fanciful spiral forms above the display windows that are reminiscent of sea shells, complex linear forms suggesting an abstract foliage design in a narrow band above transom grille, and asymmetrical circles, spirals, and swirls on the parapet's central panel. Local experts have credited the design to Gladding, McBean artist J. E. Stanton, who also worked on the Pasadena Civic Auditorium.[8] Prior to the Warner Building project, Gladding, McBean had financed a six-month overseas sabbatical for Stanton, enabling him to study tile precedents in the old world centers of the art–Spain, Italy, Algiers, and Tunis, as well as in Constantinople and southern France. Stanton subsequently published a book with the alluring title: *By Middle Seas*.[9] Stanton's educational journey probably influenced the Warner Building's design. Its decorative tiles are so unfamiliar and intriguing that it is easy to imagine they were inspired by such exotic locales.

California Southland touted the Warner Building as the best example of commercial construction that would hasten Pasadena's destiny as the nation's premier vacation city.[10] In 1930, Marston & Maybury received an award of "exceptional merit" for this commission from the Southern California Chapter, AIA.[11]

7.3 G. L. Morris Building (1924); Marston, Van Pelt & Maybury occupied the entire second floor

G. L. Morris Building

The Southern California Chapter of the AIA honored Marston & Van Pelt in 1924 for its design of the G. L. Morris Building, calling it that year's most distinctive mercantile building in the region.[12] The building, now demolished, was located at 25 S. Euclid Avenue, and Marston relocated his office there, taking over the second floor. Retail stores were located on the ground floor.

This structure was brick clad, with ornamental accents of cast stone trim used in quoins, on the piers of the ground level arcade, and for the projecting stringcourse that divided upper and lower stories. The front facade's central focus was the second story three-part arched opening with a false balcony.

The building displayed an eclectic combination of styles: Italian arcading and fenestration, Gothic arches employed in the arcade, and distinctly Moorish overtones in the flat roof, the coping, the cast stone frieze with cut-outs below the second story balcony, and the decorative diamond design brickwork over the main entry. This eclecticism no doubt explains why the structure was subject to such enigmatic descriptions at the time.[13]

The Arcade Building

Designed in 1927, the Arcade Building at 696 E. Colorado Boulevard was intended (and continues presently) to house multiple luxury retail shops and is an early example of what would become the shopping mall. The architects created an interior open courtyard around which numerous small shops are clustered. The center area is a narrow pedestrian street, enabling patrons to walk unimpeded by vehicular traffic from store to store. The building has been called "a commercial parallel to the bungalow court concept."[14]

This asymmetrical, stucco-over-brick building is designed in the Spanish Colonial Revival style. The inside courtyard is flanked by a double row of arches with a decorative fountain and small garden in the center. One can still view some of the original glass doors with steel frames and ornamental brass door handles, wrought-iron light fixtures, and decorative tile panels on the second floor.

7.4 The Arcade Building (1927), circa 1920s

Don Lee Building

As Keith Marston notes in the Afterword, in 1925 Don Lee Corporation invited his father to its San Francisco headquarters for a consultation. As a result of Marston's presentation, the company selected him to design an automobile dealership and showroom, called Don Lee Cadillac, located at 655 E. Green Street in Pasadena.[15]

This unusual Spanish building is situated at

7.5 Don Lee Building (1925), circa 1920s

a forty-five degree angle at the corner of Green and El Molino Streets, and enjoys a flamboyant entrance. High above the front door there is a Mission-style shaped parapet wall with a cast stone decoration at its center, incorporating sun rays, scrolls, and other elements, crowned with a finial. The entrance door surround is composed of decorative faience tile by Gladding, McBean. A 1927 advertisement by that company featured this entrance detail and commented on the striking effect of blank walls accentuated by decoration.[16]

Along the sides of the building is a series of large and transomed display windows set between piers. Alternating piers extend beyond the parapet roof and are capped with sizable finials that match the one above the front entry. Stylized cast stone cartouches are located between the piers. This eclectic building remains substantially intact, but its use has changed: it is now Jacob Maarse Florist.

The William Wilson Building

Pioneering realtor William Wilson, who began his business in Pasadena's civic center area, "wanted to contribute to the beauty of the public structures grouped around,"[17] and in 1927 commissioned Marston & Maybury to draw plans for his new office complex, to be built at 40 N. Garfield Avenue.

The William Wilson Building (since demolished) embodied the Italian Renaissance style, with its red-tiled roof, stately pilasters, and wood-paneled doors. Its special feature was the sgraffito panel located along the facade just below the roof line. "Sgraffito," meaning "scratched" in Italian, is a decoration produced by covering a plaster surface of one color with a thin coat of a similar material of another color and scratching through the outer coat to show the color beneath.[18] Upon seeing the frieze, former Princeton University architecture professor Julian Ellsworth Garnsey declared it "the finest sgraffito frieze not only in California but in the United States."[19]

Garnsey went on: "The firm sells real estate which consists of land and buildings....[It] boasts of its speed in such transactions....In the center panel...is a map of California upon a scroll, representing 'land'...a column surrounded by an olive branch, representing architecture, and hence 'building.' To the right, is the staff of the god Mercury, messenger from the gods, representing 'speed.' The cornucopias, or horns, filled with fruits, stand for the opulence of California."[20]

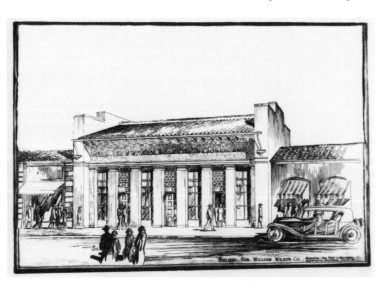

Wilson was born in Ireland in 1877 and arrived in Pasadena in 1908.[21] He shaped his company into one of the leading real estate firms in Southern California.

7.6 Architects' rendering of the William Wilson Building (1927)

Pasadena National Bank

Two of the six commercial banks Marston designed should be mentioned before leaving the Colorado Boulevard corridor. The first, the Pasadena National Bank, now demolished, was built in 1913 and located at 132 E. Colorado. Classical Revival themes prevailed: strict symmetry, an imposing facade of full-height Ionic columns supporting a triangular pediment, a flat roof with a parapet, and a wide frieze band beneath the cornice. The monumentalism of this style, prevalent in commercial bank construction, was intended to signal stability and security. This commission, reflecting Pasadena's early assuredness and self-importance, is featured in the *Los Angeles Architectural Club Year Book* for 1913[22] and in a 1916 issue of *Architect and Engineer*.[23]

Pacific-Southwest Trust and Savings Bank

Built at Colorado and Lake Streets in 1927, the Oak Knoll branch of Pacific-Southwest Trust & Savings Bank (now demolished) was primarily Italian Renaissance in design and featured a row of arched transom windows on the top floor below the eaves and an intricate frieze fronting the second and top stories. The exterior cladding was architectural concrete stone made by Brooks Art Stone Corporation; it was displayed in that company's advertisement in a 1928 architectural journal.[24]

7.7 Pasadena National Bank (1913); note Marston's signature in the lower right corner

Architect Robert Bennett singled out this commission when discussing Marston's unique talents. Marston "was very convincing, he was very good—he enticed them into building the structure." Bennett observed how Marston engaged the client about the building's proposed architectural features. "His sincerity for the client's job is the thing that made him,"[25] Bennett thought.

Pasadena Athletic Club

Marston's connection with the Pasadena Athletic Club organization actually began in 1913, when he was selected to design "a new athletic club house"[26] which involved the merger of the existing Overland and the proposed Pasadena Athletic Clubs. Marston's business colleague, Frank G. Hogan, was the most active booster for the merger and for its new headquarters. Marston drew up plans for a four-story structure that was to be "one of the finest club houses on the coast."[27] A knotty issue concerned how to accommodate women members. The local newspaper reported in 1913 that: "Tonight Mr. Marston leaves on a business trip to San Francisco and while there will visit the leading athletic clubs, for the purpose of determining what accommodations for women exist in the northern club houses, and what privileges are granted them."[28] This structure was never built.

The Pasadena Athletic Club (now demolished) was finally built in 1925 at 435 E. Green Street at the instigation of businessmen inspired by "what this beautiful building will represent in community spirit, in a social way and in the traditions of American well-being and sportsmanship."[29] A banquet with more than two hundred guests was held at the Hotel Huntington in January of 1925 to raise funds for its construction. World-famous sprinter Charlie Paddock proclaimed to the guests that the club "will hand on to youth the American 'fighting spirit,' the spirit of

7.8 Architects' rendering of the Pacific-Southwest Trust and Savings Bank (1927)

sportsmanship and the virtues of soundness and definite purpose."[30] The local press also noted that Marston and building committee chairman W. F. Creller were featured in the evening's program in order to make a presentation: "the piece de resistance — 'Our Building, With Lantern Slides.'"[31]

Creller and Marston explained that plans called for a nine storied building, with retail stores on the street frontages; a main entrance and lobby on Green Street; elevators leading to men's and women's sections; dormitories for men; an artistically tiled swimming pool; a gymnasium with a running track; stylishly old-world lounges and adjacent social rooms; a large main dining room; private dining rooms; a separate gymnasium, dining room and lounge for women; and squash and tennis courts. After the two men ended their talk, "the assemblage cheered."[32]

The club's doors opened in October of 1926. Prominent businessmen and civic leaders were especially fond of the dining room, which had one of the city's best menus. One notable entrée was squab stuffed with pate de foie gras and accompanied by truffle sauce.[33] Membership during the first year swelled to 1500.[34]

The club made athletic history. Marston's oldest son Paul was a regular and recalled the first-rate swimming program and its many Olympic-team members.[35] Johnny Weissmuller, who won countless world records and five gold medals at the 1924 and 1928 Olympic Games, frequently swam at the club. In 1926, member Lillian Copeland established world records in the shot put, javelin throw, and discus throw; and Carol Fletcher won the national springboard diving competition. Member Dr. Sammy Lee won gold medals in high-tower diving in the 1948 and 1952 Olympics. Juno Stover competed in the 1948 Olympics at the age of sixteen, and became the only woman at that point in Olympic history to

7.9 Architects' rendering of the Pasadena Athletic Club (1925)

make four Olympic teams—in '48, '52, '56, and '60. She managed to have a child between each competition, and won medals at each of the games.

Stylistically, the building was regarded as essentially Mediterranean. Its placement was deemed significant: "The club rises in ever upward steps to the intermediate and crowning roofs of red tile high above the surrounding buildings of the time...."[36] The exterior material was reinforced concrete with a pinkish hue which can appear monolithic, although here surface texture was supplied by the wood form boards in which the concrete was cast. The concrete was counterpointed by the finely detailed cast moldings, brackets, columns, blind arcades, cornices, entrance arches, a club insignia over the entry, hand-carved mahogany front doors, and large banks of arcaded windows on the second and third floors.[37] The design and combination of materials gave the club a Romanesque semblance, with touches that were almost Byzantine: massive plain walls relieved by richly decorative ornamental elements.

The sumptuous interior, seen in photographs in a 1928 issue of *Pacific Coast Architect*,[38] reveals decorative stone work, exposed and rustic beamed ceilings, tiled floors, and vaulted ceilings. Upon entry, one was greeted by a mezzanine balcony supported by ornamented brackets. The sizable dining room boasted a heavy beamed ceiling with a stencil design incorporating peacocks, handsome solid brass chandeliers, and full-sized French doors. Former Princeton professor of architecture Julian Ellsworth Garnsey was responsible for the interior decoration of the clubhouse, including oil paintings, while George Hunt designed the furniture.[39] Both designers were faithful to the building's old-world ambiance.

The pool was a favorite place, well described in one journalist's account: "You stand quite fascinated as you get the first glimpse....The lights, the deep blue of the walls, artistic in the extreme, the deeper green of the water, all subdued yet appealing—it is quite impressive."[40] The walls contained stylized symbols for water and rain, and the ceiling revealed a cloud design with lightning, shining stars, and planets.[41]

Turner & Stevens Mortuary

Marston designed three significant public buildings in close proximity to each other on North Marengo: the American Legion and YMCA, both Mediterranean in style, and the Turner & Stevens Mortuary, which features English Gothic forms. The mortuary was the first to be built, in 1922, and its rich English tradition must have pleased the many Pasadena residents who shared that heritage. The Gothic mortuary and chapel, clad in variegated brick with cast stone trim, is tastefully decorated with exquisite tracery, occasional gargoyles, stained glass, and wood plank doors with Gothic framed glass panels, and Tudor arched door frames.

7.10 Turner & Stevens Mortuary (1922); Frank E. Brown bird's-eye-view circa 1920s

It is here that the memorial services for many old-line Pasadenans were held. The building—now a restaurant and a lawyer's office—still commands a certain reverence with its quiet beauty.

The architects' sketch of the mortuary complex appeared in the 1922 *Tournament of Roses Brochure*,[42] but the best representation of the building is in a "bird's eye view" painting prepared by Frank E. Brown in the 1920s. Brown was a Pasadena artist who specialized in the technique. He would climb a telegraph pole, take dozens of photographs and make pencil sketches, then return to his studio where he completed the final painting.

Home Laundry Company

Even a Pasadena business as pedestrian as a laundry was persuaded to select period architecture: in this instance, the Tudor Revival style. In 1922, Marston & Van Pelt designed a brick and concrete indus-

7.11 Tudor style Home Laundry Company (1922)

trial building at 432 S. Arroyo Parkway for The Home Laundry Company; it is now occupied by Thomasville Home Furnishings. Novel when built, the structure was equipped for industrial use, but designed to look like a stylish Pasadena residence, with the same architectural quality, scale, and expert craftsmanship that would be found in the luxurious houses of nearby neighborhoods. This is the only known industrial building in Pasadena to be designed in the Tudor Revival style.[43]

The front facade faces west toward Arroyo Parkway. The building is a steeply-pitched, side-gabled block, intersected by a large forward-facing gable over the front entry, with three gabled wall dormers. The appealing decorative effects include half-timbering on the second floor, cast stone quoins at the corners and as first floor window frames, and wooden finials at the apex of the gables and the parapet ends. The asymmetrical front entrance features a ten-light door with a Tudor-shaped cast stone door surround designed to resemble ashlar blocks. A photograph of this handsome facade was featured in a 1925 issue of *American Architect*.[44]

The second story on the north side still retains a remnant of the original Home Laundry sign painted on the bricks. This side is divided into seven bays separated by six false chimneys with cast stone caps. Naming a commercial laundry business "The Home Laundry" was meant to telegraph a message. In a city known for its beautiful residences, where few upper income women worked outside their homes, and where wealthy winter guests at the luxury resort hotels were used to attention, the "Home Laundry" name was chosen as an assurance of the highest quality of service, just like at home. The business was deliberately placed in close proximity to the wealthy enclaves of Oak Knoll and South Orange Grove, and the city's major resort hotels.

Churches and Cemeteries

Like his grandfather, Sylvanus Marston was a church-going man who appreciated ecclesiastical architecture. Through much of his practice, from 1910 through 1939, Marston designed well over a dozen churches and parsonages in Pasadena and surrounding areas. Marston was a life-long member of the Pasadena Presbyterian Church, serving for a time as a trustee; this undoubtedly helped him obtain ecclesiastical commissions, the majority of which, not surprisingly, were for churches of the Presbyterian denomination.

Some Pasadenans who knew Marston and were interviewed for this book did not know that he was a religious man. They were not aware of his deep involvements with his own church or his standing as a 32nd degree Mason.[45] Some of his writings that reveal a strong religious faith. Marston kept a daily diary during his nine months in France during World War I. He served under the auspices of the YMCA as a physical education director for the French Army; he also taught English to the troops. The diary provides an unusual glimpse into his faith and his sense of church design.

On Christmas eve in 1918, during the voyage to France by way of England, with a wife and three young sons at home in Pasadena, Marston wrote in his diary: "Xmas service tonight nearly made me 'spill' for could only think of my boys and wife so far away. Am so glad I have the faith to trust them to the care of our Heavenly Father." In France he read the Bible almost daily and often attended the French Protestant Church. He discussed religion with bunk mates on the voyage to Europe as well as with Frenchmen he met in his travels throughout the countryside. When visiting a cathedral in France on Palm Sunday, Marston was surprised with the "indifference" of those attending, and wrote about how it made him think of "the ceremonies Christ condemned as practiced by the pharisees and the Sadducees."

The diary certainly shows his passion for architecture. Marston refers to reading "late numbers of the [Architectural] Digest." While Marston's job was to introduce American athletics and exercise to the French troops, to "give these soldiers the right start," and to convey to the men "what the YMCA stood for," he was clearly consumed by architecture. Marston visited at least fifteen chateaus and countless churches, usually on bicycle; he often traveled up to ten miles per outing.

Upon Marston's arrival in England he was awed by Winchester Cathedral: "Its refinement of detail and general proportion in spite of its great size greatly impressed me.... Was surprised to find that the Cathedral was originally a Norman cathedral built at the time of William the Conqueror, the two transepts and east end are still of the older Norman architecture." The diary's most detailed passages concerned observations while in France: Marston's reflections on that country's historical styles, design plans, and building materials. One entry tells how he had someone direct him to the ancient city gates in Parthenay. He noted that they "were of early English architecture; quite a change from all the French buildings I've seen. Hard to realize this part of France was controlled by the English in the 9th and 10th centuries." Bicycling to Fontenay-le-Comte, west of his main assignment station at Niort, Marston "studied the entrance to the old church." Near there he discovered a chateau and from a conversation with the owner learned that it "was built at the time of Louis XVI and by one of his [the owner's] great grandfathers." The owner was a "great lover of art and had a great collection of old carved wood, marble, paintings, drawings, etc. The fire places in the large salon and in the dining room are wonders all of stone and finely carved."

Marston was eager to purchase mementos of his trip, especially watercolors and sketches. He wrote about his conversation with the chateau's owner: "When looking over all his fine old samples of carved wood I asked him if he thought I could get any such samples in Paris (had in mind Van Pelt). He disappeared only to return with four big fine old large 'gravures' [engravings] of his chateau and gave them to me."

There are abundant diary references to historical periods, with Marston commenting on churches "in the Renaissance style," or one that resembled "an older feudal castle," or those that were gothic creations; he speculated on architectural origins of ancient walls, moats, and corner round towers. On one journey Marston went into the attic of a chateau to examine the construction and the huge oak trusses.[46] This European exposure contributed significantly to Marston's church architecture.

Westminster Presbyterian Church

The Westminster Presbyterian Church is located at 1757 N. Lake Avenue in Pasadena and can be seen from great distances because its tallest spires rise 150 feet above the foundation. Built in 1927, Westminster Presbyterian follows French Gothic design and has a 1,100-person capacity.

This is the crown jewel of Marston's churches. A few individuals with connections back to that era have disagreed over whether Marston, Van Pelt, or Maybury were more responsible for this design. Unfortunately, no original drawings exist that might help resolve the issue. Keith Marston believes the design reflects his father's sensibilities.[47] Other architects have asserted that the building was Van Pelt's vision,[48] although Van Pelt left the partnership

7.12 Westminster Presbyterian Church (1927)

during the project.[49] Maybury's daughter recalls her father having been deeply involved in the project and remembers him telling her that prior to construction every single piece of the building's exterior cladding was numbered.[50] Herbert J. Powell (FAIA, 1947) was employed by the firm at the time, though this was early in his career and his contribution would have been as a draftsman.[51]

Ralph Adams Cram served as a consulting architect.[52] Cram, in partnership with Bertram Goodhue at the turn of the century, planned Gothic churches that were "vigorously composed, artistic masses enriched with expressive symbolism and built with a craftsman's attitude toward construction."[53] Cram and Goodhue designed St. John the Divine in New York City, and Cram was a prolific author writing, among other things, *The Substance of Gothic*.[54] Westminster Presbyterian is the only instance where Cram participated in the design of a Pasadena building and one of his very few projects anywhere in Southern California.[55]

7.13 **Westminster Presbyterian Church**, interior view

Westminister Presbyterian is made of reinforced concrete. Its Gothic style is revealed in the great emphasis on vertically pointed arches, steeply pitched complex gable roofs, finials, and medieval decorative motifs. Height and light are the paramount qualities of the breath-taking interior. The plaster ceilings are painted blue and red and sprinkled with stars, providing a shimmering celestial aura. Sunlight pierces through three large rose windows, with richly colored panes set in delicate tracery. These windows, which are named Sapphire, Emerald, and Ruby, represent the "grisaille style" of the thirteenth century and, along with the Christ window above the communion table,[56] were made at the local Judson Studios. Photographs in a 1929 issue of *Architectural Digest*[57] reveal many of these fine features.

Scott Chapel, Methodist Episcopal Church

The *Pasadena Star News* reported on July 26, 1929: "Dream of Negro Methodists of Pasadena about to be realized in construction of new home at 55 Mary Street...the two-unit brick building with seating for more than 300, is designed by Marston & Maybury." The building no longer exists, but nearby stands its successor structure, renamed the Scott United Methodist Church and located at 444 N. Orange Grove Boulevard.

7.14 Scott Chapel, Methodist Episcopal Church (1929) attended by baseball great Jackie Robinson

The Scott United Methodist Church celebrated its 94th Anniversary on September 21, 1997.[58] It is one of the oldest black congregations in Pasadena. Marston's 1929 structure was the church that baseball luminary Jackie Robinson and his brother Mack attended.[59] The church is named after Isaiah Benjamin Scott, the first black bishop in the Methodist Conference.

The original Scott Chapel, a variant of Mediterranean design, was clad in red brick with white trim and covered with a Spanish tiled roof. Italian-Romanesque influences were evident in the distinctive bell tower crowned with a cross, the compound and splayed arched entrance, and the exaggerated coping and fenestration. These stylistic influences were a relief from Gothic architecture, so plentiful in 1920s and 1930s church construction.

Lincoln Avenue Church

The Lincoln Avenue Church was designed in 1916 and reflected the simplicity of the Mission style with its oversized bell tower, small window openings, and tile roof. Now demolished, the only known published photograph of the structure appears in a 1917 *Ladies' Home Journal* article entitled "The Small Country Church."[60] "The interior," according to the article, "is arranged so that it would be suitable for any congregation requiring social or club rooms as well as a main auditorium. The interior woodwork is stained a light brown and the walls are plastered and tinted."[61]

7.15 Lincoln Avenue Church (1916)

Hollywood Memorial Park Cemetery

The Hollywood Memorial Park Cemetery, at 6000 Santa Monica Boulevard, Los Angeles, was the first burial ground in the then little-known farming community which became "the birthplace of the defining art form of the 20th century."[62] Many pioneers of the early motion picture era are buried in this cemetery that is situated between Van Ness and Gower Streets. When it recently went through bankruptcy and repurchase, the cemetery was featured in a variety of publications including the *New York Times Magazine*.[63]

Marston & Van Pelt designed the Park's two largest structures, its public mausoleums. The Marston job records contain five entries for "Hollywood Mausoleum," with the first appearing in 1917 and the last in 1929; they refer to two separate structures.

Hollywood Cathedral Mausoleum

The first mausoleum that was built, according to the 1917 permit, was originally called a "Community Mausoleum" and had granite exterior walls;[64] it eventually was named the Hollywood Cathedral Mausoleum. At the time, there were no other buildings on the lot. A 1921 permit authorized a large extension to the building,[65] prompting the Los

7.16 Hollywood Cathedral Mausoleum (1917, 1921)

Angeles Times to report one year later: "When finally completed, the mausoleum will be the largest in the world, with 6,000 crypts,"[66] and would cost a total of $2 million.[67]

The *Los Angeles Times* also said of this structure of concrete, granite, marble, and bronze: "Architecturally, the mausoleum is...one of the outstanding examples of Italian Renaissance in this country, combining a purity and simplicity of design with a dignity and stateliness that has given the building its prominence."[68] The recessed entry emphasizes Palladian classical detailing and is crowned with a triangular pediment.

The interior contains a sizable entry hall that features large Carrara marble statues of the Apostles that were carved in Italy. Ornate murals adorn the walls. Overhead are stained-glass skylights, and opposite the entry is a stained round window with a grapevine motif. The colored glass "softens the light and gives the entire room an air of reverence."[69]

Completed in four stages over nine years, the structure houses the remains of such Hollywood luminaries as Rudolph Valentino, Tyrone Power, Col. Griffith J. Griffith, Peter Finch, Eleanor Powell, and Peter Lorre. A set of original drawings delineate the components of the mausoleum, such as the chapel, the corridor housing the crypts, the roof trusses, the skylights, and the loggia.[70] Marston's long-time chief draftsman, James C. Wheeler, was instrumental in the preparation of these drawings.

7.17 Abbey of the Psalms Mausoleum (1929): Egyptian Revival Style

Abbey of the Psalms Mausoleum

Marston, Van Pelt & Maybury's second structure at Hollywood Memorial Park Cemetery is called the Abbey of the Psalms Mausoleum, and it is located at the Park's northern boundary. Plans were begun in 1929, and the local trade press reported that the building "would contain about 650 crypts and 20 family rooms….Construction will be reinforced concrete with a plaster and granite exterior, tile and composition roofing, marble, tile and terrazzo work, art glass, bronze work, copper and sheet metal….The cost will be about $200,000."[71]

The Abbey's front facade follows the Egyptian Revival style, the only such example in Marston's work. Its main entrance facade features an extended one-story, raised temple front with a full entablature displaying a vulture and sun disk motif. The recessed entry is flanked by two paired Egyptian columns with horizontal bands and palm capitals. Popular in the United States in the early nineteenth century, Egyptian Revival was often used in courthouses, prisons, and cemeteries. Such structures were characterized by monumental proportions, smoothly monolithic and unadorned surfaces, flat roofs, shallow porches, and scant decoration, creating the effect of ponderous swelling and bulging. The severe proportions were thought to create a sense of vastness, awe, and reverence. Such buildings gave an unmistakable impression of being "solid, stupendous and time-defying."[72] The Abbey was in good company with Hollywood's nearby Egyptian Theater (1922).

The Abbey's interior favored a more classically based style, including a domed cupola whose sides are clothed in inlaid terrazzo work with alternating Christian and yin and yang symbols.[73] The corridors feature exquisite overhead arched ceiling panels made of marble, predominantly amber in color but bordered with a flower motif highlighted on either side with a thin line of royal blue marble.

The crowning decorative element, still incomplete, is the marble frieze that graces the low exterior wall perpendicular to the front entry steps. The plan was to feature twenty-eight carved marble, life-size Biblical personages to symbolize the message of the 23rd Psalm: the ideals of religious conviction, comfort, and protection. Internationally known sculptor Nisson Tregor was commissioned to carve the design in white Carrara marble. What is in place today is Tregor's "first study": clay casts that he modeled in Rome that are one-fourth the actual size.[74] The Great Depression likely ended all construction on this second Park commission.

Those who have been buried in (or their memory honored at) the Abbey are Charlie Chaplin, Cecil B. De Mille, Edward G. Robinson, Jesse Lasky, and Clifton Webb. In nearby areas of the cemetery lie the remains of Jayne Mansfield, Woody Herman, Marion Davies, Harrison Gray Otis, Harry Chandler, John Huston, Nelson Eddy, and Carl "Alfalfa" Switzer.[75] The Hollywood Memorial Park Cemetery, where tombstones "read like Oscar ballots from other eras,"[76] has been nominated to the National Register of Historic Places.

Public Libraries

There can be no more important public architecture than libraries. Marston's firm was responsible for two of Pasadena's finest branch libraries– Hill Avenue and Santa Catalina–as well as libraries in Claremont, Arcadia, and Wilmington.

The Hill Branch Library - Pasadena

The Marston firm was commissioned in 1924 to design the Hill Avenue branch library on Pasadena's east side, at Green and Hill Avenues.[77] The library was built on a plot of land that the city bought in 1923 from the Giddings family, who had used it to grow peaches and apricots and to raise chickens.[78] This charming one-story library is one of the firm's best public buildings of the Spanish Colonial Revival style. It is symmetrical, with a taller middle section emphasizing the entry, and has varying eave lines. The front entry door surround features open books, carved faces, scrolls, and sea shells in cast stone.

7.18 Hill Branch Library, Pasadena (1924)

The interior is warm and homey. An inviting wooden vestibule opens to adult and children's reading rooms, each accommodating thirty people. There is an outdoor patio reading room "which will be suitably planted and contain a small fountain and ornamental pool of water,"[79] and a rustic pergola leading to a "story-hour" room that seats forty-five people. A large fireplace on one side of the children's area is decorated with tiles depicting scenes from well-known children's stories. Through French doors and a five-sided bay window one can view the outside gardens with tall sycamore and avocado trees.

The library's doors opened on May 2, 1925, to great local fanfare. With approximately eighty people in attendance, the starting event was a grand march and a Virginia reel, "which served to put those pres-

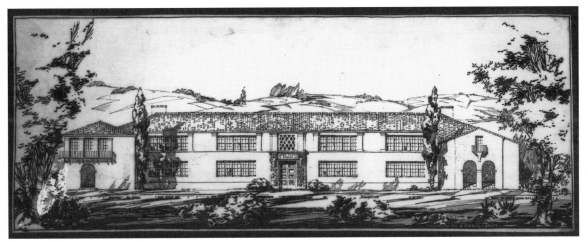

7.19 Linda Vista School, located at 1259 Linda Vista Avenue in Pasadena, was built in 1927 by Marston, Van Pelt & Maybury (now demolished).

7.20 San Rafael Elementary School, 1090 Nithsdale Road, Pasadena, was designed by Marston & Maybury in the Tudor Revival style in 1929.

7.21 Streamline Moderne blends with Spanish in Eliot Jr. High School located at 2184 N. Lake Avenue in Altadena. It was designed by Marston & Maybury in 1932 and is featured in a 1932 issue of Architectural Record.

ent...into a suitable frame of mind for the games and contests that followed.[80] The building won praise for its "light, airy and comfortable atmosphere."[81] Reportedly "one patron, who was building a new home at the time, sent her builder over to see the fireplace in order to duplicate it in her home."[82]

The Southern California Chapter of the AIA cited this commission as the best in its category of small public buildings for 1925.[83] A 1927 issue of *Pacific Coast Architect*[84] contains photographs that show its many features, such as the interior exposed beams and vestibule, the exquisite wrought iron lamps that originally flanked the front entry, and the rough wood branches used in the courtyard pergola. This neighborhood treasure is so cherished that there was a seventy-fifth anniversary party in May of 1985, and at that time the festivities were more multi-cultural, featuring a Lion Dance, a piñata, and a barbershop quartet.[85]

7.22 The Mission School, New Mexico (1910)

Public and Other Schools

In the same year Marston became a licensed architect (1908) he received commissions from the Pasadena Board of Education to prepare plans for public schools in Pasadena.[86] In all, Marston's firm would become responsible for more than twenty-five separate school jobs in Pasadena and elsewhere, particularly in Pomona. Most of these were new construction, though a few were additions, such as the Longfellow Elementary School in Pasadena, originally designed by Greene and Greene in 1911, to which the Marston firm added a new facade and considerable square footage in 1924.[87]

Marston also designed a school in a New Mexico town and an exclusive private school in Pasadena. In the realm of higher education, Pomona College selected Marston to build seven structures on its campus and UCLA tapped Marston to design one of its buildings. The firm also designed a sorority house on Hilgard Avenue across from the UCLA campus.

The Mission School - New Mexico

In 1910, the Presbyterian Church Board of Missions commissioned Marston to design a public school in Dixon, New Mexico.[88] That small, rural community of 800 people is located north of Santa Fe; its population was descended from Spanish settlers. The Board of Missions, then headquartered in Philadelphia, sought to spread the church's teachings, especially in the Southwest where the Catholic Church had a stronghold. The Board of Missions built sev-

eral schools in Northern New Mexico, including this one in Dixon, deliberately selecting a site directly across the street from the town's Catholic school.[89] At the time, the Presbyterians and the Catholics "really duked it out,"[90] but in May 1999 dignitaries from both the Catholic and Presbyterian churches held a widely publicized reconciliation service coinciding with the centennial of the Presbyterians arriving in Dixon, in an attempt to heal old wounds.

The Mission School is no longer used for instruction, but as a community center where public and private events are held.[91] This building, with "great lines," is well-preserved, and church volunteers recently stuccoed the exterior cement walls.[92] This early design was produced by Marston himself before he had any partners, and is in the Mission Revival style, rarely explored by Marston.

7.23 The Westridge School, Pasadena (1923)

Westridge School

In 1923, Marston & Van Pelt designed the Administration building for the Westridge School, at 324 Madeline Drive, which to this day remains the heart of its campus.

The client was Mary Lowther Ranney, "a forward-thinking English major from the University of Chicago,"[93] who had founded the school in 1913, at first convening a class of twenty-one students in her small house at 315 State Street.[94] Almost immediately, a sharp rise in attendance forced Ranney to locate larger quarters, in an old, two-story clapboard bungalow at 324 Madeline Drive. There, she and her parents occupied the upper floor while the lower floor and a room in the rear of the grounds were used for the school.[95] After the first few small classes graduated, it was apparent that the Ranney bungalow was too small to suit a growing student body.

7.24 The Mechanic Arts Building, UCLA, was designed by Marston & Maybury to house the then-new College of Engineering. The local newspaper reported that it "was located on Westwood Boulevard, 50 feet south of the site for the new Kerckhoff Union building, the 120 by 150 foot structure cost $35,000." It was demolished in 1964 to make room for another of UCLA's ubiquitous parking lots.

Ranney, along with her co-principal Miss Amie C. Rumney,[96] commissioned Marston in 1923 to prepare plans for a new building to be constructed on the same site after the bungalow was demolished. Plans called for "10 class rooms, assembly room, 3 offices, teachers room, collapsible [sic] iron gates, maple floors, slate blackboards, skylights; an existing building adjoining will be remodeled for a gymnasium."[97] The result was "a commodious and sightly structure, designed and constructed especially for school purposes."[98]

Designed in the Tudor Revival style, the Westridge School is a long building running east-west along the south side of Madeline Drive. The west side is two-storied to provide for its corridor plan layout. To the east is a one-story portion with a single group of classrooms. The building is decorated in plaster-finished walls, with half-timbering on the second story and exposed beams supporting the projecting upper story. The principle roof is side-gabled, with intersecting gables and dormers creating a lively roofscape.

The Unique, Beyond San Gabriel Valley

Orange County Fruit Exchange

Marston & Van Pelt was commissioned in 1921 to prepare plans for a one-story office building with stucco cladding, a clay tile roof, and art stone to house the Orange County Fruit Exchange at South Glassell and Orange Streets.[99] The small and inconspicuous building, still standing in the Old Town district of the City of Orange, has long been an integral part of the community. In the 1920s, 75 percent of the citrus fruit of that district[100] passed through this building on its way to market. Today, the building has been handsomely transformed into The Exchange, a gallery featuring the work of California artists.

Designed in the Italian Renaissance style, the structure was said to rank "among the foremost buildings of this type not only in Orange county but in other sections of the Southland,"[101] The new building was declared to be "the last word in office construction."[102] This asymmetrical structure has a recessed front entrance that consists of wrought-iron gates with an overhead grille transom bearing the words "Sunkist." The gates guard the wood-paneled front doors. There is a cast stone surround, flush to the front facade, while overhead are the original words carved in stone, "Orange County Fruit Exchange." A projecting stringcourse, often incorporated in Italian Renaissance design, accentuates the elevated roof which provides space for the roundels flanking the stone carved building name. The current owner, who cherishes the building as "one of Orange's architectural treasures,"[103] has steadfastly followed the architects' original plans (not previously executed) for construction of the masonry and iron fence that surrounds the building.

Some of the building's original interior features still remain, including two offices on either side of the entry, one with a cast stone fireplace, and both with handsome barrel ceilings. The exchange's central atrium now incorporates a ceiling entablature supported by four large Honduras mahogany columns of the Tuscan order. This was not part of the original design, but befits an art gallery.

7.25 Orange County Fruit Exchange (1921)

Padua Hills Theater

> Leaving the boulevard near Claremont, California, and veering toward the hills, a part of the San Gabriel Range, a paved but quiet road leads past orange and lemon groves; by intimate homes within stone walls....By this time you assume your guess is correct, you have reached the little theater in the Padua Hills and you note the architects, Marston and Maybury, have achieved the ambition of all architects and made their building a part of the land.

So wrote Ellen Leech in a 1931 issue of *California Arts & Architecture*[104] about the Padua Hills Theater. Located in the Claremont foothills, the theater was added to the National Register of Historic Places in 1998. The complex rests on more than six acres of property and functioned for decades as "one of Southern California's oldest cultural exchange programs."[105]

7.26 Padua Hills Theater (1930), shown as it appeared in the 1930s in the Claremont foothills

Herman H. Garner was a Pomona College graduate and local resident who made his fortune in air filters.[106] He and his associates had purchased nearly 2,000 acres of land in the Mt. San Antonio foothills. In 1930 they hired Marston & Maybury to build a complex of buildings to serve as a community theater. Garner's group chose the Spanish Colonial Revival style.[107] The plans called for three buildings: a theater and dining room, a caretaker's cottage, and an artist's studio.

The theater's evolution was a curious one. Initially, American and British plays constituted the entertainment, with Mexican-American teenagers from the surrounding area serving dinner and singing before each performance. These talented youths began to attract attention, and during the depression they literally took center stage with their popular Mexican songs, dances, and plays. By 1935, the Mexican Players, coming both from Mexico and Southern California, became full-time performers at the theater, while managing to wait tables after their evening's program ended.

Along the way, Mr. and Mrs. Garner, together with the Claremont-Pomona College President Joseph Blaisdell, college trustees, and faculty,[108] formed the Padua Institute, a non-profit entity committed to nurturing better relationships between Americans and Mexican-Americans "at a time when anti-immigrant sentiment was high and thousands of Mexicans...were being sent back to their native country."[109] The group launched an ambitious exchange program, in which actors and educators from America and Mexico temporarily switched locations in order to broaden cultural understanding.

Padua Hills Theater became well known in the social landscape of Southern California during the 1930s. Back then, this was a distant and rustic destination where deer and bear made an occasional visit, far away from the bustle of Los Angeles.[110] Notable Hollywood personalities began to visit in 1932 when Los Angeles social life flourished during the

7.27 Members of the famed "Mexican Players" flanked by the pergola that defines the Padua Hills Theatre, circa 1930s

7.28 Las Olas Beach Club (1926), Venice. This 1927 photograph of the architects' rendering was taken by Harold A. Parker, and depicts the "Las Olas Beach Club." Marston, Van Pelt & Maybury designed this club in 1926. On July 18, 1926, the Los Angeles Times announced: "New Beach Club Started - Latest Ocean Front Project." Now demolished, the club was built on a "strip of ocean frontage midway between Venice and Playa del Rey," and was projected to cost $350,000. The article featured an architects' rendering that is similar though more consolidated that the photograph. In 1926, Venice was annexed to the City of Los Angeles, undoubtedly sparking this and a great deal more development.

Olympic games. Gregory Peck and Edward G. Robinson visited as guests; Walt Disney filmed "The Three Caballeros" there.[111] One former dancer recalled "having to apologetically seat Gregory Peck outside because the place was so packed."[112] *Stage* magazine named the Mexican Players as one of the ten best little theater groups in the United States.[113]

The entire complex is clad in brick and painted white. Warmth is generated by the rich red-tiled roofs, the generous use of thick, exposed wood beams, low eave lines, and an interior courtyard with its stamped earth flooring and plentiful olive trees. The primary building, 6,700 square feet and housing the dining room, kitchen, and theater, is approached through a wood-roofed pergola supported by four paired and rounded brick columns. The dining room features double oak entry doors, an inglenook with a fireplace, a wooden cross-beamed ceiling, oak plank floors, and wrought-iron wall sconces with colored hand-blown glass shades. The wrought-iron work was done by Hayrold Glick whose house and studio were just down the road. The theater closed in 1974, but still stands on six acres in an open, serene, and largely untouched foothill setting. It is used for private social gatherings and for cultural programs put on by the Claremont Historical Society. This complex is an unassuming example of Spanish Colonial architecture—a particularly lucky stylistic choice for the theater's eventual role in celebrating Mexican culture.

Conclusion

I N THE TWILIGHT OF HIS LIFE, SYLVANUS MARSTON, whose "face was lined and distinguished and very old Pasadena,"[1] liked nothing more than the simple pleasures of playing with his grandchildren and working among the roses in his garden. But it must have brought a sense of repose that he could look back on more than thirty years of an architectural practice that he had founded and led during Pasadena's and Southern California's most phenomenal period of growth. His firm had achieved sustained acclaim from the nation's most prestigious architectural reviews for its stylistic breadth, understated elegance, and timeless designs.

Marston, shaped and fortified by his Pasadena roots, was the ultimate gentleman, who is remembered reverentially today by a fellow architect who knew him well as "a great man."[2] Marston's dignified manner and professional talents led clients to flock to him.

When Marston died on November 16, 1946, a memorial service was held at Turner and Stevens Chapel in Pasadena. "If you would find his monument, look around you," the minister told an overflow crowd,[3] referring to Marston's impressive legacy that demonstrates his role as a powerful force in architectural design during Southern California's three finest decades of building.

Afterword

Keith Palmer Marston (1914-2001)

THE FIRST GLIMMER I HAD OF MY FATHER'S PROFESSIONAL STATURE came in the mid-1920s when the Don Lee Corporation–the first Cadillac distributor in California–invited him to its San Francisco headquarters for a consultation. The whole family went along. On the basis of that meeting, Dad was selected as the architect to design the Cadillac showroom, eventually built on Green and El Molino streets in Pasadena, now housing Jacob Maarse Florist.

I acquired an even better window into my father's world beginning at the age of twelve years old, when I started going with my father to his office. He promptly put me to work drawing Ionic, Doric, and Corinthian columns, which I now believe involved the Italian Renaissance styled mausoleum intended for the renowned Hollywood Cemetery. These early experiences no doubt influenced my later decision to become an architect, and in 1936 I obtained a degree in architecture from the University of Southern California. Between my graduation and World War II, I joined my father in his practice and we collaborated on projects such as the Alpha Phi sorority across from UCLA and Mark Keppel High School in Alhambra.

Serious reflection upon my father's career came only after my own retirement in 1974, when I embarked upon the project of putting together a compendium of Dad's works based on the original job records. The project helped me recall so many of the structures as works in progress years earlier. I remember especially clearly the Westminister Presbyterian Church, which I believe conveys the design sense my father acquired when he was in France with the French Army during World War I. Dad visited many chateaus and churches and brought back amazing sketches. I've always figured that the Presbyterian Church was influenced by that unforgettable exposure. I also have a vivid memory of the Ellis Bishop mountaintop ranch in Rancho Santa Fe that was one of Dad's larger residential commissions.

I do not know where my father got his design ideas. I know that Dad loved architecture and greatly valued his Cornell education which was very wedded to historical precedent. I also know from our many conversations in the 1930s that as an architect he placed the greatest importance on balance, symmetry, and the relationship of masses. Perhaps most importantly, I know that my father had great intuitive sense and strived to give clients all that they desired in a given project.

I cannot speak of my father's career successes without mention of my mother, who brought a profound sense of well-being and calm to his life. While she concerned herself mostly with raising the family, there was the occasional client who I believe she had much to do with cultivating. Grace Nicholson is a case in point. My father designed a most unusual structure for her in the 1920s. My mother and Nicholson had much in common: they were learned women, especially for their time (my mother was a graduate of Cal '06, and Nicholson was well-read). Both were aware and alert to the larger world, my mother through her religious work and missionary outreach, and Grace Nicholson through her intense study of the Far East.

While my father's greatness is obvious to me now, as a boy growing up in Pasadena in the 1920s, I knew him mainly as a terrific Dad. Dinner conversation was not taken up with his office talk, project designs, or client difficulties. Rather, he was very involved in the upbringing of myself and my two brothers. To this day, it is my father's goodness and humanity especially that I shall never forget. On the eve of World War II, his business dried up and staff had to be laid off. Dad informed me that I would have to leave, which would save him from having to terminate Jim Wheeler, who had been his loyal and talented chief draftsman since back in the 1920s. Although this decision initially was a little difficult for me to accept, my father's devotion to close colleagues was quite extraordinary.

I hope that this book is treasured by our family and that it serves as a perpetual memory of my father—a man who reached the pinnacle of his profession, yet was down-to-earth and honest, and who loved life. I also hope this book will be enjoyed by many other readers who might draw from these pages an esthetic appreciation and inspiration from one man's life and contributions.

Keith Palmer Marston
Montecito, California
September, 2000

Acknowledgments

I N THE FALL OF 1996 I ATTENDED A SOCIAL GATHERING that was sponsored by the Pasadena Historical Museum and held at a French manor house along the edge of the Arroyo. Guests came to celebrate the city's rich architectural heritage and to hear Keith Palmer Marston speak about his architect father Sylvanus Marston, who had designed the house. Keith, himself an accomplished architect, and then eighty-two years old, talked movingly about his father. The scene became a metaphor for how easily the fabric and texture of a community can fade. I approached Keith after his remarks and suggested we work on a book about his father. This volume is the result of that effort.

Although Keith Marston read and commented upon the manuscript in its final stages, I deeply regret that he did not live to see the published product. His fondest wish was to hold the book in his hands and to attend book-signing events and speak about his father's life and career. I am profoundly grateful to Keith for many things: his invaluable assistance; providing a window into the Marston family; sharing treasured stories, rare photographs, and his father's diary from World War I; for his decency, his kindness, and his trust. Many thanks to his wife Nancy Marston, who appreciated this project's importance to Keith. Thanks also to his children William and Linda, and grandson Keith Palmer Marston II, for their avid interest.

A book about a man born in the nineteenth century and thus beyond the reach of most living memories imposes special challenges. The writer must dig deeply to ensure that what is presented is more than merely a snapshot of the person. There is the further need to come to know the broader panorama of Marston's era in order to accurately place him in it. Finally, with no writings or memoirs by Marston save his World War I diary, portraying him as a man and personality can be complicated, involving making assumptions based on facts that are known. In this process countless individuals and institutions provided assistance. I am beholden to them for the treasures they shared. I was especially honored to speak with two eminent architects who knew Marston and whose careers intersected his: A. C. Martin, Jr., and Robert E. Bennett. I also thank Richard Thomas who, as a boyhood friend of the Marston sons and as their next-door neighbor, saw Sylvanus Marston at close range; to friends and relatives of Garrett Van Pelt: Louise Kellogg, Marian Lacey Bassett, Marie Van Pelt Clark, and Walter P. White, Jr.; and to Edgar Maybury's children Marjorie Maybury Kellogg and Allen N. Maybury, who shared with me their vivid memories.

I want to herald the unexpected wonders found in local and regional libraries, those from Bangor, Maine, to Los Angeles—they are the repositories of historical secrets and are a writer's best friend. In particular, deep thanks to Carolyn Garner of the Pasadena Central Library; Dr. Alan Jutzi, Curator of Rare Books, and Jennifer Watts and Kate McGinn, Curators of Rare Photos at the Huntington Library; the late Tom Owens, as well as Carolyn Cole and Kathy Kobayashi of the Los Angeles Public Library's California Files; Charlotte Brown, Special Collections, University Research Library, UCLA; Dennis Bitterlich of the UCLA Archives; USC's marvelous Helen Topping Architecture and Fine Arts Library (especially Jason Stieber); Lydia Emard, Arts Library, U.C. Santa Barbara; Tompkins County Public Library, Ithaca, New York; Oakland Public Library; The Burton History Collection at the Detroit Public Library; Bangor Public Library; Barbara Richmond of the Menaul Historical Library of the Southwest; John Moulton, Embudo Library, Dixon, New Mexico; Katherine Reagan, Rare and Manuscript Collections, University Library, Cornell University; and the Library of Congress.

Museums, historical societies, preservation groups and governmental entities were crucial to this project. My thanks to John Cahoon, Seaver Center for Western History Research, Natural History Museum, Los Angeles County; David Kamansky, Executive Director and Senior Curator, Pacific Asia Museum; Edward R. Bosley, Director of the Gamble House in Pasadena; Altadena Heritage; Bangor Historical Society; Claremont Historical Society; Phyllis Paul of the Rancho Santa Fe Historical Society; and the U.S. Lighthouse Society in San Francisco. Appreciation, too, to Richard N. Quacquarini, Chief Cadestral Engineer of the Los Angeles County Assessor's Office; to Betsy Figueira of the California State Board of Architectural Examiners who found some remarkable material in ancient files; and to Cynthia A. Howse of the California State Office of Historic Preservation, which holds the nomination papers for state historical landmark status and for listing on the National Register of Historic Places.

Unquestionably, this book would not have been possible without the enthusiasm, support and resources of two groups. The first is the Pasadena Historical Museum, where the Marston Collection and Pasadena's past are preserved; special thanks to Jeannette L. O'Malley, Jane Irwin Laudeman, Tania Rizzo, Kirk Myers, Ardis Willwerth, Patricia Sims, and Jaclyn Palmer. Pasadena Heritage, the second group, has fought many a good fight to preserve Marston structures and shared invaluable historical files with me; special thanks to Susan Mossman, Sheree Sampson, and Nancy Carlton.

The coverage of Marston's works would not have been as comprehensive, nor as architecturally descriptive, were it not for the impressive earlier work on individual Marston buildings, in the form of historic structure inventories, proposals for nomination as state or national historical landmarks, or scholarly publications. Authors who prepared reports or articles relied upon in this book include: Ann Scheid Lund, William W. Ellinger, III, Becky Bishop, Alson Clark, Edward R. Bosley, Diane Williams, Jeanne Perkins, Robert Winter, Kathleen Flanigan, Linda Peters, Jane Apostol, Ginger Eliott, Thirtieth Street Architects, Inc., Charles Hall Page & Associates, Denver Miller, Christy J. McAvoy, Lauren Bricker, Janet Tearnen, John Christopher Terell, and Pamela Lee Gray.

The American Institute of Architects locally and its headquarters in Washington, D.C., were important resources, and I wish to thank Janet White, FAIA, national vice president, for her assistance with access to the AIA archives and library in Washington; and Adolfo Miralles, past president of the Pasadena-Foothill Chapter and Diana Barnwell, the organization's executive director. Thanks also to architect Dwain Lind, and to James De Long, AIA, editorial director of the Journal of the Taliesin Fellows.

Enormous thanks go to Donald L. Parker, now deceased son of the notable Pasadena photographer Harold A. Parker, who provided generous access to a collection of his father's photographs featuring early Pasadena people and buildings. From these photographs and preserved architects' renderings, I was able to "see" some Marston buildings that had been demolished. For his photographic assistance, sensitive approach, and love of the subject, I also want to thank Tavo Olmos of Positive Image Photography in Pasadena.

I am profoundly grateful to past and current Marston homeowners who welcomed me into their houses with enthusiasm and a measure of curiosity. I want to extend special thanks to Shawn Libaw, at whose splendid house I became inspired to write this book about Marston; to Nancy H. Sokol who lives near Cornell University in Marston's very first residential commission; and to Margaret Brooks who lives in

Phineas Marston's house in Bangor, Maine. Homeowners and I puzzled over their dwellings' histories, the architects' blueprints, and the occasional eccentric demands placed upon the architects (e.g., secret passageways and hidden door panels). Appreciation is extended to local enthusiasts who provided some introductions: Charles Livingstone, Dave Sturges, Brett Furrey, Esther Tan, and Peggy Dickson.

John Ripley, an exoatmospheric aeronautical engineer by day, who on weekends savors his eighty-five year old Pasadena bungalow, contributed priceless information for the Arts and Crafts chapter. My thanks to him for his remarkable research and for generously giving of his time in numerous conversations.

No one embarks upon a project such as this without uncommon inspiration and the faith of friends and family. These individuals, who I thank most warmly, include: my excellent editor at Hennessey + Ingalls, Robert Barrett, who first encouraged this work; Mark P. Hennessey, for his confidence in the project; Edward R. Bosley, for letting me in the circle; William F. Deverell, Jr., who pointed me toward the Huntington Library; friend and architect, David Greenwood, who years ago introduced me to Hennessey + Ingalls; Mary Doyle, who buoyed me with her enthusiasm; Kathryn and Neal Showers as well as Kathleen Keaton and Edward Murphy, who endured every twist and turn; Katherine McDaniel, Neil Barker, and Patrick Del Duca, whose intelligence and equanimity were crucial; Ann Gray, of Balcony Press; Anne and Kevin Smith, Daniel Borenstein, Charles March, Don Whitehead, Libby Breen, and Romy Wylie; friends at the office: John Hopkins-Luder, Stuart Lytton, Dana Aratani, Lisa Kaas Boyle, Olga Correa, Stanley Williams, Thomas Papageorge, Joseph Scott, and Rich Llewelyn; and great friends on and off the tennis courts: Nick and Gerry Williams, Eric and Martha Malnic, Lynn T. Jewell, Diane Kanner, and Karen Wada; and finally, heartfelt thanks to wonderful family farther away–Doug, Nancy, and Josh, and the young ones who I promise to spend more time with, Rebecca and Hannah; and to Charlotte Josephine Boecker, my great-aunt (1909-1999), who lived and loved history, and whose uncommon kindness eased this effort.

My deepest appreciation goes to four people I hold dear. This book is dedicated to the memory of my father, Burt Joseph Tuttle, whose 47-year life was far too brief. He loved his native California and shared many favorite places with his family–from national parks and ghost towns to historic sites in Southern California. These travels introduced me to the richness of our golden state. I owe a special debt of gratitude to my mother, Dolores Tuttle, to my stepfather, Gilbert Geis, and to my brother, John A. Tuttle, for their steadfast faith in me, their encouragement and loving support, their unflagging enthusiasm for this project, their sacrifice of time, and their unceasing wise counsel, criticism, and reflection upon all aspects of this effort. They sustained me in what has been an incredible journey.

Kathleen Tuttle
Altadena
June 2001

List of Structures

References

AA *American Architect*
AD *Architectural Digest*
AIA American Institute of Architects
A&D *Arts & Decoration*
A&E *Architect and Engineer*
AF *Architectural Forum*
AR *Architectural Record*
B&C *Builder and Contractor*
CA&A *California Arts & Architecture*
CL *California Life*
CG *California Gardens*
CS *California Southland*
CR *The Craftsman*
HB *House Beautiful*
H&G *House & Garden*
LHJ *The Ladies' Home Journal*
LAT *Los Angeles Times*
LABC *Los Angeles Builder and Contractor*
LAN *Los Angeles News*

MD *Mediterranean Domestic Architecture in the US*
MM *Mediterranean to Modern: Residential Architecture in Southern California*
NYT *New York Times*
PCA *Pacific Coast Architect*
PDU *Pasadena Daily Union*
PEP *Pasadena Evening Post*
PSN *Pasadena Star News*
PP *Picturesque Pasadena*
SCQ *Southern California Quarterly*
SWCM *Southwest Contractor and Manufacturer*
SWBC *Southwest Builder and Contractor*
TB *Tournament of Roses Brochure*
WA *Western Architect*
YB *Year Book of the Los Angeles Architectural Club*

Building Status

D Demolished
AA Alteration and/or addition to existing structure

Structures that appear in the book are in **boldface type**.

Marston Structures Not Listed in Original Job Records

Year	Job No.	Client/Project	Address	Notes/References
1910	~~	**Arts and Crafts Portals**	Prospect Park Entrance at Orange Grove Ave., Pasadena	See architect's blueprint at Pasadena Historical Museum
1910	~~	**Arts and Crafts Entrance Gates**	Linda Vista Park, Santa Monica	PSN 12/15/1911; LABC 12/14/1911
1911	~~	**Curtis-Kendall Co. Bungalow**	599 S. Mentor Ave., Pasadena	CR 11/1914; LHJ 5/1915
1930	~~	Dr. Stacy Clapp	4442 E. Live Oak Dr., Claremont	See architects' blueprint
1934	~~	Arnold White	Pasadena	AR 7/1935; AF 1938
1939	~~	Jack Armstrong	419 W. Armsley Sq., Ontario	See California State Office of Historic Preservation, Marston Database

Marston Structures Listed in Original Job Records Located at the Pasadena Historical Musuem

Year	Job No.		Client/Project	Address	Notes/References
1908	1		C. R. Seaver		
1908	2	D	G. S. Hinckley	542 S. Oakland Ave	LABC 4/2/1908
	3		A. G. Merriam	648 S. Oakland Ave.	
1909	7		**C. P. McAllaster**	658 S. Hudson Ave	
	8		Citizen's Realty Co.	681 S. Oakland Ave.	
	9		Rev. E. H. Gilian	1003 Atchison St	
	10	D	A. M. Jones	236 S. Madison Ave.	
	11	D	E. Horstman	1590 Las Tunas	
1909	12		**C. P. McAllaster**	516 S. Oakland Ave.	TB 1910
1909	13	D	S. N. Frey	496 S. Madison Ave.	LABC 2/18/1909
1908	14		**St. Francis Court**	777 E. Colorado Blvd. [see 709, 717, 725 S. Catalina Ave.]	SWBC 9/17/1908; AA 1/6/1909; *Bungalows;* YB1910; 1911; *Sunset,* December 1911; TB 1910, 1911, 1912; LHJ, 2/1914, 4/1914, 2/1915, 6/1915; *The Building Age,* Oct. 1919; PSN 10/29/1914, 12/19/1925; *The California Bungalow,* 1980; *Toward A Simpler Way of Life,* 1997.
1909	15		Isaac R. Morris	230 S. Grand Ave.	PSN 12/3/1929
	16		C. P. McAllaster	500 S. Oakland Ave.	
	17	D	G. A. Backus	98 S. Euclid Ave.	
	19	D	A. F. Mills	83 S. Orange Grove Blvd.	
	20	D	W. J. Hogan	115 N. Madison Ave.	
	21		A. F. Mills	see #19	
1909	22		**Ella M. Barnes**	120 N. Madison Ave.	LABC 6/3/1909
1910	23	D	**Maryland Hotel Bungalow**	96 N. Euclid Ave.	TB 1911
1910	24	D	**Maryland Hotel Bungalow**	99 N. Euclid Ave.	
	25		J. S. Maltman	3036 Santa Rosa Ave., Alt.	
	26		Harold Breakey	520 E. Mariposa St., Alt.	
	27		J. S. Maltman	see #25	
	28		W. A. McCormick	325 E. Alvarado St., Pomona	
	29	D	F. C. Beidler	160 N. Madison Ave.	
	30		Mary H. Burg	4925 Pasadena Ave. Terrace, LA	
	31	D	Hogan Bungalows	744-46 Herkimer St. (Union)	
	32		T. A. Schnitzlein	560 E. Mariposa St., Alt.	Now Senior Center
1911	33		A. A. French	Madison Ave.	LABC 5/11/1911
1910	34		**H. C. French, Jr.**	1011 S. Madison Ave [father]	LABC 2/3/1910
	35		A. A. French	1000 S. Madison Ave.	
	36	D	John Baker	231 W. California Blvd.	
1910	37		Edward Eliot	469 California Terrace	
1910	38		**S. B. Marston**	661 S. El Molino Ave.	
	39	D	F. G. Hogan	91 S. Los Robles Ave. [apt]	
	40	D	F. G. Hogan	127 N. El Molino Ave [Col. W.J. Hogan home]	
1910	41	D	**Maryland Apartments**	95 S. Los Robles Ave. [Hogan]	WA 1/1911
1910	42		**J. E. Hinds**	695 Prospect Blvd.	PSN c.1913; PS 5/13/1915; PSN 1924
1910	43	D	F. A. Marston	560 E. California Blvd.	
	44	D	M. H. Lord	181 S. Madison Ave.	
	45		C. C. Hudson	1707 Oak St., S. Pas. [façade is new]	
1910	46		West Side Congregational Church	535 S. Pasadena Ave	
	47	D	M. J. Hill	376 N. Raymond Ave. [AA]	
1910	48		West Side Congregational Church Parish House	535 S. Pasadena Ave.	*B&C 9/1910; B&C 3/13/1913* Now Sequoia School
1910	49		**Dr. D. F. Fox**	993 N. Madison Ave.	LABC 9/1/1910; PSN 12/3/1924

1909	50	D	J. E. Parker	125 S. Orange Grove Ave.	TB 1913
1910	51		**Mission School**	Dixon, New. Mexico	Now Community Center
	52	D	McKinley School Kindergarten	S. El Molino Ave.	TB 1913
	53	D	Dr. G. D. Fundenburg	727 E. Colorado. Blvd.	
	54	D	Hogan Co.	99 N. Euclid Ave. [AA]	
1911	55		**Dr. G. Roscoe Thomas**	574 Bellefontaine Place	PDU 10/20/1887; PSN 1/1918; YB 1912; *Trolley Days in Pasadena*, 1982
	56		A. F. Mills	see #19	
	57	D	Tujunga Rock Co. Plant	Tujunga Canyon	
	59		W. J. Hogan	see #20	
	60		W. J. Hogan	see #20 [garage]	
	62		J. E. Coggshall	655 N. Los Robles Ave.	
	63		H. R. Slayden	237 W. Colorado Blvd. [community garage]	
	64		J. P. Phillips		
	66		J. Brettingham		
	67		Mrs. Warne		
	68	D	L. M. Pratt	164 N. Hudson Ave.	
	70	D	Washington School Manual Training		
	71		G. S. Hinkley	see #2	
1911	75		**W. M. Eason**	630 Prospect Boulevard	
	116		Stacy W. Clapp		
	150		T. C. Lee	1255 S. Oak Knoll Ave.	
	151	D	J. J. Bleecker	40 S. Los Robles Ave. [AA]	
	152		Henderson	516 S. Oakland Ave. [A]	
	153	D	F. C. Beidler	[AA]	
	154		N. D. Hinckley	Redlands	
1910	155		Mrs. Fenyes	170 N. Orange Grove Blvd. [AA]	LABC 11/24/1910
	156		Backus - #1	contractor	
1910	157		**Curtis-Kendall Co. Bungalow**	623 S. Mentor Ave.	TB 1912; YB 1912; *Scribners* 1912
1912	158		**Curtis-Kendall Co. Bungalow**	606 S. Mentor Ave.	CR 11/1914; LHJ June 1915
1911	159		**Mrs. Robert Anderson**	695 S. Madison Ave.	YB 1912
	160		Curtis-Kendall Co.	665 S. Mentor Ave.	
	161	D	W. J. Hogan Stables	744 Union St.	
	162		Dr. G. Thomas Roscoe	see #55	
	163		Dr. C. H. Parker	55 W. Altadena Dr. [AA].	
1911	163a		A. S. French (Brooks)	946 S. Madison Ave.	
1911	164		A. S. French	932 S. Madison Ave.	
1911	165		**Maitland Bishop**	422 California Terrace	LABC 5/18/1911; PS 8/7/1965 PSN 9/6/1985
1911	166		**George B. Ellis**	1440 N. Los Robles Ave.	TB 1913
	167	D	Columbia Elementary-Kindergarten	N. Mentor Ave.	
	168		C. H. Paddock	746 S. Madison Ave. [AA]	
1911	169		Andrew Jackson Elementary School	593 W. Woodbury Rd., Alt.	PP
	170	D	Lincoln Avenue School	600 N. Lincoln Ave.	
	171		J. W. Coleman	1625 Casa Grande St.	
1911	172	D	**Robert A. Swink**	400 N. Los Robles Ave.	
	173	D	Kendall-Curtis Co. (National Biscuit Co.)	445 S. Raymond Ave.	
	174	D	C. B. Scoville	56 N. Grand Ave.	
	175	D	Lon Chapin	597 Drexel Place	
	176		E. S. Armstrong	920 S. Madison Ave.	
	177	D	Kendall-Curtis Co	634 S. Lake Ave.	
	178		C. P. McAllaster	535 S. Catalina Ave.	
	179	D	Emma M. Grossman	565 S. Catalina Ave.	
1912	180		**H. R. Lacey**	1115 Woodbury Rd	LABC 11/2/1911
1911	181		**L. G. Haase**	1185 N. Marengo Ave.	LABC 11/23/1911
1911	182		F. E. Day	656 S. Oakland Ave.	
	183		City Reality Co.		
1912	184		H. L. Joannes	1036 S. Madison Ave. [original porch was cobblestone]	LABC 12/28/1911

	185		Mrs. C. Hanna	803 S. Oakland Ave.	
	186		Rev. E. H. Gilian	see #9	
	187		Porter Memorial	Korea	
	188		Frank Brackett	140 E. 4th St., Claremont [AA]	
1912	189		**W. D. Petersen [Villa Sarah]**	1095 Rubio Drive, Alt.	YB 1913; PSN 5/10/1912; LABC 2/29/1912; SWCM 5/11/1912; A&E 1913, 1914
	190	D	H. S. Carhart	277 N. El Molino Ave.	
	191	D	H. M. Parsons	1620 Monterey Rd., S.Pas.	
1913	192		W. W. Gerlach	985 N. Los Robles	
1911	193		**Kendall-Curtis Co. Bungalow**	636 S. Mentor Ave.	
	194	D	E. F. Hahn	175 S. El Molino Ave.	
	195	D	Munger Store	194-96 E. Union St.	
	196	D	O. K. Hines	190 S. Oakland Ave. [was 90 Ford Place]	
1912	197		**William Hespeler**	239 N. Orange Grove Blvd.	LABC 8/29/1912; YB 1913; A&E 6/1913 and 9/1914
	198	D	Pasadena City School Warehouse	577 Worchester Ave.	
	199	D	Joseph Wolfenstetter	415 S. Madison Ave.	
1913	200	D	**Pasadena National Bank**	132 E. Colorado Blvd.	A&E 6/1916; YB 1913
1913	201		G. L. Andrews	1303 Rubio Dr., Altadena	LABC 11/26/1913
	202		W. B. Bentley	La Canada	
	203	D	Joseph McManus	745 E. California Blvd.	
	204		A. A. Nottmeyer	985 S. Oakland Ave.	
1913	205		**Arroyo Park Co. [Henry Newby]**	1015 Prospect Blvd.	AA 2/191915;TB 1915; AR 10/1916; PSN 9/18/1929
	206		I. R. Morris	see #15	
	207		W. S. Adams	873 N. Hill Ave. ["Pine Hill"]	
1913	208	D	Mrs. Francis White	336 Palmetto Drive	
	209	D	M. C. Treat	98 N. El Molino Ave.	
1913	210		**H. E. Bidwell**	1047 S. Madison Ave.	TB 1922, AR 10/1917; CL 11/29/1913
	211		W. H. Spurgeon, Jr.	1704 Main St., Santa Ana	
	212		Congregational Church Parish House	531 S. Pasadena Ave.	
	213	D	Pasadena National Bank	124-30 E. Colorado Blvd.	YB 1913
1913	214	D	**T. E. Hicks**	255 Madeline Drive	LABC 8/29/1912, AR 10/1917
	215		Pasadena High School Gym	1570 E. Colorado Blvd.	Now Pasadena City College
	216		H. A. Baldridge	761 N. Fair Oaks Ave.	
	217		H. N. Anderson	817 S. Madison Ave	
	218	D	Pasadena High School Agriculture Bldg.	1570 E. Colorado Blvd.	
	219		C. C. Stanley	326 Congress Place	
	220	D	Turner & Stevens Mortuary	Chapel & Main Sts, Alhambra	
	221		Harvey Newby	456 Ford Place	
	222	D	J. W. Lawrence	160 N. El Molino Ave. [AA]	
1915	223		Leo G. MacLaughlin	1010 Armada Dr.	
	224		R. H. Pyle		
	225	D	St. Francis Court Annex	777 E. Colorado Blvd.	
	226	D	Roosevelt School	320 Rosemont Ave. [AA]	
	227		Lamanda Park Elementary School	2690 E. Colorado Blvd	
	228		Altadena School	743 E. Calaveras St., Altadena	
1913	229		Henry Newby	see #205	
	230		C. B. Summer	500 La Loma Rd.	
	231		I. G. Pattinson	487 California Terrace	
	232		C. M. Davis		
	233		Roy Anderson		
	234		Woodworth & Son	1064 N. Chester Ave	
	235	D	A. M. Johnson	475 E. California Blvd.	
	236	D	Miss Loop	473 Kensington Place	
	237		Henry Newby	see # 205 [garage]	
	238		W. S. Adams	873 N. Hill Ave. [garage]	
	239	D	Rice Bungalow	40 S. Los Robles Ave.	

	240	D	C. G. Scoville	534 Linda Vista Ave. [greenhouse]	
	241		Mrs. Eva Fenyes	see #155	
	242	D	Mexican Mission	153 Filmore St. (Ritzman) [Methodist Church]	
1915	243		**W. K. Jewett**	1145 Arden Rd.	AD 1924; AR 7/1922; PSN 8/27/1935; CS 10/1927
1915	244	D	**J. E. Meeker**	397 N. Raymond Ave.	WA 1/1918; PSN 2/2/1928
1915	245		**S. S. Hinds**	880 La Loma Rd.	AR 11/1916, 7/1922; A&E 1920; CS 6/1919; NYT 10/13/1948
	246	D	Throop Dormitory	1220 San Pasqual St. [this job was a relocation]	
	247		Franklin Thomas	685 S. El Molino Ave. [new front portico]	
	248	D	Hospital Dispensary	36 Congress St.	
	249	D	J. H. McKellar	693 E. California Blvd.	
	250	D	Brick Store	169-71 N. Fair Oaks Ave.	
	251	D	Pasadena High School Club House	1570 E. Colorado Blvd.	
1915	252		Jeremiah M. Rhodes	195 S. Hill Ave.	CS 4/1919; Now Knox Presbyterian Church Annex
1916	253		**F. H. D. Banks**	1210 Chelten Way, S. Pas	LAT 4/13/1980
	254		Mrs. H. M. Dobbins	1300 S. Los Robles Ave	
	255		George Jr. Rep - Gymnasium	Chino	
1916	256	D	**Lincoln Avenue Church**	2601 N. Lincoln Ave.	LHJ 1/1917
	257		Altadena School – West	593 W. Woodbury Rd., Alt.	
	258		Altadena National Bank	N. Lake Ave.	
	259		Lincoln Avenue School	600 N. Lincoln Ave.	
	260		S. S. Hinds	see #245 - garage	
	261		W. K. Jewett	see #243 - garage	
	262		W.K. Jewett	see #243 - driveway	
	263		F. H. Ohrmund		
	264	D	Joseph Burkhard	2100 Brigden Rd.	
	265		George E. Hall	1254 Oak Knoll Ave. [since remodeled]	
	266		C. I. Baxter	1199 Wentworth Ave.	
1916	267		W. G. Palmer	859 S. Oakland Ave.	
	268		G. W. Gildehaus	2699 E. California Blvd	
	269		S. S. Hinds	see #245 – retaining wall	
	270	D	George A. Weber	1627 San Pasqual St.	
1916	271		A. C. Buttolph	1140 New York Dr.	
	272	D	E. E. Webster	139 N. El Molino Ave.	
	273		Fowler Museum		
1916	274		**Arthur L. Garford**	1126 and 1132 Hillcrest Ave.	AR 9/1919; PSN 4/26/1916; CS 1/1922; WA 8/1923; PEP 4/18/1916
	275		Charles Shade	485 S. Euclid Ave.	
	276	D	Shade & Wold Garage	707-717 E. Colorado Blvd.	
1916	277		Altadena Country Club Co. #1	2290 Country Club Dr. [now Holliston] Altadena	Now Private Residence
	278		Altadena Country Club Co. #2	1973 Mendocino Lane, Alt	Now Private Residence
	279		Altadena Country Club Co. #3	2029 Mendocino Lane, Alt	Now Private Residence
1915	280		Mrs. H. M. Dobbins	1300 S. Los Robles Ave. – garage	LAT 9/22/1962
	281		C. I. Baxter	see # 266 - garage	
	282		W. G. Palmer	see # 267 - garage	
	283		G. W. Gildehaus	see # 268 - garage	
	284		A. C. Buttolph	see # 271 - garage	
	285		Dr. Upjohn		
	286		Altadena Country Club - Wall	2290 Country Club Dr., Alt.	
	287	D	Pasadena High School Swimming Pool	1570 E. Colorado Blvd.	
	288	D	Pasadena High School - Music Hall	1570 E. Colorado Blvd.	
1917	289		Westminster Presbyterian Church	1757 N. Lake Ave.	
	290		Crown Apartments	675-677 E. Colorado Blvd. [AA]	

1917	291		**W. DeWitt Lacey**	1105 Arden Rd.	
	292		Altadena Country Club Co. #2	see #278 – garage	
	293		Altadena Country Club Co. #3	see #279 – garage	
	294	D	Marcey	Newport Ave. @ Marcey Dr. [tractor shed]	
	295		Marcey	East Tustin – prop continuous w/ westly line of Irvine Ranch [barn]	
	296		Marcey	[ranch house]	
	297		Walkover Boot Shop	36 E. Colorado Blvd. [has been remodeled]	
	298		F. M. Hicks	1315 S. Oakland Ave. [AA] Known as "Wistaria House"	
1917	299		E. L. Roberts	509 Prospect Blvd	
	300		R. J. Bassett	see #297	
	301		George Jr. Rep. - Hospital	Chino	
	302		C. W. Gates	1025 Arden Rd. [AA]	
	303	D	Rare Metals Refinery	309 S. Arroyo Pkwy	
	304	D	Fowler Playground Cottage	295 Grove St.	
	305		F. G. Hogan		
	306		Marcey	service porch	
	307	D	Dr. Hicks	969 San Pasqual St.	
	308		Rufus P. Spaulding	349 S. Grand Ave. [AA]	
	309	D	Joseph Scott	1199 S. Orange Grove Blvd. [AA]	
	310		Gerald Waterhouse	585 N. Marengo Ave. [AA]	
1917	311		**Hollywood Mausoleum**	6000 Santa Monica Blvd., Los Angeles [Phase 1]	LAT 9/17/1922; LAT 11/12/1922 SWBC 3/21/1930 *NYT Magazine* 11/15/1998
1918	312		W. A. McNally Store	106 W. Colorado Blvd.	Now Commercial Bldg in Old Town
	313		Gaylord	[AA]	
	314		W. K. Jewett Mausoleum	601 Roses Rd., San Gabriel	
	315		S. L. Van Pelt (contractor)	1272 N. Catalina	
	316		Shade & Wold Garage	see #276 [addition]	
	317		Thomsen	[AA]	
	318		Colin Stewart	450 Ford Place	
	319		Richard Gaud		
	320		Marcey	see #296 [pumphouse]	
	321	D	G. A. Buckingham	1909 S. Harvard Blvd., LA. [AA]	
	322		W. A. McNally Store	see #312	
	323		Arthur Noble	550 W. California Blvd. [AA]	
	324		W. D. Petersen	see #189 [fence]	
	325	D	Frank Harwood	San Dimas	
	326		Bessie A. Wilson	250 S. Hill Ave.	
	327		David Blankenhorn	E. California Blvd.	
	328	D	George Day	610 S. Orange Grove Blvd.	
	329	D	Holstrum Warehouse	350 S. Arroyo Parkway	
	330		C. H. Branaman	2901 Waverly Drive, LA	
	331	D	E. F. & S. E. Hahn Store	329-335 E. Colorado Blvd.	
	332		H. O. Ayers		
	333	D	C.W. Dorsey	5330 Russell Ave., LA	
	334		J. E. Hinds	851 S. Oakland Ave.	
1920	335	D	**S. L. Bird**	251 S. Orange Grove Blvd.	PSN 2/28/1920
1921	336	D	**W. T. Jefferson**	35 N. Grand Ave.	HB 2/18/1922; CS 1/1922; AR 7/1922; MD; PP; WA 8/1923; PSN 5/10/1924
1921	337		Robert Casamajor	883 S. Oakland Ave.	
	338		Henry A. Doty	841 S. Oakland Ave.	
	339		Garfield Jones	1224 Arden Road	
1920	340		**J. E. Tilt**	455 Bradford St. [was 707 S. Orange Grove Blvd.]	SWBC 5/28/1920; HB 1/1922; AR 7/1922; PSN 9/29/1930
1920	341		T. C. Eggleston	1484 E. California Blvd.	CS 1/1922

1922	342		**John N. Van Patten**	282 S. San Rafael Ave.	AA 6/3/1925
	343	D	M. Sweet	1665 San Pasqual St.	
	344		Hogeland		
	345		Sheehan		
1920	346		**McMurtry-Meyers** **(J.H. Meyer) "Villa Alegre"**	1021 Oak Grove Ave., San Marino	AR 7/1922; SWCB 5/21/1920; CS 1/1922; HB 1/1922; AD 8/1924; MD; WA 8/1923; CL 5/1/1925
	347		Garfield Jones Store		
	348		Marcey-Ravels Co.	Santa Ana	
	349		W. K. Jewett	see #243 – tennis courts	
	350	D	Claude M. Griffith	745 S. Orange Grove Blvd.	
	351		C. C. Stanley	1325 Lombardy Rd	
1920	352		**Vista del Arroyo Hotel** **1920s Hotel Structure**	125 S. Grand Ave	PP; TB 1921;WA 8/1923; CL 12/12/1924; CL 5/13/1922; CS 11/1921; AA 8/1923; Now Federal Appellate Courthouse
	353		Jones & Keck residence		
1921	354		Colin Stewart	281 S. San Rafael Ave.	PSN 8/4/1910; CL 2/18/1922
	355		J. H. McKellar	725 S. Oak Knoll Ave.	
	356	D	California Laundry	1025 Vine St., LA	
	357	D	R. J. Bassett	322 Elevado Dr.	
1922	358		**Hollywood Mausoleum**	6000 Santa Monica Blvd., LA [Phase 2]	
	359		Inglewood Cemetery	720 E. Florence Ave., Inglewood	
	360	D	George A. Weber	1649 San Pasqual St.	
	361		Lee K. Stewart		
	362		W. H. Mann	777 S. Oak Knoll Ave	
	363	D	Harold A. Parker Co. Store	570 E. Colorado Blvd.	
	364	D	Pasadena Presbyterian Church Kirkhouse	E. Union St.	
	365		H. O. Cunningham	770 Oak Knoll Circle	
	366	D	Ben Hahn	550 N. Santa Bonita	
1922	367	D	Staats Bank & Office Bldg.	305 E. Colorado Blvd.	
	368	D	Garfield Avenue Stores	10-38 N. Garfield Ave.	
1922	369		**Turner & Stevens Mortuary**	95 N. Marengo Ave.	Now Holly Street Grill
1922	370		**James Scripps Booth**	1066 Charles St. [was 1771 Linda Vista]	CS 2/1923; A&E 3/1923; PCA 7/1924; AR 11/1923; MD
1922	371		**Bertha Holt Clark**	587 S. Hill Ave	PSN 1/7/1928; MD
	372	D	First Methodist Church	see #242	
	373		John Simpson	685 S. Euclid Ave	
	374	D	Pasadena Boy's & Girl's Library	190 N. Raymond Ave.	
	375		R. B. Rickenaugh	287 S. Hill Ave.	Now Caltech Administration Bldg.
	376	D	G. A. Ogle	217 S. Orange Grove Blvd. [AA]	
	377		Andrew Jackson Elementary School	See #169	
1921	378		**Orange County Fruit** **Exchange**	Glassell and Orange Sts., Orange	SWBC 11/11/1921; AA 4/22/1925; Now The Exchange Gallery; *Orange Daily News* 12/28/1922
	379		Mrs. H. M. Dobbins	see #254	
	380		Hogan Co	1999 Brae Burn Rd., Altadena	
	381		L. P. Freer	381 Meadow Grove, Flintridge	
1922	382		Guido A. Vincenti	242 S. Hill Ave.	
	383		McMurtry-Meyers	see #346	
	384		C. W. Dorsey	see #333	
	385		Preston Apartment House #1	589-599 S. Oakland Ave	
	386		John L. Storrow	see #205	
	387		Munn "X"	4301 Commonwealth Ave., Flintridge	HB 1/1924
	388		W. D. Morse	1030 Armada Dr.	
	389		Munn "L"	Commonwealth Ave., Flintridge	
	390		George Midland		
	391		Hogan Co.	2034 Glenview Terrace, Alt	
1922	392	D	**G. L. Morris Building**	21-45 S. Los Robles Ave.	AA 6/23/1925; PSN 6/17/1922

	393		Lowery		
	394		Mrs. W. Warne	1104 Montrose Ave., S. Pas	
	395		J. E. Tilt	see #340	
	396		Eton	Santa Barbara	
	397		American National Bank	S. Garey Ave., Pomona	AA 12/5/1927
1921	398		Pomona Country Club ("Mt. Meadows")	Ganesha Blvd., Pomona	SWBC 3/28/1924
1922	399	D	Mary C. Scotten	107 S. Orange Grove Blvd.	PP
	400		Storrow	see #386 [alteration]	
1922	401		Gerlach Store	466 E. Colorado Blvd. [has been remodeled]	AA 6/23/1925
	402		Fraser & Son Nursery	1000 E. Colorado Blvd.	AA 4/22/1925
	403		Westminster Presbyterian Church	1757 N. Lake Ave.	
	404		Mann Service Station		
	405		I. R. Morris	320 S. Orange Grove Blvd	
	406		Emma E. Laughrey	1222 E. Calaveras St	
	407	D	Frank Harwood	San Dimas – gatelodge	
	408		Sharp	451 San Gabriel Blvd.	
	409		George Hunt	cancelled	
	410		A. O. Preston	884 S. Oakland Ave.	
1922	411		**Home Laundry Company**	432 S. Arroyo Parkway	AA 4/8/1925 Now Thomasville Home Furnishings
1924	412	D	**T. W. Warner**	891 S. Orange Grove Blvd.	PSN 10/24/1919 and 1/10/1925; LAT 12/3/1947
1924	413	D	**G. L. Morris Office Building**	23-29 S. Euclid Ave	PSN 6/17/1925; SWBC 10/6/1922
	414		McNally Warehouse	106 W. Colorado Blvd. (behind store)	
	415	D	Root Store Bldg	S. Fair Oaks Ave., S. Pas.	
	416	D	Carrillo Hotel	Santa Barbara	
	417		Charington Store		
1924	418		**George Hunt**	1415 Park View Ave.	HB 6/1925; A&E 9/1924; PSN 2/14/25; AA 3/11/1925; H&G 5/1925
	419		Paul M. Gregg	825 Oak Knoll Circle	
	420		W. H. Mann		
	421		Gerlach Store	see #401	
	422		R. Fehr	2333 Midlothian Dr	
	423	D	Munger & Munger	174 E. Union St.	
1923	424		**W. H. Peters**	70 S. San Rafael Ave.	PSN 4/7/1923; SWBC 4/13/1923; AR 11/1925; A&E 5/1927; A&D 8/1926; PP
1923	425		Edgar W. Maybury	1375 New York Dr.	AA 3/1925; SWBC 4/23/1923
1923	426		**Dr. Roy Thomas**	523 Muirfield Rd. (Hancock Park) LA	
	427		J. S. Mather	1555 Brae Burn Rd., Altadena	
1922	428		**Turner & Stevens Chapel**	95 N. Marengo Ave.	TB 1922 Now Holly Street Grill
1923	429	D	Marshall Neil Factory	1010 E. Green St.	A&E 4/1927; AD 1927
1923	430		**Westridge Administration Building**	324 Madeline Dr.	SWBC 6/22/1923; PSN 2/14/1954; PSN 9/20/1988
	431		Dr. Upjohn		
	432	D	A. Brand	890 S. Orange Grove Blvd.	
	433		Blankenhorn-Hunter	Bung. #1	
1923	434		**Mark Reeves Bacon**	60 S. San Rafael Ave.	
	435		Community Bldg.	Third & Garey, Pomona	
	436		Blankenhorn-Hunter	Bung. #2	
1924	437	D	**Ferdinand R. Bain**	Palms (West LA)	AA 3/22/1925
	438		Blankenhorn-Hunter	Bung. #3	
	439		W. A. Brackenridge		
	440		Blankenhorn-Hunter	Bung. #4	
1922	441		**Hollywood Mausoleum**	6000 Santa Monica Blvd., LA [Phase 3]	
	442		McKevett-Converse Nursery		

	443		Norman Eastman	1245 Wentworth Ave.	
	444		H. M. Keck	7 Oak Knoll Circle (770 Oak Knoll)	
	445		E. C. Corey (McKevett)		
	446		J. E. Tilt	see #340 – pool	
	447		Preston Apt. House #2	590-600 S. Oakland Ave.	
1924	448		**Hannah N. Shaw**	335 Wigmore Dr.	SWBC 3/21/1924
	449		Waterhouse		
	450		Herman T. Koerner	1915 Park View Ave	
	451		Store Bldg.	Balboa	
	452		Ferdinand R. Bain	Palms - cow barns	
	453		Ferdinand R. Bain	Palms – ranch house	
	454		Light posts/art concrete works		
1923	455		Charles H. Hermann	975 Oak Grove Ave., San Marino	PP
	456		Robert Staats	468 Allendale Rd.	
	457		Samarkand Hotel	Santa Barbara County [AA]	CS 1924
	458		Steele	[entrance]	
	459		Frank J. Thomas		
	460		Wellington S. Morse	450 S. San Rafael Ave. [AA]	
	461		Julius Fried Store		
	462		McKevett St. Paul's Bungalow		
	463		Victor H. Doyle		
1924	464		**Grace Nicholson Treasure House**	46 N. Los Robles Ave. [Phase 1]	WA 7/1929; CS 4/1925; LAN 12/13/1925; SCQ Fall1999
	465		Stewart – pergola		
	466		Orrin White Studio	1205 Linda Vista Ave.	
	467		Roy F. Reinnman	1430 Morada Place	
	468		R. B. Hull	Lake Arrowhead	
1924	469		E. A. Shedd	908 Rexford Dr., Bev. Hills	SWBC 4/25/1924
	470		Fred R. Harris	560 S. San Rafael Ave.	
	471		Herbert Hahn	2606 Deodar Circle	
	472		Turner & Stevens Crypt	95 N. Marengo Ave	
	473		Lewis B. Stone	Toluca Lake, N. Hollywood	
	474		Pasadena Humane Society Kennels	361 S. Raymond Ave.	
1924	475		Mrs. A. C. Stewart	1215 Garfield Ave., S. Pas.	
	476		Misses Thilo		
1925	477	D	United Presbyterian Church	201 S. Lake Ave.	
1924	478		**Misses Fannie & Helen Hamilton**	445 Prospect Square	
	479		Miss Henrietta Brockman		
	480		K. H. Roby	1661 E. Mendocino St., Alt	
	481		First National Bank of Chino	Sixth and "B" St., Chino	AA 12/5/1927
	482		Turner Store		
1924	483		**W. R. Staats**	293 S. Grand Ave	SWBC 10/31/1924; PSN 7/2/1926
	485		Westminster Presbyterian Church School	1757 N. Lake Ave	
1924	486		**Hill Avenue Branch Library**	55 S. Hill Ave	SWBC 4/11/1924; SWBC 11/21/1924 PSN 10/8/1924CS 7/1926 PCA 7/1927; A&E 4/1927
1924	487		American Legion Bldg	131 N. Marengo Ave	PSN 5/28/1923; PSN 1/13/1925 SWBC 11/28/1924
1924	488		**R. A. Pratt**	336 Sturtevant Dr., Sierra Madre	SWBC 10/31/1924
	489		H. B. Reticker	938 Bel Air Rd., Bel Air, LA	
	490		Fraser		
	491		Frederick Koch	2060 N. Berendo St., LA	
	492		S. G. McClure	770 S. El Molino [alterations]	
1926	493		Edmund K. Crittenden	600 S. Hill Ave	
	494		Rule		
	495		Palos Verdes		
	496		M. J. Ely	546 La Paz Ave., San Marino	
	497		T. W. Warner	see # 412	
	498		Ferdinand R. Bain	Palms – [pavillion]	
	499		Washington Street Methodist Church		

	500		Longfellow School	1065 E. Washington Blvd. [AA]	
	501		Todd Ford	garden [for CP Day]	
	502	D	Security National Bank	132 E. Colorado Blvd	
	503		Alhambra Presbyterian Church		
	504		Grace Nicholson	46 N. Los Robles Ave. [phase 2]	
	505	D	Frank Harwood	San Dimas	
	506		R. T. Shea	429 S. Santa Anita Ave.	
	507		Barnes		
	508	D	Pasadena Presbyterian Church		
	509		Thomas C. Gillespie	101 S. Plymouth Blvd., LA	
	510		E. A. Culbertson	1321 Virginia Rd., San Marino	A&E 5/1929
	511	D	Midwick Country Club	200 Hellman Ave., Alh.	
	512		Marsh Garage		
	513		Eaton Mausoleum		
	514		W. H. Peters	see # 424 – driveway	
	515	D	Blankenhorn Pacific Properties	54 S. Los Robles Ave.	
	516		**Hollywood Mausoleum**	6000 Santa Monica Blvd., LA [Phase 4]	SWBC 3/21/1930
	517		Chamber of Commerce		
	518		C. P. McAllaster	sun porch	
	519		Slater Stores		
1925	520		Pasadena YMCA	120 N. Marengo Ave	SWBC 11/14/1924; PSN 11/24/1937
1925	521	D	**Pasadena Athletic Club**	435 E. Green St.	PSN 1/10/1925; PSN 10/18/1926; PCA 3/1928
	522	D	Mount Washington School, LASD	4000 San Rafael Ave., LA	
	523		Stevens		
1925	524		**Wiley W. Stephens**	484 S. San Rafael Ave.	AR 11/1926
	525		Fisk		
1925	527		**E. S. Skillen**	1905 Lombardy Rd	
	528		Henry A. Doty	841 S. Oakland Ave. [AA]	
	529		Thomas & Stephenson #1 Stephenson	2005 San Pasqual St.	
	530		L. B. Guyer	1401 Rubio Dr., Alt.	
	531		Paul Wold	611 Landor Lane	
	532		R. B. Hull	360 Waverly Drive [AA]	
	533		Kelley		
	534		Hornby		
	535		McNulty		
	536		O'Melveny		
	537		Ferdinand R. Bain	[wind screen]	
	538		Thomas		
	539		Evans		
	540		Andrew Jackson Elementary School	see #169	
	541		Charles Howland	Glendale	PCA 9/1928
	542		Woodbury		
	543		H. T. Koerner	1915 Park View Ave. [porch]	
1926	544		Thomas & Stephenson #2 **Catherine Sturgis**	2015 San Pasqual St.	CA&A 3/1931; *Calif. Gardens, Landscaping the American Dream, 1989.*
	545		Turner		
	546		George B. Sherwood	986 Cornell Rd	
	547		Grace Nicholson	46 N. Los Robles Ave. [Phase 3]	
1926	550		Gordon Hatch	1565 E. California Blvd	
1925	551		**Don Lee Bldg. (Cadillac Garage)**	655 E. Green St	PCA 3/1927 Now Jacob Maarse Florist
	552		Charles Howland	Beach Cottage	
	553	D	Hogan Garage	379 E. Colorado Blvd.	
	554		Adams Mausoleum	2400 N. Fair Oaks Ave. (Mt. View, Alt.)	
	555		Morris Wilson	(cancelled)	
1925	556		**Vista del Arroyo Hotel**	125 S. Grand Ave.	Now Western Justice Center

		H. I. **Stuart Bungalow**		Foundation
	557	McDonald		
	558	Robert Casamajor	see #337	
	559	Pomona Masonic Temple	Pomona	
	560	Rancho Leucadia	Manager's Office	
	561	W. R. Staats	see #483 – formal garden	
	562	Stewart Machine Shop		
1928	563	**Douglas Morris**	725 Holladay Rd.	
	564	Gordon Hatch	1565 E. California Blvd (see #550)	
1927	565	Thomas & Stephenson #3	1947 San Pasqual St. [AA]	
	566	S. L. Van Pelt	(contractor)	
	567	Jefferson Elementary School	1500 E. Villa St. [alter #1]	
	568	Kelley		
	569	Thomas & Stephenson #4 Jennison	433 S. San Marino Ave.	
	570	Hobbs Nursery		
	571	J. E. Tilt		
	572	Noble	W. California Blvd.[AA]	
	573	Mark Reeves Bacon	60 S. San Rafael Ave.	
	574	Jefferson Elementary School	1500 E. Villa St. [alt #2]	
	575	Standard Mfg. Co.		
	576	Don Wells (Jenks)		
1926	577	**Huntington Hotel Cottages Finleen**	1401 S. Oak Knoll Ave.	Now Private Residence
1926	578	Thomas & Stephenson **Crawford**	423 S. San Marino Ave.	
	579	Thomas & Stephenson Condon	405 S. San Marino Ave.	
1926	580	Frederick C. Porter	2202 La Mesa Dr., Santa Monica	
	581	S. L. Van Pelt	[contractor]	
1926	582	Thomas & Stephenson **Diggs**	395 S. San Marino Ave.	PSN 1/19/1934 and 1/24/1999
	583	Harding Store (Mrs. T.E.)	Bakersfield	
	584	Hoffman Beach House	Balboa	
	585	T. W. Warner	driveway	
1928	589	Blacker, Dotten & Fay Bldg J. H. Biggar	680 E. Colorado Blvd.	
	590	DeWitt Gorman	1905 Altadena Dr.	
1928	591	**H. F. Haldeman**	711 N. Maple Dr., Bev. Hills	PCA 1/1929; AR 11/1929; HB 2/1931
	592	Thomas & Stephenson Daggett	410 S. Berkley Ave.	
	593	Martin		
	594 D	Pasadena Holding Co. Auto Sales	350 W. Colorado Blvd.	
	595	A. B. Stevens	1295 Lombardy Rd.	
	596	Harding	see #583	
	597	Thomas & Stephenson Wilson	416 S. Berkley Ave.	
	598	Mrs. E. N. Bender	2995 Lombardy Rd.	
	599	C. Temple Murphy	1260 Wentworth Ave.	
	600	Wilmington Library	309 W. Opp St., LA	Now Wilmington Community Center
	601	Southern Counties Gas Co.	Tustin	
	602 D	Harry B. Brooks	725 S. Hobart Blvd., LA	
	603	Thornton Hamlin	1485 N. Michigan Ave.	
	604	S. S. Hinds	see #245	
	605	F. H. Booth		
	606	K. L. Carver	1365 St. Albans Rd, San Marino	
1926	607	**Huntington Hotel Cottages Ferncroft**	1401 S. Oak Knoll Ave.	Now Private Residence
	608	Southern Counties Gas Co	Orange	
1926	609	**Vista del Arroyo Hotel**	125 S. Grand Ave.	

			Bungalow Apts.	[4 apt units]	
	610		Allyn Barber	955 Old Mill Rd.	
	611		H. K. Barber		
1928	612		John B. F. Bacon	65 S. San Rafael Ave.	
1926	613		**Edward C. Harwood**	905 Orlando Rd., San Marino	AD 1929
	614		Thomas & Stephenson Stimson		
1926	615		**Huntington Hotel Cottages Clovelly**	1401 S. Oak Knoll Ave.	CL 11/18/1922; CS 9/1926; Now Private Residence
	616		George Hunt	see #418	
	617		Southern Counties Gas Co	Ventura [office]	
	618		Southern Counties Gas Co	Ventura [warehouse]	
1926	619		**Huntington Hotel Cottages Spalding**	1401 S. Oak Knoll Ave.	Now Private Residence
1926	620		**Huntington Hotel Cottages Mariner**	1401 S. Oak Knoll Ave.	Now Private Residence
	621		L. B. Mathis		
1927	622	D	Carl F. Johnson	4330 Meadow Grove Pl., Flintridge	
1927	623	D	**William Wilson Building**	40 N. Garfield Ave.	CS 4/1928; PSN 3/25/51
1927	624		La Vista Co.	1545 E. Altadena Dr	
1927	625		**Huntington Hotel Cottages Chance View**	1401 S. Oak Knoll Ave.	Now Private Residence
	626		George E. Dudley	790 Pinehurst Drive	
	627	D	Midwick Country Club	1200 W. Hellman Ave., Alhambra [AA]	
	628		La Vista Co.	1471 E. Altadena Dr. [sales office]	Now Dickson Real Estate Office
	629		Southern Service Co.	Pomona	
1926	630	D	**Las Olas Beach Club**	Speedway, Venice	LAT 7/18/1926
1926	631		Redlands YMCA	Redlands	
	632		Judge W. J. Wood	1490 Chelsea Rd., San Marino	
	633	D	E. R. Murphy	27 N. Grand Ave.	
	634		Hahn Warehouse		
	635		Hogan Co. Gateway	1471 E. Altadena Dr.	
1927	636	D	**Mrs. Francis E. Stevens**	807 Las Palmas Rd.	AD 1929; MM
	637		C. Temple Murphy	see # 599	
	638		Southern Counties Gas Co.	Santa Barbara	*A&E July 1928;* Now Wells Fargo Bank
	639		Southern Counties Gas Co.	Ventura	
	640		Kenneth Colburn #1		
	641		Kenneth Colburn #2	860 Chester Ave., San Marino	
	642		Southern Counties Gas Co	Santa Barbara	
	643		Edwin Hahn		
1927	644		**Huntington Hotel Cottages Howard**	1401 S. Oak Knoll Ave.	Now Private Residence
1927	645	D	**Pacific-Southwest Trust and Savings Bank**	880 E. Colorado Blvd.	AD 1928
	646		T. W. Banks	641 S. Hill Ave.	
	648		Carroll Paige Fisk	2529 N. Marengo Ave.	
	649	D	Leroy Sherry, M.D.	675 S. San Gabriel Blvd.	
	650		Pasadena Humane Society	361 S. Raymond Ave. [acctng. bldg.]	
	651		E. R. Murphy	Vine & Romaine, Hollywood [market]	
	652		G. D. Hoffman	[AA]	
1927	653	D	**Linda Vista Elementary School**	1259 Linda Vista Ave.	
1927	654	D	Pasadena Holding Co.	725 E. Colorado Blvd.	Was J. Herbert Hall Jewelers
1927	655		**Westminster Presbyterian Churc**	1757 N. Lake Ave	AD 1929
	656		H. F. Haldeman	see # 591 - garage	
	658		LA Cal Tile Products		
1927	659		**Pasadena Holding Co. The Arcade**	696 E. Colorado Blvd.	
	660	D	Riverside High School	Riverside	
	661		Davis [Baker Co.]	[Arroyo Crest Tract- on LaCresta	

				Dr.]	
1927	664		**F. A. Hardy "Villa Verde"**	800 S. San Rafael Ave.	AD 1929
	667		Roy Munger	2290 Lombardy Rd., San Marino	
1927	669		**T. W. Warner Building**	469-483 E. Colorado Blvd.	CS 4/1928 Now Linden Optometry
	672		Westridge Administration Bldg.	see # 430	
	673		C. F. Braun	1025 Oak Grove Ave., San Marino [AA]	
	674		Ferdinand R. Bain		
	675		W. A. Johnstone	San Dimas [AA]	
	676		A. P. Nichols	Pomona	
1927	677		**Harold V. Ogden**	1125 Armada Dr.	HB 2/1931, AD Vol. 8; CA&A July 1930
	678		F. A. Hardy	see # 664 - garage	
1928	681	D	Claremont Library	Second and Harvard Streets, Claremont	
	683		Louise Hately	1620 Lombardy Rd.	
	684		Edward Kauth	548 Athens St. [contractor]	
	685		Morris Wilson	176 Painter St.	
	687		Ferdinand R. Bain	Stockton [ranch house]	
	688		Otto Thum	never built	
	691		Otto Thum	246 S. San Rafael Ave. [garage; never completed; concrete framing and brick walls only]	
	692		E. M. McKenna	Eleventh & Berkley, Claremont	
	694	D	Mrs. A. M. Dole	270 Grant, Pomona	
	695		F. A. Hardy	see # 664	
	696		E. M. McKenna	Eleventh & Berkley, Claremont [garage]	
1928	697		**Mrs. H. A. Everett**	171 S. Grand Ave.	PSN 7/5/1937 Now Shakespeare Club
	698		C. Temple Murphy		
1928	699		Carl Parker, M.D.	3255 N. Lincoln Ave., Alt.	SWBC 8/3/1928
1926	702		**Vista del Arroyo Hotel Hamilton Bungalow**	125 S. Grand Ave. [8 apt units]	LAT 3/27/1926
	703		Dr. Clifford Harn		
	704		Mrs. Mable (Rev. John) Carruthers	La Quinta	
	705		Don Nichols	Claremont	AR 3/1935
	706		Ferdinand R. Bain	Stockton [garage]	
	707		R. M. Modisette		
	708		Wilshire Presbyterian Church	5211 W. Olympic Blvd., LA	
	709		Benedict & Ginrich	1443 E. Colorado Blvd. [has been altered]	
	710		Tustin Presbyterian Church	Main & C Streets., Tustin	
	711		C. S. Holman		
	712		Mutual Bldg. And Loan Association		
1928	713		**Ellis Bishop**	4802 E. Arco Iris Ave., Rancho Santa Fe	CS 3/1926, A&D 1/1941, C&AA October 1931
	714		Paschall Funeral Chapel		
	715		W. M. Keck	745 Oak Knoll Circle	
1929	716	D	**Scott Chapel, Methodist Episcop Church**	Mary Street	PSN 7/26/1929
	717		Harry P. Hammond	1816 Midlothian Dr.	
	718		Ellis Bishop	see #713 [stables]	
	719		J. S. Mather	1555 Brae Burn Rd., Alt.	
	720		Joseph L. Stanton	2026 Oakdale St	
1928	721		**Herbert M. Vanzwoll**	4230 Chevy Chase, Flintridge	AD January 1930
	722		Pomona College	Claremont [infirmary]	
1929	723		**Hollywood Mausoleum**	6000 Santa Monica Blvd., LA [phase 5]	
	724		Ellis Bishop	See #713 [gate lodge]	
	725		Mrs. G. W. Gildehaus	2955 E. California Blvd	
	726		C. F. Braun	1000 S. Fremont Ave., Alhambra	

			[powerhouse + gate]	
1928	727	President's House (Blaisdell House)	Pomona College, Claremont	
	728	Fred C. Smith	[AA]	
	729	George C. Hinckley		
	730	Mrs. C. W. Dobbins	1215 Chelten Way, S. Pas.	
1929	731	**Vista del Arroyo Hotel Maxwell Bungalow**	125 S. Grand Ave.	Now Western Justice Center Foundation
	732	Haradon	[AA]	
	733	Lewis B. Perry		
1929	734	Arcadia Public Library	First St. and Huntington Dr, Arcadia	PSN 2/11/1929
	735	Adolph F. Linden		
	736	Collis Store		
1929	737	Alpha Phi Sorority (UCLA)	Hillgard Ave., Westwood	
	738	General Lansing H. Beach	690 Bradford St.	
	739	Herbert Wise	Chateau Rd.	never built, cancelled Oct. 28, 1929
	740	Washington St Meth Ch	see #499	
1929	741	**San Rafael Elementary School**	1090 Nithsdale Rd.	
	742	Mrs. C.W. Dobbins	[Beach House]	
1929	743	**J. J. McCarthy**	1199 Chateau Rd.	
1929	744	**Herbert E. Bell**	243 N. San Rafael Ave.	
	745 D	Claude Griffith	745 S. Orange Grove Blvd. [AA]	
	746	Pomona College	Claremont [heating plant]	
	747	Samuel H. French	2596 S. Oak Knoll Ave., San Marino	
	748	Turner & Stevens	95 N. Marengo Ave. [AA]	
	749	Otto Thum	S. San Rafael Ave. [retaining wall]	
	750	Bell-Welter Tract Development	Chateau Rd & Bridge	
	751	H. F. Haldeman	[AA]	
	752	Dr. James Hasbrouch	1065 Armada Dr. [AA]	
	753	Pomona College	[swimming pool]	
1929	754	**Helen D. Chandler**	2124 Midlothian Dr., Alt.	
	755	A. C. Stewart	1215 Garfield Ave., S. Pas. [tea house]	
1929	756 D	**Mechanic Arts Bldg., UCLA**	Westwood	
	757	C. F. Braun Co. – Office Bldg.	1000 S. Fremont Ave., Alhambra	
	758	Mrs. Milton Stewart	[[AA]	
	759	C. F. Braun Co	1000 S. Fremont Ave., Alhambra [laboratory]	
	760	Dr. Leon G. Campbell, MD	1506 E. California Blvd. [AA]	
1928	761 D	**Vista del Arroyo Hotel Jenks Bungalow**	125 S. Grand Ave. [10 deluxe apts]	PSN 4/3/1928; PSN 3/27/1926
	762	Frank Harwood	see #505, San Dimas [AA]	
	763	Vista del Arroyo	[garage] S. Arroyo Blvd.	
	764	Sidney Franklin	711 Maple St., Burbank	MM
	765	F. A. Hardy	[garden alterations]	
	766	Zubietta Apartments		
	767	Brydolf	[beach house]	
	768	L. B. Guyer	beach house alteration	
	769	Dr. Robert Freeman	cabin, Mt. Baldy	
	770	James L. Beebe	1060 Roanoke Rd., San Marino	AR 1933
	771	San Dimas School	San Dimas	
	772	I. G. Pattinson	1224 Arden Rd (see #339) [AA]	
	773	Paul F. Johnson	(cancelled)	
1931	774	Santa Catalina Branch Library	999 E. Washington Blvd.	
	775	Thornton Hamlin	Balboa Island [beach house]	
	776	Gordon L. Hatch	1565 E. California Blvd. [AA]	
1931	777	Henley & Haynes Bldg	713 E. Green St.	Now Akira, French-Japanese restaurant
	778	Paul F. Johnson (Bates)	3100 Maiden Lane, Alt.	
	779	Thompson Smith	5035 Louise Dr., Alta Canada	
	780	J. W. Bates	1155 Dolores Dr., Alt.	
	781	Holland Apt. House		

	782	Paul F. Johnson	Beach house, Laguna Beach	
	783	McDonald		
	784	Sunday School Bldg. Congregational Church	393 N. Lake Ave.	
1932	785	**Charles Paddock**	985 Linda Vista Ave	LAT 1/20/1922; AR 9/1933
	786	**Eliot Jr. High School**	2184 N. Lake Ave., Alt.	AR 8/1932
	787	John E. Porter	532 Brewinton, Watsonville	
	788	Walter E. Cockcroft	Santa Cruz Rd, Watsonville	
1930	789	**Padua Hills Theater**	4400+ Padua Ave., Claremont	CA&A 2/1931; *Sunset* 8/1967; PSN 8/3/1997; Now Owned by Claremont Historical Society
1931	790	**Joseph B. Erkenbrecker**	750 Chester Ave., San Marino	PSN 5/22/1931
	791	H. L. Dunn	260 California Terrace	
	792	McKee	[AA]	
	793	William T. Kester	Kester Ranch House, Potrero Rd, Ventura Cnty	
	794	Isabel Turner	107 S. Orange Grove Blvd [AA]	
	795	W. Kester	[gate lodge] Potrero Rd., Ventura County	
	796 D	Ferderick H. Bartlett	1020 Oak Grove Ave.	
	797	Warehouse – City of Pasadena	1103 Glen Ave.	
	798	W.P. Durkee, Jr.	beach house Balboa Island	
	799	J. T. Durkee		
	800	Mrs. F.A. Burnham		
	801	Patee	beach house	
	802	Knights of Pythias	[AA]	
	804	Moore		
	805	Mrs. M. E. Morris	Emerald Bay [beach house]	
1933	806	Reading Room – First Church of Christ, Scientist	550 E. Green St.	AD 1931
	807	Stewart Market	E. Colorado Blvd.	
	808	Pomona College	Field House, Claremont	
	809	Mrs. R. L. Lucas	[beach house]	
	810	Arthur N. Stewart	3001 Lombardy Rd.	
	811	Col. John W. Barnes	109 Picacho Lane, Montecito	
	812	Paul M. Gregg	825 Oak Knoll Circle (see #419)	
	813	A. G. Stewart		
	814	Mark Reeves Bacon	[elevator]	
	815	Mrs. W. Keck	745 Oak Knoll Circle	
	816	Mrs. W. L. Stewart	[garage] 2870 E. California Blvd	
	817	B. G. White		
	818	Pasadena Post Office	281 E. Colorado Blvd. [AA]	
	819	Mrs. M. E. Morris	[alterations] see #805, Emerald Bay	
	820	Health Bungalow, Eliot Jr. Hi	2184 N. Lake Ave., Alt.	
	823	F. H. Booth	[alterations] see #605	
	824	Andrew Jackson Elementary School		
	825	San Dimas School	San Dimas [AA]	
	826	Longfellow Elementary School	see #500 [AA]	
	827	John B. F. Bacon	[cottage alt], Montecito	
	828	Rathbun	1330 Wentworth Ave. [AA]	
	829	San Rafael Elementary School	see #741	
1935	830	Pomona College	Pearson Hall, Claremont	
	831	Pasadena City College	Sexton Auditorium 1570 E. Colorado Blvd.	
	832	A. H. Sturtevant	1244 Arden Rd. [AA]	
	833	Jefferson Elementary School	Primary Bldg; 1500 E. Villa St	
	834	W. W. Stephens	see #524, [elevator]	
	835	Vista del Arroyo Hotel	125 S. Grand Ave, [AA]	
	836	Robert and Helen Ransome	Palm Springs	
	837	Vista del Arroyo Hotel	125 S. Grand Ave., [shops]	
	838	Edward P. McMurtry	2479 Vista Laguna Terrace	

	839	Methodist Church	Choir Rm., 500 E. Colorado Blvd.	
	840	C. F. Braun Co	Club Bldg., 1000 S. Fremont Ave., Alhambra	
	841	Ralph L. Jones	1430 Morada Pl., Alt.	
	842	Donald McKenna	4611 Live Oak Canyon Rd., Claremont	AD Vol. 9
	843	Southern Properties	Greer [AA]	
	844	John B. F. Bacon	see #612 [AA]	
	845	Van Houten Spec. House #1	39 Wallis St	
	846	Benedict & Gingrich	Warehouse	
	847	Vista del Arroyo	125 S. Grand Ave.; [Pergola]	
	848	Lincoln Elementary School	N. Garey Ave., Pomona	
	849	John McLauchlan	1935 Midwick Dr., Alt	
	850	C. F. Braun Co.	1000 S. Fremont Ave., Alh. [AA]	
1935	851	**Vista del Arroyo Hotel A. G. Cox Bungalow**	125 S. Grand Ave.	Now Western Justice Center Foundation
	852	William Wilson Jr	530 Bellmore Way	
	853	F. C. Beetson	1029 Flintridge Ave., Flintridge	AF 10/1939
	854	Dr. Robert Freeman	Magnolia Ave., [Library]	
	855	Norbert Hensler	3600 San Pasqual St	
	856	Joy #1		
	857	H. L. Dunn	512 Arroyo Sq., S. Pasadena	
1935	858	**Vista del Arroyo Hotel W. Cady Griffith Bungalow**	125 S. Grand Ave.	Now Western Justice Center Foundation
	859	David Walter #1	235 W. Foothill Blvd., Arcadia	AD Vol. 9
	860	Joy #2		
	861	Van Houten Spec. House #2	390 E. Glenarm St.	
	862	Van Houten Spec. House #3	1034 Nithsdale Rd.	
	863	Carmelita Grandstand		
	864	Pomona Public Library	Pomona [AA]	
	865	San Dimas School	auditorium	
	866	John L. Burnham	3575 Yorkshire Rd	
	867 D	O. M. Smith	2044 Allen Dr., Alt	
	868	Mrs. Lillian Flood	219 Annandale Rd.	
	869	Sherwin Williams	casework	
	870	Van Houten Spec. House#4	1052 Nithsdale Rd.	
	871	Mrs. R. Hibben	1631 Oakdale St	
	872	David Walter #2	477 W. Foothill Blvd., Arcadia	
	873 D	Pomona Jr. College	Holt Ave., Pomona; Gymnasium	
	874	Sidney Franklin	Lake Arrowhead	
	875	C. S. Lytle		
	876 D	Hahn Store Bldg	see # 331	
	877	Misses McIlvried	495 E. Jefferson Ave., Pomona	
	878	Dick Powell	[AA]	
	879	Miss Louise Crawford		
	880	C. F. Braun Co.	1000 S. Fremont Ave., Alh., Admin. Bldg.	
	881	Van Houten Spec. House #5, Spec. House #6	1077 S. Los Robles Ave., 1087 S. Los Robles Ave.	
	882	C. F. Braun Co.	1000 S. Fremont Ave., Alh., [draughting]	
	883	C. F. Braun Co.	[garage]	
	884	C. F. Braun Co.	yard improvements	
	885	Donald Cutler	3618 San Pasqual St	
	886	C. W. Isbell	1975 Lombardy Rd	
	887	F. H G. Stevens	2721 Windsor Ave., Alt	
	888	D. H. Martin	2200 Chaucer Rd., San Marino	
	889 D	California Teachers Association, Apartment Bldg.	808 E. Villa St.	
1938	890	Pomona College	Student Union Bldg., Claremont	
	891	C. B. Cooper	1000 Hillside Terrace	
	892	Stern	[AA]	

	893		James M. Taft	1016 S. Arroyo Blvd.	
	894	D	Munger Store	see #195	
	895		Herbert Hahn	2606 Deodar Circle [AA]	
	896		Herbert	[AA]	
	897		Pomona Christian Science Church	Pomona	
	898		T. W. Warner Store	[AA]	
	899		Judge R. T. Bishop	1345 Park View Ave.	
	900		Keith P. Marston	3541 San Pasqual St	
	901		Horace Mann	3609 Thorndale Rd	
	902		Frank H. Sellers	see #683	
	903		LaCanada Christian Science Church		
	904		John B. F. Bacon	674 E. Valley Rd., Montecito, [gate lodge]	
	905		Graser	[AA]	
	906		Richard Davis	Los Gatos	
	907		Hebron Center	Winter & Evergreen Ave., LA	
	908		Knowles Ryerson		
	909		Carl Hinshaw	3053 Lombardy Rd	
	910		Richard Davis	Big Sur	
	911	D	Norman & Ginny Johnson	590 Castano Ave	
	913		Lee Davis	2155 Orlando Rd., San Marino	
	915		Blennerhasset	2150 S. El Molino Ave., San Marino	
	916		Mark Keppel High School	501 E. Hellman Ave., Alh	SWBC 9/20/1940
	917		H. L. Miller	395 San Marino Ave.	
	918		Fremont Jr. High School	S. Garey Ave., Pomona [classroom bldg.]	Now District and Administrative Service Center
	919	D	Pomona School District Administration Bldg.	Pomona	
	920		Rucklos Co	E. Colorado Blvd.	
	921		Bedell	[AA]	
1939	922		**Nelson Eddy**	485 Halvern Dr., Brentwood	
	923		Southern Properties		
	924		Benedict & Gingrich	1443 E. Colorado Blvd., [AA]	
	925	D	First Methodist Church	94 W. Colorado Blvd. [AA]	
	926		W. R. Staats Bldg.	see # 367 [AA]	
	927		Pomona First Federal Savings and Loan	Pomona	
	928		Sidney Franklin		
	929		Alcott Kindergarten	S. Towne Ave., Pomona	
	930		Pomona College	Claremont [fountain]	
	931	D	Pasadena Presbyterian Church Choir Room	585 E. Colorado Blvd	
	932		Donald Keith		
	933		Dorothy Allen		
	934		Jungmeyer Apartment Bldg		
	935		F. O. Campe	Glendora	
	936		H. L. Miller Store	[AA]	
	937		Fred Wonser	1098 Palm Terrace	
	938	D	J. Harriman	E. Colorado Blvd, hamburger stand	
	939		E. M. Baillie	3180 San Pasqual St	
	940		Fremont Jr. High School	S. Garey Ave., Pomona [auditorium]	Now District and Administrative Service Center
	941		William Thum	787 Canterbury Rd., San Marino	
	942		McHaffi	Alh [AA]	
	943		California Teachers Association Apartment Bldg	808 E. Villa St	Now "Villa Gardens" Retirement Center
	944		UCLA, Alpha Phi Sorority	Hillgard Ave., Westwood [AA]	
	945		Hale Elementary School	2550 E. Paloma St	Formerly Lamanda Park Elementary School
	946		Eliot Jr. Hi Gymnasium	2184 N. Lake Ave., Alt	
	947	D	Roy Munger State Bldg	751 E. Green St	

	949	Graser Store Bldg	2506-2510 Huntington Dr., San Marino [AA]	
	951	WH & RW Duff	Hampton & Inverness, Flintridge	
	952	Arthur Stewart	[AA]	
	955	H. P. Jeannerette		
	956	National Marine & Engineering		
	967	Sturdevant	Ashley Store	
	958	Mary F. Bacon Mausoleum	601 W. Roses Rd., San Gabriel	
	960	Pasadena First Federal Savings		
	1000	B. W. Photo Utilities	1346 E. Walnut St.. [office]	
	1001	Rucklos Auto Sales	cancelled	
	1003	Stokesbury	Alhambra	
	1004	Babcock	Prince Albert Dr., Riverside	
	1005	Peteler-Pearson Auto Sales	270 N. Lake Ave	
	1006	C. S. Mead Auto Sales	1355 E. Colorado Blvd	Now Loud Auto Sales
1946	1112	Emerson Jr. High School	East Lincoln Ave., Pomona	Completed by KPM and Eugene Weston
1946	1113	Hamilton Elementary School	Hamilton Blvd., Pomona	Completed by KPM and Eugene Weston
1946	1115	Schuyler Joyner	Cherry Drive	

The author has made every effort to locate and document structures designed by Sylvanus Marston and his firm; she has attempted to ascertain from public records, firm archives, and contemporary publications the earliest reported date for each structure. When Keith Palmer Marston reconstructed the original job records in the 1970s, he was able to provide the year for many of the projects, but for some he could only estimate the date within a range of years, as indicated above. The projects are in the proper chronological order as they were developed and built. The author would greatly appreciate hearing of any corrections and additions, which may be addressed to her publisher.

Sylvanus Marston   1908-1913
Marston and Van Pelt   1914-1923
Marston, Van Pelt & Maybury   1923-1927
Marston & Maybury   1927-1942

Photographic Credits

Altadena: The Community of the Deodars
    (Altadena: Altadena Chamber of Commerce, c. 1932):   5.19

American Architect
    February 17, 1915:   3.30, 3.31
    April 22, 1925:   7.25
    June 3, 1925:   4.26, 4.27

Architectural Digest, 1925:   4.8

Architectural Record
    September 1919:   5.2
    November 1926:   5.22

Arts & Decoration, January 1941:   5.16

Author's Collection: 2.5, 2.13, 3.24

The Heirs of Mary Ford Bacon and Mark R. Bacon: 4.12, 4.13, 4.14

Marian Lacey Bassett: 4.7

Robert E. Bennett: 1.2

Edward R. Bosley: 3.23, 3.25

California Arts & Architecture, July, 1930:   4.31

Chateau Owner: 4.36

Louis Cocanougher: 4.3

The Craftsman, November, 1914:   3.12, 3.13, 3.14, 3.15

Pauline B. Deuel, *Mexican Serenade: The Story of the
    Mexican Players and the Padua Hills Theatre*
    (Claremont: Padua Institute, 1961):   7.26, 7.27

William W. Ellinger III: 3.16, 3.17

Joseph Edwin Hinds IV: 4.10

Orville Hoag: 4.1

House Beautiful, January 1922:   4.16

The Huntington Library: 4.18, 6.2, 6.3, 6.4, 6.8, 7.8, 7.14

Kelley Gallery: 7.10
Marjorie Maybury Kellogg: 1.4, 4.5
The Ladies Home Journal, January 1917: 7.15
Library of Congress: 4.17
Dr. Marianne McDonald: 5.15
Marston Family Collection: 1.1, 1.9, 1.13
National Archives, National Park Service
(Eadweard Muybridge): 1.6
Rexford Newcomb, *Mediterranean Domestic Architecture in the
United States* (Cleveland: J. H. Jansen, 1928),
reprinted by Acanthus Press, New York (1999): 5.6, 5.7, 5.8, 5.11, 5.12, 5.13, 5.23, 5.24, 5.27
Harold A. Parker (Parker specifically, or his studio): 2.8, 2.14, 2.15, 2.16, 2.17, 2.22, 4.15, 7.1, 7.2, 7.6, 7.9, 7.19, 7.28
Pasadena Heritage: 2.6, 2.7
Pasadena Historical Museum: 2.2, 2.3, 3.1, 3.18, 3.25, 3.27, 4.19, 4.21, 4.29, 4.30, 5.3, 5.14, 5.25, 6.5, 7.3, 7.4, 7.5, 7.12, 7.13, 7.22, 7.24
Picturesque Pasadena (Pasadena: Star News, c. 1925): 4.40, 4.41, 5.10
Rancho Santa Fe Historical Society: 5.17
Real Estate Brochure: 4.20
Nancy H. Sokol: 1.2
Southern California AIA, *Mediterranean to Modern:
Residential Architecture in Southern California, 1939*,
reprinted by Hennessey + Ingalls, 1998: 5.20
Tournament of Roses Brochure (Pasadena: Star News): 2.4, 3.8
Kathleen Tuttle: 1.7, 2.1, 2.10, 2.11, 2.12, 2.18, 2.19, 2.20, 2.21, 3.2, 3.3, 3.4, 3.5, 3.7, 3.9, 3.11, 3.19, 3.20, 3.21, 3.22, 3.29, 4.2, 4.4, 4.6, 4.9, 4.11, 4.22, 4.24, 4.25, 4.28, 4.32, 4.33, 4.34, 4.35, 4.37, 4.38, 439, 5.1, 5.4, 5.5, 5.9, 5.18, 5.21, 5.26, 6.1, 6.6, 6.7, 7.11, 7.16, 7.17, 7.18, 7.20, 7.21, 7.23
University Archives, Division of Rare and Manuscript
Collections, Cornell University Library,
Cornell University: 1.10, 1.11
UCLA Special Collections: 3.16, 3.26, 7.7
Western Architect, November, 1918: 3.10
Larry Williams: 1.3
M. W. Wood, *History of Alameda County* (Oakland:
Pacific Press, 1883): 1.5, 1.8
Year Book of the Los Angeles Architectural League
(Los Angeles: Kingsley, Mason & Collins Co., 1912): 3.6, 3.26
Year Book of the Los Angeles Architectural League
(Los Angeles: Kingsley, Mason & Collins Co., 1913: 3.28, 4.23

Frequently Used Citations

Publications

AIA	American Institute of Architects
A&E	*Architect & Engineer*
CA&A	*California Arts and Architecture*
CL	*California Life*
CS	*California Southland*
H&G	*House and Garden*
HB	*House Beautiful*
JSA	*Journal of the Society of Architectural Historians*
LABC	*Los Angeles Builder and Contractor*
LAN	*Los Angeles News*
NYT	*New York Times*
PCA	*Pacific Coast Architect*
PDU	*Pasadena Daily Union*
PEP	*Pasadena Evening Post*
PES	*Pasadena Evening Star*
PP	*Pasadena Post*
PS	*Pasadena Star*
PSN	*Pasadena Star News*
SCQ	*Southern California Quarterly*
SWBC	*Southwest Builder and Contractor*
AA	*The American Architect*
AD	*The Architectural Digest*
AR	*The Architectural Record*
CR	*The Craftsman*
LHJ	*The Ladies' Home Journal*
LAT	*The Los Angeles Times*
NYT	*The New York Times*
TB	*The Tournament of Roses Brochure*
WA	*The Western Architect*
YBLAAC	*Year Book of the Los Angeles Architectural League*

Individuals

KPM	Keith Palmer Marston

Notes

–Chapter 1– Shaping Influences

1. S.B. Marston was elected to the Southern California Chapter on December 1, 1909, Annual Report of Chapter, 1911; AIA Archives, Washington, D.C.

2. Southern California Chapter, 1910-1911 File; AIA Archives, Washington D.C.

3. Ibid.; also Chapter Minutes, 25 June 1920; 12 April 1921; AIA Archives, Washington, D.C.

4. Chapter Minutes from 11 October 1921, 10 May 1921, and 9 March 1920; AIA Archives, Washington D.C.

5. Chapter Minutes, 13 September 1921; AIA Archives, Washington, D.C.

6. Chapter Annual Report for 1910; AIA Archives, Washington, D.C.

7. Chapter Minutes, 10 July 1920; AIA Archives, Washington, D.C.

8. Albert C. Martin, Jr., interview, Pasadena, 3 September 1998.

9. *American Architects Directory*, ed. George S. Koyl (New York: R.R.Bowker Company, 1955) p. 373.

10. *SWBC*, 20 September 1940.

11. Robert E. Bennett, interview, Pasadena, 20 October 1998; Richard E. Thomas, interview, Pasadena, 26 October 1998.

12, Marjorie Maybury Kellogg, interview, 30 June 2000.

13. Albert Frey, Arthur C. Evans, Robert E. Alexander, and Wallace Neff; Van Pelt's Fellow's File; AIA Archives, Washington, D.C.

14. Walter P. White, Van Pelt relative, interview, Pasadena, 13 December 1997.

15. Ibid.

16. Robert E. Bennett interview, Pasadena, 20 October 1998.

17. *A&E*, December 1929, p. 11.

18. Ibid.

19. Aside from the name partners, the architects and draftsmen known to have worked at one time for the firm include: Herbert E. Mackie, Burgo Purcell, Raymond M. Hobbs, J. Cyril Bennett, Leslie H. Lippiatt, James C. Wheeler, Jr., James W. McClymont, Herbert J. Powell, Herb Moses, Mark W. Ellsworth, Robert H. Ainsworth, Richard F. King, Aubrey St. Clair, Theodore Pletsch, John Porter Clark, and Keith Palmer Marston.

20. Apparently Neff began all his own drawings and then turned over the details to Robert Ainsworth, his chief draftsman. See *Wallace Neff: Architect of California's Golden Age* (Santa Barbara: Capra Press, 1986), p. 21; the A.C. Martin firm worked similarly; Albert C. Martin, Jr., interview, Los Angeles, 3 September 1998.

21. Albert C. Martin, Jr., interview, Los Angeles, 3 September 1998.

22. Ibid.

23. *PSN*, 10 January 1925.

24. See *Diary, Army Young Men's Christian Association*, by S.B. Marston, 24 December 1918–19 June 1919 [several months lost], *PSN*, 10 May 1924.

25. KPM interview, Montecito, California, 30 August 1997.

26. Ibid.

27. *SWBC*, 21 October 1938.

28. *SWBC*, 18 September 1942.

29. Charles Sumner Greene, *TRB* (Pasadena: Star News, 1907).

30. *SWBC*. 19 May 1944.

31. By 1927 Wallace Neff confined himself to houses costing more that $50,000. See *Wallace Neff: Architect of California's Golden Age* (Santa Barbara: Capra Press, 1986), p. 25.

32. John Galen Howard, *AR*, Vol. 40, October 1916, p. 38.

33. *LABC*, 24 November 1910.

34. *SWBC*, 24 June 1921; Nicholas C. Polos, *San Dimas: Preserving the Western Spirit* (San Dimas, 1990), p. 138.

35. Conrad and Nelson, *Santa Barbara: El Pueblo Viejo* (Santa Barbara: Capra Press, 1983), p. 130.

36. Sumner P. Hunt was recorded as absent. Minutes of the Meeting of the State Board of Architecture, Southern District, January 28, 1908, from the Archives, California State Board of Architectural Examiners, Sacramento, California.

37. Ibid.

38. Ibid.

39. Ibid.

40. Henry F. Withey, "History of the California Chapter of the AIA," *SWBC*, Vol. 104, 20 October 1944, pp. 28-34.

41. Ibid.

42. Henry F. Withey, *Biographical Dictionary of American Architects* (Los Angeles: New Age Publishing Co., 1956), p. 275.

43. KPM, interview, Montecito, California, 30 August 1997; this was corroborated by James DeLong, a Los Angeles Architect associated with Marston in a defense-related project during World War II. James DeLong, interview, Altadena, California, 19 August 1997.

44. KPM interview, Montecito, California, 30 August 1997.

45. Robert E. Bennett, interview, Pasadena, 20 October 1998.

46. Paul Orban, Jr., telephone interview, 21 October 1998.

47. Ibid.

48. KPM, interview, Montecito, California, 30 August 1997.

49. Robert E. Bennett, interview, Pasadena, 20 October 1998; Richard E. Thomas, interview, Pasadena, 26 October 1998.

50. It was not until July of 1914 that Marston and Van Pelt's names appeared together as a partnership on a project–the residence for C.B. Sumner at 500 La Loma Road. See John Ripley, Pasadena Houses of the Craftsman Era–Marston," unpublished paper, 8 July 1998.

51. Van Pelt Application for Examination for Certificate, State of California, January 12, 1912, Board of Architectural Examiners, State of California.

52. John Ripley, *Pasadena City Directory* unpublished research, July 1998.

53. Van Pelt Application for Examination for Certificate, State of California, January 12, 1912, Board of Architectural Examiners, State of California.

54. Walter P. White, Jr., Van Pelt relative, interview, Pasadena, 13 December 1997.

55. Ibid.

56. Ibid.

57. Marie Van Pelt Clark, interview, 20 April 1998.

58. Ibid.

59. Walter P. White, Jr., Van Pelt relative, interview, Pasadena, 13 December 1997.

60. Ibid

61. Ibid.

62. Ibid.

63. Ibid.

64. Van Pelt Application for Examination for Certificate, State of California, 12 January 1912; Van Pelt Application for Membership, AIA, Washington, D.C., 14 July 1916.

65. *Who's Who in California: A Biographical Directory*, 1928-29 (San Francisco: Who's Who Publishing, 1929), p. 195.

66. Van Pelt Correspondence, Author's collection.

67. Van Pelt Application for Examination for Certificate, State of California, 12 January 1912.

68. Ibid.

69. Ibid.

70. Walter P. White, Van Pelt relative, interview, Pasadena, 13 December 1997.

71. (Cleveland: J.H. Jansen, 1928).

72. Robert E. Alexander, interview by Marlene L. Laskey, *Architecture, Planning and Social Responsibility*, Vol. 1. Oral History Program, UCLA, 1989, pp 36-37.

73. Ibid.

74. *Pasadena Community Book* (Pasadena: Arthur H. Cawston, 1943), Vol. 1, p. 406.

75. *PSN*, 2 February 1917.

76. *PSN*, 1 April 1914.

77. *PSN*, 2 February 1917,

78. Marjorie Maybury Kellogg, interview, 30 June 2000.

79. Maybury File, California State Board of Architectural Review, Sacramento.

80. Ibid.

81. Henry Withey, *Biographical Dictionary of American Architects* (Los Angeles: New Age Publishing Co., 1956), pp. 34-45.

82. Marjorie Maybury Kellogg, interview, 30 June 2000.

83. Henry Withey, op. cit.

84. Maybury File, California State Board of Architectural Review, Sacramento.

85. Ibid.

86. *SWBC*, 7 May 1920, p. 12, col. 3.

87. Thornton and Richard Hamlin, interview, San Marino, California, 9 June 2000.

88. Kellogg interview, op. cit.

89. For a general understanding of architectural education in the U.S., see Arthur Clason Weatherhead, *The History of Collegiate Education in the United States* (Los Angeles, 1941).

90. Joan Draper, "The Ecole des Beaux-Arts and the Architectural Profession in the United States: The Case of John Galen Howard," *The Architect*, ed. Spiro Kostof (New York: Oxford, 1977), p. 214.

91. Gertrude Atherton, *California: An Intimate History* (New York: Harper & Brothers, 1914), pp. 123-24.

92. S.B. Marston, *Journal–Bangor,* Nov. 1st, 1849.

93. Ibid.

94. This framed certificate is now part of the Rare and Manuscripts Collection, The Huntington Library, San Marino, California.

95. M.W. Wood, *History of Alameda County, California* (Oakland: Pacific Press, 1883), pp. 932-33.

96. Ibid.

97. "Plan of Union Street Brick Church," *Year Book of the Independent Congregational Society* (Bangor: Press of

J.H. Bacon, 1892), pp. 21-23.

98. M.W. Wood, op. cit.

99. Deborah Thompson, *Bangor, Maine 1769-1914: An Architectural History* (Orono: University of Maine, 1988), p. 256, 328.

100. Ibid.

101. KPM interview, Montecito, California, 21 September 1997.

102. M.W. Wood, op. cit.

103. Ibid.

104. Ibid.

105. Ibid.

106. "Up to the Wilderness," *NYT*, 28 September 1986.

107. Point Reyes and Bolinas Bay Brochure, pp. 21-2, Point Reyes Lighthouse file, United States Lighthouse Society, San Francisco; Dewey Livingstone, "Point Reyes," *The Keeper's Log*, Vol. VII, Winter 1991, pp 2-14.

108. Point Reyes Light Station Application, National Register of Historic Places, 5 November 1990, section 8, page 1.

109. Livingston, op. cit.

110. Pigeon Point Lighthouse Landmark Application, 30 November 1979.

111. *San Mateo County Times-Gazette*, 10 June 1871.

112. Ibid.

113. M.W. Wood, op. cit.

114. "Alice Marston Hastings Remembers," *Pasadena Community Book*, ed. C.F. Shoop (Pasadena: Arthur H. Cawston, 1955), pp. 115-19.

115. Ibid.

116. Obituary, *Oakland Enquirer*, 24 March 1896.

117. Ibid.

118. KPM, telephone interview, 6 January 1998.

119. *PSN*, 30 January 1922.

120. "Alice Marston Hastings Remembers," op. cit., pp 115-19.

121. KPM interview, Montecito, California, 21 September 1997.

122. Charles Cherniss, *Pasadena Star News* columnist, telephone interview, October 1997.

123. *PSN*, 15 July 1931.

124. "Alice Marston Hastings Remembers," op. cit.

125. Ibid.

126. Thurston's Pasadena City Directory, 1893-1894.

127. Ralph Arnold, "Edna Gearhart Remembers," *Pasadena in the Gay Nineties* (Pasadena: Star News, 1955), p. 94.

128. "Alice Marston Remembers," op. cit., pp. 115-119.

129. Edith Hatfield Marston, interview by Betty Barton Shafer, Pasadena, 23 April 1970; transcript with Marston Collection, Pasadena Historical Museum.

130. Ibid.

131. Ibid.

132. Joan Draper, "John Galen Howard," *Journal of Architectural Education*, Vol. 33, November 1979, p. 32.

133. "125 Years of Achievement," *The History of Cornell's College of Architecture, Art, and Planning*, (Ithica: Cornell University, 1996), Preface.

134. Gertrude S. Martin, "The College of Architecture: Cornell Universit5." *AR*, Vol. 22, July 1907, p. 47.

134. Ibid.

136. A.D.F. Hamlin, "The Influence of the Ecole des Beaux-Arts on Our Architectural Education," *AR*, Vol. 23, April 1908, p. 243.

137. Ibid, p. 246.

138. Gertrude S. Martin, op. cit., p. 50.

139. Grade Card for Sylvanus Boardman Marston, Cornell University, Rare and Manuscript Collections, Kroch Library, Cornell.

140. Ibid.

141. Richard Chafee, "The Teaching of Architecture at the Ecole des Beaux-Arts," *The Architecture of the Beaux-Arts*, ed. Arthur Drexler (New York: Museum of Modern Art, 1977), p. 112.

142. Paul Cret, "The Ecole Des Beaux Arts: What Its Architectural Training Means," *AR*, Vol. 23, May 1908, p. 369.

143. Ibid., p. 370.

144. J. Stewart Barney, "The Ecole des Beaux Arts, Its Influence on Our Architecture," *AR*, Vol. 22, November 1907, p. 342.

145. *The Cornell Class Book*, 1907, p. 353.

146. Ibid., p. 123.

147. Faculty Biography Folder, The Late Clarence A, Martin, Department of Architecture, Cornell University.

148. Ibid.

149. Albert C. Martin, Jr., interview, Los Angeles, 3 September 1998.

150. Gertrude S. Martin, op. cit., pp 42-43.

151. *PSN*, 2 July 1907.

152. Ibid.

153. Roster of Licensed Architects and Meeting Minutes, 1908, Board of Architectural Examiners, State of California.

154. "Katherine Nash (Mrs. Carl) Thomas Remembers," *Pasadena Community Book* (Pasadena: Arthur H. Cawston, 1955), p. 237.

155. *PSN*, 17 July 1937.

156. Ibid.

157. *PP*, 6 June 1938.

158. Ibid.

159. *PS*, 17 July 1937.

160. *PP*, 6 June 1938.

161. Nancy H. Sokol, owner of Thomas's house in Ithaca, telephone interview, 10 May 1977.

163. Ibid.

163. *PSN*, 9 February 1910

164. Ibid.

–Chapter 2– A Winter Colony

1. "Architecture as a Profession," *A&E*, Vol. 25, July 1908, p. 54.

2. Video, "Pasadena: A Heritage to Celebrate," distributed by the Arroyo Arts Association, 1987; "Pioneer List Loses L.J. Merritt," *PSN*, 21 March 1929.

3. Morrow Mayo, *Los Angeles* (New York: A.A. Knopf, 1933), p, 212.

4. "Architecture in Southern California," *AR*, Vol. 8, July

1905, p.1.

5. Ibid.

6. "Why I Live in Pasadena," *TRB* (Pasadena Star News, 1911). No pagination.

7. *AR*, Vol.8, January 1905, p. 7.

8. Billy M. Jones, *Health-Seekers in the Southwest, 1819-1900* (Norman: University of Oklahoma, 1967), viii.

9. Ibid., vii.

10. Ibid., viii.

11. See Newton H. Chittenden, *Health Seekers', Tourists', and Sportsmens' Guide to Health and Pleasure Resorts of the Pacific Coast* (San Francisco: C.A Murdock & Co., 1884; Billy M. Jones, op. cit., p. 152.

12. F.C.S. Sanders, *California as a Health Resort* (San Francisco: Bolte & Braden, 1916).

13. Ibid., preface.

14. Ibid, p. 169.

15. Ibid.

16. Ibid., p. 171

17. Morrow Mayo, op. cit., p. 213.

18. *Los Angeles Herald*, 7 November 1904, p. 4, with illus.

19. *PSN*, 10 January 1922.

20. Grace Hortense Tower, "Two Famous Boulevards," *TRB* (Pasadena Star News, 1905). No pagination.

21. City of Pasadena Librarian Carolyn L. Garner, "Great men & Their Grand Hotels, speech at Pasadena Historical Museum, 18 October 1998.

22. "Midwick Papers," *CL*, Vol. 22, 1 December 1925, pp. 6-7.

23. Ibid., p. 7.

24. Lon F. Chapin, *Thirty Years in Pasadena* (Los Angeles: Southwest Publishing Co, 1929), p 178.

25. Ibid., p. 176

26. J.W. Wood, *Pasadena–Historical and Personal* (Pasadena: J.W. Wood, 1917), p. 266.

27. *PS*, 4 August 1910.

28. "D.M. Linnard Mourned as Man of Vision," *PSN*, 2 September 1949.

29. Ibid.

30. Ibid.

31. J.W. Wood, op. cit., p. 268.

32. *LABC*, 17 November 1910.

33. Ibid.

34. Eleanor Gates, "Paradise Regained," *Sunset Magazine*, Vol. 27, December 1911, pp. 609-610.

35. Ibid., p. 609.

36. Marston Collection, Pasadena Historical Museum.

37. "Pasadena Portico of Paradise," *TRB* (Pasadena: Pasadena Star News, 1911). No pagination.

38. Ibid.

39. Ibid.

40. Ibid.

41. *LABC*, 10 November 1910.

42. Advertisement. *TRB* (Pasadena: Pasadena Star News, 1911). No pagination.

43. *LABC*, 10 June 1909.

44. Vol. 17, January 1911.

45. Thomas D. Carpenter, *Pasadena: Resort Hotels and Paradise* (Pasadena: Castle Green Times, 1984), p. 71.

46. Ibid.

47. Ibid.

48. The Huntington Hotel Historic District Application for the National Register of Historic Places, 15 August 1985, Item 8, p. 7.

49. *PSN*, 29 June 1958.

50. Donald M. and Mary L. Decker, *Reflections on Elegance* (Laguna Niguel: Royal Literary Publications, 1991). p. 10.

51. Final *Environmental Impact Report for Huntington Hotel*, August 1986, by Cotton/Beland Associates, Inc., pp. III-36-37.

52. Thomas D. Carpenter, op. cit., p. 94.

53. 9 January 1914.

54. J.W. Wood, op. cit., p. 269.

55. Thomas D. Carpenter, op. cit., p. 90.

56. Donald M. and Mary L. Decker, op. cit., p 23.

57. Final *Environmental Impact Report for the Huntington Hotel*, op. cit., III-36-37.

58. Thomas D. Carpenter, op. cit., p. 90.

59. Donald M. and Mary L. Decker, op. cit., p. 25.

60. Thomas D. Carpenter, op. cit., p. 88.

61. Donald M. and Mary L. Decker, op. cit., p. 25.

62. See Vol. 81, *CS*, p. 24; also Vol. 6, *AD*, 1927, p. 152, indicating pool contractor was Thomas & Stephenson, further evidence that the pool was designed by Marston.

63. Ibid., *CS*, p. 27.

64. Donald M. and Marty L. Decker, op. cit., p. 27.

65. September 1926, p. 24.

66. Ibid.

67. The Marston Job Records indicate that each cottage was built by Thomas & Stephenson, one of Pasadena's earliest contractors. Marston's already established relationship with that firm, stemming from earlier work, may have assisted Marston in acquiring these commissions.

68. Donald M. and Mary L. Decker, op. cit., p. 35.

69. The Huntington Hotel...Historic Places, op cit, Item 8, p. 12.

70. Donald M. and Mary L. Decker, op cit, p. 35.

71. Ibid.

72. September 1926, p. 24.

73. Ibid.

74. Ibid.

75. Thomas D. Carpenter, op. cit., pp. 95-7.

76. Ibid.

77. Ibid, p. 104.

78. Ibid.

79. Carol Pretty, "Boarding House to Courthouse: A Brief History of the Vista Del Arroyo," *Pasadena Heritage Magazine*, Vol. 13, October 1991, pp. 6-7; *Historic Structures Report Vista Del Arroyo Hotel*, prepared for the General Services Administration, by Charles Hall Page & Associates, Inc., July 1980, p. 17.

80. *SWBC*, 17 September 1920.

81. Ibid.

82. Vista del Arroyo File, Pasadena Heritage.

83. Thomas D. Carpenter, op. cit., p. 106.

84. *Historic Structures Report Vista Del Arroyo Hotel*, op. cit., p. 15.

85. Ibid., p. 19.

86. Advertisements (Pasadena: Pasadena Star News, 1921 and 1922).

87. Vol. 32, August 1923, plate 7.

88. (Pasadena: Star News, c. 1925), p. 40.

89. *Historic Structures Report Vista Del Arroyo Hotel*, op. cit., p. 41.

90. Ibid., p. 16.

91. *CL*, 13 May 1922, p. 14.

92. Ibid.

93. Ibid.

94. *CL*, 12 December 1924, p. 10.

95. Vol. 25, 15 January 1929, p. 37.

96. *CL*, 15 November 1924, p. 13.

97. "Pasadena Hostelry Sold," *LAT*, 27 March 1926.

98. *SWBC*, 22 June 1928.

99. Gebhard & Winter, *Architecture in Los Angeles* (Salt Lake City: Peregrine Smith, 1985), p. 351.

100. *CL*, Vol. 28, 13-17 May 1922, p. 14.

101. *Alternative Reuse Feasibility Study for the Vista del Arroyo Hotel Bungalows*, prepared for General Services Administration by Thirtieth Street Architects, Inc., July 1980, p. 23.

102. *Historic Structures Report Vista Del Arroyo Hotel*, op. cit., p. 23.

103. *PSN*, 20 November 1998.

104. *Vista del Arroyo Hotel & Bungalows Nomination to National Register of Historic Places*, 10 September 1980, Item 8.

105. *Historic Structures Report Vista Del Arroyo Hotel*, op. cit., p. 20

106. *Alternative Reuse...Study...*, op. cit, p. 5.

107. *Historic Structures Report Vista Del Arroyo Hotel*, op. cit., p. 21.

108. Thomas D. Carpenter, op. cit., p.115.

109. Ibid.

110. *Historic Structures Report Vista Del Arroyo Hotel*, op. cit., p. 23.

111. *PSN*, 15 November 1998.

112. Vista del Arroyo File, Pasadena Heritage.

113. Ibid.

114. Carol Pretty, op. cit., p. 7.

115. *LAT*, 27 March 1926.

116. Ibid.

117. Ibid.

118. *PSN*, 3 April 1928.

119. Ibid.

120. Ibid.

121. Ibid.

122. *LAT*, 27 March 1926.

123. "Seeing Stars at the Vista del Arroyo," *CL*, 12 December 1924, p. 10.

124. *Vista del Arroyo Hotel and Bungalows Nomination to National Register of Historic Places*, 10 September

125. *Pasadena Community Book* (Pasadena: Arthur H. Cawston, 1943), p. 545.

126. Ibid.

127. Ibid.

128. Renovation firm cost estimate, Vista del Arroyo File, Pasadena Heritage

129. *Pasadena Community Book*, op. cit., p. 231.

130. Ibid.

131. *PSN*, 16 September 1932.

132. *Arizona Republic*, 17 September 1932.

133. *Pasadena Community Book*, op. cit., p. 231.

134. *PSN*, 16 September 1932.

135. *Arizona Republic*, 17 September 1932.

136. See *PSN*, 16 September 1932; *Arizona Republic*, 17 September 1932.

137. History of Hotel Vista del Arroyo: Historical Significance, copy available at library, U.S. Courthouse, Vista del Arroyo, p. 5.

138. *Historic Structures Report Vista Del Arroyo Hotel*, op. cit., p. 25.

139. Carol Pretty, op. cit., p. 7.

140. *Historic Structures Report Vista Del Arroyo Hotel*, op. cit., p. 26.

141. See *PSN*, 15 July 1974, 14 February 1975, 14 March 1975, and 9 August 1976.

142. *PSN*, 4 February 1986.

143. Ibid.

144. Ibid.

145. Ibid.

146. 4 February 1986.

–Chapter 3– Embrace of the Arts and Crafts

1. Barry Sanders, *A Complex Fate: Gustav Stickley and the Craftsman Movement* (New York: Preservation Press, 1996), p. 84.

2. Kenneth Miedema, Lecture on Pasadena Arts and Crafts Period 1900-1920, organized by Pasadena Heritage, 2 September 1998; see also F.C.S. Sanders *California as a Health Resort* (San Francisco: Bolte & Braden Co., 1916).

3. Charles Sumner Greene, *TRB* (Pasadena: Star News), 1907.

4. *AR*, Vol. XVII, August 1905, p. 222.

5. *CR*, Vol. XII, October 1907, p. 79.

6. Ibid.

7. (New York: The Macmillan Company, 1929), pp. 2-8.

8. Ibid.

9. Robert E. Bennett, interview, Pasadena, 20 October 1998.

10. The Cornell Class Book, 1907, p.123.

11. Robert Winter, *The California Bungalow* (Hennessey + Ingalls, 1980), p. 60; Edward R. Bosley, "Sylvanus B. Marston," *Toward a Simpler Way of Life*, ed. Robert Winter (Berkeley: University of California, 1997), p. 169; Charles Alma Byers, "The Popular Bungalow-Court Idea," *The Building Age* (April 1915); Henry L. Saylor, *Bungalows* (New York: McBride, Winston & Co., 1911).

12. Robert Winter, interview with Larry Mantle, radio station KPCC, Pasadena, 25 July 1997.

13. *TRB* (Pasadena: Star News, 1920).
14. *LABC*, 23 November 1911.
15. Virginia and Lee McAlester, *A Field Guide to American Houses* (New York: Knopf, 1996), p. 439.
16. James DeLong, interview, Altadena, California, 19 August 1997.
17. Public Television Series on Frank Lloyd Wright, 12 November 1998.
18. Ibid.
19. Pasadena Heritage Files.
20. *Pasadena Community Book* (Pasadena: Arthur H. Cawston, 1943), pp. 273-74.
21. Ibid.
22. *YB, LAAC*, Third Exhibition (Los Angeles: Kinglsey, Mason & Collins Co., 1912) [no pagination].
23. *LABC*, 18 May 1911.
24. *PSN*, 6 September 1985.
25. Ibid.
26. *PSN*, 7 August 1965.
27. Ibid., 6 September 1985.
28. *PSN*, 1 December 1985.
29. *Orange Heights: The Treasures on Your Block*, [undated].
30. 3 December 1924.
31. Harold Kirker, Foreword; Karen Weitze, *California's Mission Revival* (Los Angeles: Hennessey + Ingalls, 19840), p. ix.
32. *WA*, Vol. 27, October 1918.
33. Ibid., p. 99.
34. Ibid., p. 98.
35. Ibid.
36. *TRB* (Pasadena: Star News, 1913).
37. *YB, LAAC*, op. cit.
38. *Scribner's Magazine*, Vol. LII, July-December 1912, p. 40.
39. *CR*, Vol. 27, November 1914, pp. 209-212.
40. Ibid., pp 209-210.
41. Ibid.
42. Ibid.
43. *Scribner's Magazine*, op. cit.
44. "The Young Folks' First Home," by Carey Edmunds, *LHJ*, Vol. XXXII, May 1915, p. 36.
45. *CR*, Vol. 27, November 1914, p. 209-212.
46. (Pasadena: Star News, 1910).
47. John Ripley, "Pasadena Houses of the Craftsman Era–Marston," unpublished paper, 8 July 1998.
48. *LABC*, 2 November 1911.
49. John Ripley, op. cit.
50. Robert Judson Clark and Thomas S. Hines, *Los Angeles Transfer: Architecture in Southern California*, 188-1980 (Los Angeles: William Andrews Clark Memorial Library, UCLA, 1983), p. 22.
51. *PS*, 13 May 1915; *PSN*, 15 December 1924.
52. *PSN*, c. 1913.
53. Randall L. Makinson, *A Guide to the Work of Greene & Greene* (Salt Lake City: Peregrine Smith Books, 1970), p. 147.
54. Prospect Park Gates Blueprint, Marston Collection, Pasadena Historical Museum.

55. *LABC*, 14 December 1911.
56. 15 December 1911.
57. Randall L. Makinson, op cit., p. 147.
58. (Pasadena: Star News, 1911).
59. *SWBC*, 17 September 1908, is the earliest dated material indicating that Marston was "making plans" for the bungalow court. A New York based publication picked up this as well, although slightly later in time: "Building News," *AA*, XCV, 6 January 1909, p. 26, noted that "S.B. Marston, as architect for the Frank G. Hogan Realty Company, has prepared plans for a number of bungalows to be erected here at a probable expense of $30,000. Bids for the construction are soon to be taken." See also for a comprehensive account of this commission Edward Bosley, "Sylvanus B. Marston," in *Toward a Simpler Way of Life*, ed. Robert Winter (Berkeley: U.C. Press, 1997), pp. 169-180.
60. Henry H. Saylor, *Bungalows* (New York: McBride, Winston & Co., 1911), p. 23.
61. Robert Winter, *The California Bungalow* (Los Angeles: Hennessey + Ingalls, 1980), p. 60.
62. Henry H. Saylor, op. cit.
63. Ibid., p. 25.
64. Ibid., P. 23.
65. Ibid.
66. Henry H. Saylor, *Bungalows* (New York: McBride, Winston & Co., 1911); Charles Alma Byers, "The Popular Bungalow-Court Idea," *The Building Age*, April 1915, p. 21.
67. Helen Lukens Gaut, "The Little Money Bungalow," *LHJ*, Vol. XXXI, February 1914, p. 27; Helen Lukens Gaut, "The Six-Room Bungalow," *LHJ*, Vol. XXXI, February 1914, p. 100; Carey Edmunds, "The Bungalow That Has Proved its Worth," *LHJ*, Vol. XXXII, February. 1915, p. 28' Carey Edmunds, "Bungalows That Other Women Have Built," *LHJ*, Vol. XXXII, June 1915, p. 26.
68. *YB, LAAC*, Fourth Edition (Los Angeles: Geo. Rice & Sons, 1910).
69. Eleanor Gates, "Pasadena–Paradise Regained," *Sunset*, Vol. XXVII, December 1911, p. 612.
70. *PSN*, 19 December 1925.
71. Ibid., 22 October 1919.
72. Ibid., 13 July 1933.
73. Ibid., 29 October 1914.
74. National Register of Historic Places Multiple Property Documentation Form, prepared by Thirtieth Street Architects, Inc., 26 May 1993, p. F-6.
75. *TRB* (Pasadena: Star News, 1912).
76. See *LABC*, 23 December 1910.
77. See *SWBC*, December 1923 and 12 December 1924.
78. *Notables of the West* (New York: International News Service, 1915), Vol. II, p. 455.
79. Ibid.
80. Ibid.
81. *PSN*, 19 May 1960.
82. *TRB* (Pasadena: Star News, 1913).
83. J.M. Guinn, *Los Angeles and Environs* (Los Angeles: Historic Record Company, 1907), Vol. II, p. 1055.
84. Ibid.
85. *PDU*, 11 November 1918.
86. *PSN*, 11 November 1918.

87. Charles Siems, *Trolley Days in Pasadena* (San Marino: Golden West Books, 1983), p. 30.

88. *LABC*, 29 August 1912.

89. *YB, LAAC*, Fourth Edition, op. cit.

90. *A&E*, Vol. 28, September 1914, p. 88.

91. *AR*, Vol. XL, October 1916, pp. 330-332; *AA*, Vol. 107, 17 February 1915, plates and plans.

92. City of Pasadena Cultural Heritage Landmark Application, September 1987, p. 3.

93. Vol. 107, 17 February 1915, plates and plans.

94. (Pasadena: Star News, 1915).

95. *PSN*. 18 September 1929.

96. Ibid.

–Chapter 4– Revival Architecture

1. Merry Ovick, *The End of the Rainbow* (Los Angeles: Balcony Press), pp 156-77.

2. "Field Day for Lookie-Loos," *LAT*, 13 April 1980.

3. Ibid.

4. *LAT*, 10 August 1997; the Pasadena Showcase of Interior Design is sponsored each year by the Pasadena Junior Philharmonic, and it selects an annual "Showcase House" which is decorated by the leading local interior decorators and opened to the public for viewing.

5. Marston Job List, #214, Pasadena Historical Museum.

6. A.D.F. Hamlin, *AR*, Vol. 42, October 1917, pp. 291, 360.

7. *LABC*, 29 August 1912.

8. John Ripley, "Pasadena Houses of the Craftsman Era–Marston," unpublished paper, 8 July 1998.

9. James A Culbertson Day Book, Greene and Greene Library, Gamble House, Pasadena.

10. Edward R. Bosley, *Greene & Greene* (London: Phaidon Press, 2000).

11. KPM, interview, Montecito, California, 21 September 1997; June Haver, interview, Brentwood, California, Summer 1997.

12. A. Lawrence Kocher and Howard Dearstyne, Colonial Williamsburg: Its Buildings and Gardens (New York: Holt, Rinehart & Winston, 1976), p. 79.

13. Marjorie Maybury Kellogg, interview, 30 June 2000.

14. Ibid.

15. Death Records, Mountain View Cemetery, Altadena; Thurston's *Pasadena City Directories* 1925, 1927, 1930.

16. Virginia and Lee McAlester, *A Field Guide to American Houses* (New York: Alfred A. Knopf, 1996), p. 156.

17. Marian Lacey Bassett, interview, 28 October 1998, Pasadena.

18. *AA*, Vol. 125, 22 March 1925, Plate 67.

19. 1925, p. 13.

20. Virginia and Lee McAlester, op. cit., p. 343.

21. Ibid., p. 344.

22. *AR*, Vol. 40, November 1916, pp. 479-81; Prentice Duell, "Some Recent Works of Marston & Van Pelt," *AR*, Vol. 52, July 1922, p. 33.

23. *AR*, Vol. 52, July 1922, p. 33.

24. *A&E*, Vol. 62, August 1920, p. 93.

25. KPM, interview, Montecito, California, 29 August 1997.

26. Harold D. Carew, *History of Pasadena and the San Gabriel Valley* (New York: S.J. Clarke Publishing Co., 1930), Vol. III, p. 364.

27. *The Phi Delta Gamma*, Vol. 57, February 1935, pp. 371-74.

28. *PSN*, 22 March 1916.

29. Ibid.

30. *PSN*, 8 July 1941.

31. *NYT*, 14 October 1948.

32. Ibid.

33. Ibid.

34. *Pasadena Community Book* (Pasadena: Arthur H. Cawston, 1947), p. 476.

35. Ibid.

36. Ibid.

37. Vol. 8, January 1930, pp. 122-25.

38. Grace Hortense Tower, "Two Famous Boulevards," *TRB* (Pasadena: Star News, 1905), pp. 32-34.

39. *SWBS*, 28 May 1920, p. 16.

40. *PSN*, 19 April 1984.

41. *PSN*. 7 October 1930.

42. Vol. 52, July 1922, P. 34.

43. *PSN*, 29 September 1930.

44. *PSN*, 10 January 1925.

45. *PSN*, 24 October 1919.

46. Ibid.

47. Ibid.

48. *AD*, Vol. 6, 1927, pp. 76-8.

49. *LAT*, 3 December 1947.

50. Bryant Properties Brochure, copy on file, Pasadena Historical Museum.

51. *PSN*, 3 February 1928.

52. Pasadena City Building Permit #1569B, 1921.

53. *PSN*, 3 February 1928.

54. Vol. 1, 1924, p. 43.

55. Vol. 52, July 1922, pp. 34-35.

56. See *CS*, Vols. 90, 91; June, July 1927, pp. 12, 13 respectively.

57. *PSN*, 20 February 1998.

58. *CS*, Vol. 94, October 1927.

59. *PSN*, 20 February 1998.

60. *PSN*, 27 August 1935.

61. Ibid.

62. *PSN*, 5 July 1937.

63. Ibid.

64. Ibid.

65. KPM, interview, 21 September 1997.

66. *PSN*, 5 July 1937.

67. Ibid.

68. Shakespeare Club History, unpublished papers, Shakespeare Club Files.

69. Lon F. Chapin, *Thirty Years in Pasadena* (Pasadena: Southwest Publishing Co., 1929), Vol. 1, p. 77.

70. *LABC*, 29 February 1912.

71. *PSN*, 14 May 1912.

72. *SWCM*, 11 May 1912.

73. *A&E*, Vol. 33, June 1913, pp. 47-72; *A&E*, Vol. 38, September 1914, pp. 61-87.

74. Vol. 33, June 1913, pp. 47-48.

75 (Pasadena: Star News, 1922) [no pagination].

76. *AR*, Vol. 42, October 1917, pp. 291, 361.

77. "Entre es sa [sic] casa, Amigo," *CL*, Vol. 10, 29 November 1913.

78. *PSN*, 30 August 1938.

79. Ibid.

80. (Chicago: The Lakeside Press, 1928).

81. *PSN*, 30 August 1938.

82. *AA*, Vol. 127, 3 June 1925, plates 141-44.

83. *AR*, Vol. 66, November 1929, pp. 397-445.

84. Ibid., p. 407.

85. *PCA*, Vol. 35, January 1929, p. 3.

86. Vol. 33, 1928, p. 36. See also HB, Vol. 69, February 1931, p. 142.

87. "H.R. Haldeman Dies," *Washington Post*, 13 November 1993.

88. Ibid.

89. Bruce Henstell, *Sunshine and Wealth: Los Angeles in the Twenties and Thirties* (San Francisco: Chronicle Books, 1984), p. 42.

90. (Berkeley: University of California, 1994).

91. Professor Jules Tygiel, telephone interview, 4 April 2001.

92. *LAT*, 20 January 1922.

93. *Pasadena Community Book* (Pasadena: Arthur H. Cawston, 1943), pp. 305-6.

94. *Residential Architecture in Southern California* (Washington: AIA, 1939; reprinted by Hennessey + Ingalls, 1998).

95. Ibid., p. 58.

96. Vol. 74, September 1933, pp. 224-5.

97. *SWCB*, 21 March 1930, p. 31.

98. Ibid.

99. Vol. 8, pp. 56-7.

100. Vol. 39, July 1930, pp. 24-5.

101. *HB*, Vol. 69, February 1931, pp. 140-41.

102. Ibid., p. 141.

103. Virginia and Lee McAlester, op. cit.

104. See Terry Silo and John Manion, *Around Pasadena* (Pasadena: Gallery Productions, 1976), pp. 50-3.

105. Original architect's record, Job Number 483, in possession of Dr. Shawn Libaw.

106. *SWBC*, 31 October 1924.

107. *Pasadena Community Book* (Pasadena: Arthur Cawston, 1943), 612-13.

108. Ibid.

109. *PSN*, 2 July 1926.

110. See Carol Green Wilson, *California Yankee* (Claremont: Saunders Press, 1946).

111. Ibid; *PSN*, 1 January 1929.

112. Garrett Van Pelt AIA Fellow's File, AIA Archives, Washington.

113. KPM, interview, Montecito, California, 29 August 1997.

114. See S.B. Marston, "Diary–Army Young Men's Christian Association," 24 December 1918–29 June 1919 [last pages lost], Marston family collection.

115. *PSN*, 22 May 1931.

116. *AD*, Vol. 7, 1929, pp. 99-101.

117. *PSN*, 25 June 1932.

118. Ibid.

119. *HB*, Vol. 67, April 1930, pp 441-44.

120. AD, Vol. 6, 1927, pp. 46-51.

121. James J. Yoch (New York: Harry N. Abrams, Inc., 1989), p. 55.

122. Winifred Starr Dobyns (New York: Macmillan Company, 1931), plates 196-197.

123. *CA&A*, Vol. 39, March 1931, pp. 25-27.

124. Ibid.

125. Ibid.

126. James J. Yoch, "Harmony and Invention in the Gardens of Florence Yoch," *Pacific Horticulture*, January 1989, pp. 12-29.

127. *PSN*, 19 January 1934.

128. *PSN*, 24 January 1999.

129. *PSN*, 14 February 1925; *HB*, Vol. 56, August 1924, pp. 133-35; *HB*, Vol. 57, June 1925, pp. 67-78.

130. Ibid.

131. *A&E*, Vol. 78, September 1924, pp. 53-74.

132. *PSN*, 24 April 1924; 14 February 1925.

133. Ibid.

134. *H&G*, Vol. 47, May 1925, p. 95.

135. Ibid.

136. Ibid.

137. *HB*, Vol. 57, June 1925, p. 678.

138. Ibid,

139. *AA*, Vol. 125, 11 March 1925, plates 63-66.

140. Vol. 1, 1925, p. 14.

141. Ibid.

142. *HB*, Vol. 56, August 1924, p. 133.

–Chapter 5– The New Regional Idiom

1. *A&E*, Vol. 19, November 1909, p. 44.

2. Reyner Banham, introduction; Randell L. Makinson, *Greene & Greene: Architecture as Fine Art* (Salt Lake City: Gibbs M. Smith, 1977), p. 23.

3. Clarence S. Stein, "A Triumph of the Spanish-Colonial Style;" Bertram Grosvenor Goodhue, *The Architecture and the Gardens of the San Diego Exposition* (San Francisco: Paul Elder, 1916), p. 12.

4. (Boston: Art Library Publishing Co, 1902).

5. Ibid., p. 509

6. David Gebhard, "The Spanish Colonial Revival in Southern California (1895-1930)," JSAH, Vol. 26, May 1067, p. 136.

7. Ibid., p. 131.

8. See e.g., Robert Judson Clark, "Los Angeles Transfer: Romanticism and Integration, 1880-1930," *Los Angeles Transfer: Architecture in Southern California* (Los Angeles: William Andrews Clark Memorial Library, 1983), p. 3.

9. Clarence S. Stein, op. cit., p. 13; see also "The California Mission and Its Influence Upon Pacific Coast Architecture," *A&E*, Vol. 24, February 1911, p. 63.

10. David Gebhard, op. cit.

11. Professor Robert Winter, quoted by Leon Whiteson, "20s Spanish Style Needs No Revival," *LAT*, 5 March 1989.

12. David Gebhard, op. cit.

13. *WA*, Vol. 32, August 1923, p. 88; se also Merry Ovnick, *Los Angeles: The End of the Rainbow* (Los Angeles: Balcony Press. 1994), pp. 154-228.

14. Merry Ovnick, *Los Angeles: The End of the Rainbow* (Los Angeles, 1994), p. 194.

15. Sam Hall Kaplan, LA Lost & Found (New York: Crown Publishing, Inc., 1987), p. 84.

16. Merry Ovnick, op. cit.

17. *LAT*, 5 March 1989.

18. Vol. 60, November 1926, p. 390.

19. Vol. 52, July 1922, p. 18.

20. *CS*, Vol. 46, October 1923, p. 16.

21. Garrett Van Pelt, Jr., *Old Architecture of Southern Mexico* (Cleveland: J.H. Jansen, 1926).

22. Ibid.

23. Ibid., introduction.

24. *American Architecture Since 1780: A Guide to the Styles* (Cambridge, Mass: MIT Press, 1969, 1981), p. 227.

25. (Cleveland: J.H. Jansen, 1928); reprinted by Acanthus Press (New York: 1999).

26. Alson Clark, *Wallace Neff: Architect of California's Golden Age* (Santa Barbara: Capra Press, 1986), p. 24.

27. Merry Ovnick, op. cit., p. 181.

28. *AR*, Vol. 52, July 1922, p. 35.

29. *AR*, Vol. 46, September 1919, p. 196.

30. *CS*, Vol. 25, January 1922, p. 11.

31. *AR*, Vol. 52, July 1922, p. 18.

32. Alson Clark, op. cit., p. 21.

33. Ibid., foreword by David Gebhard.

34. *Johnson. Kaufman & Coate*: Partners in the California Style (Claremont: Scripps College, 1992).

35. *LAT*, 5 March 1989.

36. *AR*, Vol. 46, September 1919, p. 196

37. *PSN*, 26 April 1916.

38. *AR*, Vol. 45, September 1919; PSN, 26 April 1916.

39. Vol., 46, January 1922, p. 10.

40. *SWBC*, 16 April 1920, p. 11.

41. *PEP*. 18 April 1916, p. 10.

42. *AR*, Vol. 46, September 1919, p. 202; see also *WA*, Vol. 32, August 1923, plate 14.

43. *PSN*, 26 April, 1916.

44. *Bulb Horn*, January-March 1987 (Lorain County Historical Society), pp. 22-30.

45. Ibid.

46. Ibid.

47. Ibid., p. 29.

48. "Arthur L. Garford and the Roosevelt Years," unpublished paper, files of Keith Palmer Marston.

49. Ibid.

50. Ibid.

51. Ibid.

52. Villa Verde Application, National Register of Historic Places, 13 September 1983, Item 7, p. 1.

53. Vol. 7, 1929, pp. 108-9.

54. "The Garden," brochure by owner.

55. Ibid.

56. Summary of F.A. Hardy, as prepared and provided by Edward K. Hardy, Jr., grandson; copy with current owner.

57. Ibid.

58. Ibid.

59. *SWBC*, 31, October 1924.

60. *AR*, Vol. 52, July 1922, p. 35.

61. *SWBS*, 21 May 1920, p. 15.

62. *CS*, Vol. 25, January 1922, p. 10.

63. *AR*, Vol. 52, July 1922, p. 36; see also *HB*, Vol. 51, January 1922, p. 19.

64. *AR*, Vol. 52, July 1922, p. 26.

65. *CL*, Vol. 21, 1 May 1925, p. 49.

66. *AR*, Vol. 52, July 1922, p. 29.

67. Ibid., p. 36.

68. (Cleveland: J.H. Jansen, 1928).

69. *WA*, Vol. 32, August 1923, plate 1.

70. Advertisement, *PSN*, 24 January 1999.

71. J.E. Pleasants, *History of Orange County* (Los Angeles: J.R. Finnell & Sons, 1931), Vol. III, pp. 306-7.

72. Ibid.

73. *Pasadena Community Book* (Pasadena: Arthur H. Cawston, 1943), pp. 673-76.

74. Ibid.

75. *HB*, Vol. 51, January 1922, p. 20.

76. *AR*, Vol. 52, July 1922, pp 37-38.

77. Ibid, p. 36.

78. Ibid, p. 38.

79. *CS*, Vol. 25, January 1922, p. 11.

80. (Cleveland: J.H. Jansen, 1928), pp. 26-29.

81. *AR*, Vol. 52, January 1922, p. 11.

82. (Pasadena: Star News, c. 1925), p. 20.

83. "Originally Well-Designed Homes Remain Unaffected By Changes of Recurring Cycles of Architectural Style," 10 May 1924.

84. *WA*, Vol. 32, August 1923, p. 87 and plate 5.

85. *AR*, Vol. 52, July 1922, p. 38.

86. Thurston's *Pasadena City Directory*, 1922-1934.

87. Ibid., 1935-1938.

88. *CS*, Vol. 38, February 1923, p. 9.

89. Ibid.

90. *Detroit Press*, 14 September 1954.

91. Obituary, *New York Herald Tribune*, 14 September 1954.

92. *American Art Annual* (Washington, D.C.: American Federation of Arts, 1919), Vol. 16, p. 314.

93. *Detroit News*, 11 April 1949 and 2 June 1937.

94. Ibid.

95. George D. Booth, Brief Biography, Burton Historical Collection, Detroit Public Library; *Detroit News*, 11 April 1949.

96. Ibid.

97. Vol. 72, March 1923, p. 62.

98. *A&D*, Vol. 31, July 1929, pp. 37-39.

99. Vol. 26, July 1924, p. 20.

100. *AR*, Vol. 54, November 1923, pp. 393, 394, and 396.

101. *WA*, Vol. 52, August 1923, plate 3.

102. (Cleveland: J.H. Jansen, 1928), pp. 34-37.

103. Robert Judson Clark, op. cit., p. 29.

104. Ellis Bishop House, National Register of Historic Places Application, 15 July 1998.

105. Advertisement, CS, Vol. 60, December 1924, p. 23.

106. *PSN*, 24 May 1929.

107. *A&D*, January 1941, p. 13.

108. Rancho Santa Fe Art Jury Minutes for 1928, RSF Historical Society.

109. Ibid.

110. Original Job Record, Job #713, RSF Historical Society.

111. *SWBC*, 30 November 1928.

112. *San Diego Union*, 24 November 1928.

113. "Splendid Home for Bishop Estate," *Rancho Santa Fe Progress*, October 1928, p. 2.

114. October 1931, p. 28.

115. "Splendid Home..." op. cit.

116. *SWBC*, 14 January 1933, p. 13.

117. *SWBC*, 14 May 1944.

118. *Rancho Santa Fe Progress*, October 1928, p. 7.

119. Ibid., p. 2.

120. "At the End of the Road," *A&D*, January 1941.

121. October 1931, pp. 28-31.

122. "At the End of the Road," *A&D*, January 1941.

123. Ibid.

124. Marianne McDonald, interview, Rancho Santa Fe, 8 January 1998.

125. John Steven McGroarty, *History of Los Angeles* (Chicago: American Historical Society, 1923), Vol. II, pp. 50-51.

126. Ibid.; "Wealthy Rancho Resident Expires," *San Diego Union*, 29 February 1933.

127. John Steven McGroarty, op. cit.

128. Ibid.

129. "Wealthy Rancho Resident..." op. cit.

130. *PSN*, 16 March 1929.

131. Vol. 75, March 1926, p. 43.

132. *San Diego Union*, 29 February 1933.

133. *Rancho Santa Fe: A California Village* (Rancho Santa Fe Historical Society, 1993), p. 122.

134. *PSN*, 8 February 1933.

135. "John Burnham Dies; Banking Firm Founder," *San Diego Union*, 15 April 1963.

136. "Many Notables Own Dwellings in 110-Home Rural Community," *San Diego Union*, 20 October 1960.

137. Ellis Bishop House, National Register of Historic Places Application, 15 July 1998.

138. Ibid.

139. "Early Ranch Abode Home for Greek Scholar," *Rancho Santa Fe Review*, 24 March 1992; and *NYT*, 16 May 1958.

140. Sylvester Baxter, *Spanish-Colonial Architecture in Mexico* (Boston: Art Library Publishing Co., 1902), p. 30.

141. Talbot Hamlin, *Architecture Through the Ages* (New York: G.P. Putnam's Sons, 1940, p. 388.

142. *Mediterranean to Modern: Residential Architecture in Southern California* (Los Angeles: Southern California AIA, 1939; reprinted by Hennessey + Ingalls, 1998), p. 27.

143. Ibid.

144. (Altadena: Altadena Chamber of Commerce, circa 1932).

145. Nancy Rhodes, interview, Altadena, California, 6 February 1999.

146. Thurston's *Pasadena City Directory*, 1928-1929.

147. Thurston's *Pasadena City Directory*, 1930-1933.

148. *PEP*, 11 June 1933.

149. Ibid.

150. *SWBC*, 8 November 1929.

151. *Pasadena Community Book*, op. cit., p. 315; Mrs. Nina C. Bushnell, interview, South Pasadena, 1 March 1999.

152. (Los Angeles: Southern California AIA, 1939), p. 43.

153. Ibid.

154. *PSN*, 9 June 1928.

155. (Los Angeles: Southern California AIA, 1939), p. 43.

156. Vol. 7, 1929, p. 116.

157. Pasadena Building Permit #9359C.

158. *A&D*, February 1930, Vol. 32, p. 72.

159. Vol. 60, November 1926, pp. 385-474.

160. Ibid., p. 387.

161. *Pasadena Community Book*, op. cit., p. 727.

162. Ibid.

163. *PSN*, 7 January 1928.

164. See Margaret Holt Lowry Butler, *Letters to Tweeters* (Westport, Ct: Eidolon Press, 1980), p. 1.

165. (Cleveland: J.H. Jansen, 1928), pp. 38-41.

166. *Santa Barbara News Press*, 13 February 1996.

167. Deed history, in possession of current owner G.P. Wilson.

168. Marilyn Regan Sachs, interview, Pasadena, 29 November 1997.

169. Ibid.

170. Ibid.

171. *Santa Barbara News Press*, op. cit.

172. Ibid.

173. *SWBC*, 13 April 1923.

174. Vol. 58, November 1925 pp. 483-487.

175. Vol. 89, May 1927, pp. 81-83.

176. *A&D*, Vol. 25, August 1926, pp. 34-37, 70-72.

177. (Cleveland: J.H. Jansen, 1928), pp. 21-25.

178. (Pasadena: Star News Publishing Co., c. 1925), p. 50,

179. *A&D*, op. cit.

180. Heloise Bacon Power, interview, 21 September 1997.

181. Ibid.

181. Vol. 89, May 1927, pp. 81-83.

183. Ibid.

184. Docent lecture, Pasadena Heritage Home Tour, 13 April 1997.

185. Dr. Douglas Benson, interview, Pasadena, October 1996.

186. Ibid.

187. Ibid.

188. Ibid.

189. Docent lecture, op. cit.

190. John Schooler, *The Peters Cartridge Company* (December 1970), distributed by Remington Arms Company, Inc., Illen. New York.

191. Heloise Bacon Powers, interview, 21 September 1997.

192. Ibid.

193. Ibid.

194. Obituary, *PSN*, 13 December 1951.

195. Dr. Douglas Benson, interview, Pasadena, October 1996.

–Chapter 6– The Nicholson House: China in Pasadena

1. Marston Collection, Pasadena Historical Museum, Original Drawings, Job #464.

2. For the best summary of facts and architectural details see *Application for registration of Historical Landmark, Pacific Asia Museum,* by Jeanne Perkins and Linda Peters, 7 November 1988; copy available at Sever Center for Western History Research, Natural History Museum of Los Angeles.

3. M. Urmy Sears, "Grace Nicholson's Treasure House of Art," *CS*, Vol. 64. April 1926, pp. 23-26.

4. Letter to Cynthia Howe, State Architectural Historian, from Professor Robert Winter, Occidental College, 25 January 1989.

5. *Application for Registration...*, op. cit.

6. Carolyn Pearson, *LAN*, 13 December 1925.

7. Rhonda Packer, "Grace Nicholson: An Entrepreneur of Culture," *SCQ*, Vol. LXXVI, Fall 1994, p. 309.

8. Ibid., p. 310.

9. Nicholson Diary, Box 12, "Family and Building Papers," GNC, THL.

10. Box 15, "Indian Notes," GNC, THL.

11. Nicholson Diary, Box 12, "Family and Building Papers," GNC, THL.

12. Ibid.

13. Ibid; Rhonda Packer, op. cit., p. 311.

14. Rhonda Packer, op. cit.

15. Jane Apostol, "Saving Grace," *Westways*, Vol 68, October 1976, p. 70.

16. Dr. Jae Carmichael, first director of the Pacific Asia Museum, interview, 17 November 1997. Dr. Carmichael is descended from the Giddings family of Pasadena.

17. Rhonda Packer, op. cit., p. 313.

18. Box 12, "Grace Nicholson Biographical Material," GNC, THL.

19. *PS*, 28 September 1912.

20. Box 12, "Grace Nicholson Biographical Material," GNC, THL.

21. Rhonda Packer, op. cit, p. 314.

22. Notes of C.S. Hartman, Box 12, "Printed Items," GNC, THL.

23. Box 6, "Correspondence," GNC, THL; Carolyn Pearson, *LAN*, 13 December 1925.

24. *Application for Registration...*, op. cit.

25. Jane apostol, op. cit., p. 73.

26. Rhonda Packer, op. cit.

27. Nicholson Diary, Box 12, "Family and Building Papers," GBC, THL.

28. Ibid.

29. David Kamansky, Executive Director and Curator, Pacific Asia Museum, interview, 15 November 1997; see also Application for Registration..., op. cit.

30. David Kamansky, op. cit.

31. Rose Henderson, "A Chinese Treasure House," *WA*, Vol. 38, July 1929, p. 118.

32. David Kamansky, op. cit.

33. Album 56, Part II, GNC, THL.

34. Box 12, "Papers re Construction of Grace Nicholson Building at 46 Los Robles," Album 56, Part II, GNC, THL.

35. Album 56, Part II, "Building the Chinese Building–Architectural Details and Photographs in Forbidden City which served as model," GNC, THL.

36. M. Urmy Sears, op. cit., p. 24.

37. Letter to Cynthia Howse, State Architectural Historian, from Professor Robert Winter, Occidental College, 25 January 1989.

38. Notes by C.S. Hartman, Box 12, "Printed Items," Grace Nicholson Collection, The Huntington Library.

39. Rose Henderson, *WA*, Vol. 38, July 1929, pp. 116-18.

40. Ibid.

41. *Application for Registration...*, op. cit.

42. Rose Henderson, op. cit.

43. M. Urmy Sears, op. cit.

44. Rose Henderson, op. cit.

45. *Application for Registration...*, op. cit.

46. M. Urmy Sears, op. cit.

47. Ibid, quoting Laurence Binyon, *Painting in the Far East.*

48. *Application for Registration...*, op. cit.

49. Grace Nicholson, letter to Mrs. Flora, 16 March 1939; Box 6, "Correspondence," GNC, THL.

50. Dr. Jae Carmichael, op. cit.

51. David Kamansky, op. cit.

52. *PMN*, c. 1928.

53. David Kamansky, op. cit.

54. KPM, interview, Montecito, California, 21 September 1997.

–Chapter 7– Designing Community

1. The work of Wallace Neff, George Washington Smith, and Reginald Johnson was primarily residential. *Wallace Neff: Architect of California's Golden Age* (Santa Barbara: Capra Press, 1986; Santa Monica: Hennessey + Ingalls, 1999, p. 24

2. See *CS*, Vol. 9, April 1928, p. 26 for coverage of these structures.

3. Ibid.

4. *PSN*, 26 December 1923.

5. *PSN*, 26 May 1927.

6. Pasadena Athletic Club Nomination Application, National Register of Historic Places, 17 March 1977, item 8, p. 3.

7. 1979 Final Report, Historic Resources Inventory, Department of Parks and Recreation, State of California, August 1979, p. 37; prepared by Ann

Scheid.

8. See: Atholl McBean: Foreword, *By Middle Seas–Photographic Studies*, by J.E. Stanton (San Francisco: Gladding, McBean & Co., 1927).

9. (San Francisco: Gladding, McBean & Co., 1927).

10. Elizabeth St. John, *CS*, Vol. 9, April 1928, pp. 29-31.

11. "Modernistic Style Receives Recognition in AIA Architectural Honor Awards," SWBC, 21 March 1930, p. 30.

12. *PSN*, 9 April 1924.

13. Ibid.

14. Cultural Heritage Program, 1979 Final Report, Pasadena's Architectural and Historical Inventory, p. 50.

15. Pasadena Playhouse Grouping, Historical Resources Inventory, Department of Parks and Recreation, State of California, June 1984, p. 18.

16. *PCA*, Vol. 31, March 1927, p. 3.

17. "Sgraffito Frieze," *PSN*, 25 March 1951.

18. Ernest Burden, *Illustrated History of Architecture* (New York: McGraw-Hill, 1998), p. 194.

19. *PSN*, 25 March 1951.

20. Ibid.

21. *Pasadena Community Book*, 1955, p. 359.

22. (Los Angeles: Kingsley, Mason & Collins Co, 1913), [no pagination.]

23. Vol. 45, June 1916, p. 57.

24. *AD*, Vol. 6, 1928, p. 135.

25. Robert E. Bennett, interview, Pasadena, 20 October 1998.

26. *PSN*, 13 March 1913

27. *LABC*, 13 March 1913.

28. Ibid.

29. *PSN*, 10 January 1925; 16 January 1925.

30. Ibid.

31. Ibid.

32. Ibid.

33. Pasadena Athletic Club, Club History, undated (circa 1980).

34. Ibid.

35. Pasadena Athletic Club Public Hearing Regarding Its Status, Transcript, 9 August 1977, p. 10.

36. Pasadena Athletic Club, Nomination to National Register of Historic Places, 17 March 1977, item 8, p. 8.

37. Ibid.

38. Vol. 33, March 1928, pp. 37-43.

39. Pasadena Athletic Club, Club History, undated (circa 1980).

40. Ibid.

41. Ibid.

42. (Pasadena: Star News, 1922) [no pagination].

43. Home Laundry, Nomination Application for National Register of Historic Places, 1982, item 8, p. 1.

44. *AA*, Vol. 127, 8 April 1925, plate 88.

45. Richard Thomas, interview, Pasadena, 26 October 1988. Thomas grew up two houses away from Marston's house on El Molino and was best friends with the Marston sons.

46. S.B. Marston: "Diary, Young Men's Christian

Association." 24 December 1918–29 June 1919 [incomplete].

47. KPM, interview, Montecito, California, 21 September 1997.

48. See Van Pelt Fellows Application File, 1963-64; AIA Archives, Washington D.C.

49. A 1929 issue of *AD*, Vol. 7, pp. 114-115, features the church with photographs and has two credit lines, one giving credit to Marston, Van Pelt & Maybury, the other naming Marston & Maybury.

50. Marjorie Maybury Kellogg, interview, 30 June 2000.

51. David Gebhard, et al., *A Catalogue of The Architectural Drawing Collection of the University Art Museum, U.C. Santa Barbara*, 1983, p. 427.

52. *The Bungalow Reader* (Newsletter of the Urban Conservation Office, City of Pasadena, Winter 1988, No. 3, Col. 1.

53. *Master Builders*, ed. Diane Maddex (The Preservation Press: Washington, D.C., 1985), p. 114.

54. Ralph Adams Cram, *The Substance of Gothic: Six Lectures on the Development of Architecture from Charlemagne to Henry VIII* (Boston: Marshall Jones Company, 1917).

55. *The Bungalow Reader*, op. cit., Col. 2.

56. *PSN*, 8 May 1998.

57. Vol. 7, pp. 114-115.

58. Sunday Program, Scott United Methodist Church, 94th Anniversary Celebration, 21 September 1997.

59. Ibid.

60. Vol. 34, January 1917, p. 31.

61. Ibid.

62. Hollywood Memorial Park Cemetery, Nomination Application, National Register of Historic Places, 24 November 1997, p. 2.

63. Amy M. Spindler, "A Resting Place to Die For?" 15 November 1998, pp. 112-115; "New Lease on Life," *Preservation: The Magazine of the National Trust for Historical Preservation*, May-June 1998, p. 15.

64. Los Angeles City Building Records, Permit No. 5267, 11 October 1917.

65. Ibid., permit 5316, 16 March 1921.

66. 17 September 1922.

67. "Design for Imposing Mausoleum," *LAT*, 19 March 1922.

68. 12 November 1922.

69. *LAT*, 12 November 1922.

70. Marston Collection, Original Drawings, Job #311, Sheet 6, 1 October 1917; Pasadena Historical Museum Archives.

71. *SWBC*, 21 March 1930.

72. Richard G. Carrott, *The Egyptian Revival* (Berkeley: U.C. Press, 1978), p. 54.

73. Hollywood Memorial Park Cemetery, Nomination Application, National Register of Historic Places, 24 November 1997, p. 19.

74. Hollywood memorial Park Cemetery Brochure, undated.

75. Hollywood Memorial Park Cemetery, Nomination Application, National Register of Historic Places, 24 November 1997.

76. "New Lease on Life," *Preservation: The Magazine of the National Trust for Historic Preservation*, May-June

1998, p. 15.

77. *SWBC*, 11 April 1924.

78. Pasadena Public Library System Summary, Hill Branch Library, undated, p. 1.

79. *PSN*, 8 October 1924.

80. Club Summary, Pasadena Library Club, Thomas Cowles, Secretary-Treasurer, undated, copy on file at Hill Branch Library.

81. Pasadena Public Library System Summary, Hill Branch Library, undated, p. 1.

82. Ibid.

83. "Hill Avenue Branch Library," Vol. 32, August 1927, pp. 17-30 (5 plates); see also *A&E*, Vol. 89, April 1927, pp. 39-50

84. Ibid.

85. *PSN*, 14 August 1996.

86. *LABC*, 13 August 1908.

87. *PSN*, 1 November 1924.

88. Patricia McComb, Dixon resident, telephone interview, 21 February 1999.

89. John Moulton, volunteer librarian, Embudo Library, Dixon, telephone interview, 18 February 1999.

90. Ibid.

91. Ibid.

92. Ibid.

93. *PSN*, 20 September 1988.

94. *PSN*, 14 February 1954.

95. Ibid.

96. *SWBC*, 22 June 1923.

97. Ibid.

98. *PSN*, 14 February 1954.

99. *SWBC*, 11 November 1921.

100. "New $20,000 Citrus Office Ready," *Orange Daily News*, 28 December 1922.

101. Ibid.

102. Ibid.

103. "The Exchange–Fine Arts," Brochure, Orange County Fruit Exchange, undated.

104. Vol. 39, February 1931, pp. 38-39.

105. "To Padua Hills for Mexican Food, Dancing, Theater, Shopping," *Sunset*, August 1967, pp. 46-47.

106. "The Story of Padua Hills," *PSN*, 3 August 1997.

107. Ibid.

108. Judy Wright, *Claremont: A Pictorial History* (Claremont: The Claremont Historical Resources Center, 1980), pp. 166-67.

109. *PSN*, 3 August 1997.

110. Ibid.

111. Ibid.

112. Ibid.

113. Padua Hills Theater Nomination Application to National Register of Historic Places, 29 July 1997, Section 8. p. 1.

Conclusion

1. Heloise Bacon Powers, interview, Montecito, 21 September 1997.

2. Robert E. Bennett, interview, 20 October 1998.

3. "City Honors Memory of S.B. Marston," *PSN*, 19 November 1946; tribute patterned on inscription on Sir Christopher Wrens tomb, St. Paul's Cathedral, London.

Index

Individual buildings and structures designed by the firm of Marston, Van Pelt and Maybury or any of its constituent members are listed in this index under the name of the firm and the type of the commission.

ALEXANDER, ROBERT E., 7
Annandale Club, 48, 55, 59, 68, 79
Armstrong, John S., 5
Arts and Crafts movement, Pasadena, 31-32

BABCOCK, CHARLES, 12
Bachelder, Ernest, 2, 48
Bacon, Mark R., 56
Bain, Ferdinand R., 54
Bakewell, John, 97
Banks, Francis H. D., 50
Banks, Lillian Dobbins, 50
Barber, Donn, 7
Baxter, Sylvester: *Spanish-Colonial Architecture in Mexico*, 73
Bennett, Cyril, 7, 32, 97
Bennett, Robert, 3, 32, 101
Bennett and Haskell, 7
Benton, Arthur B., 2
Bergstrom, Edwin, 2, 97
Bertonneau, A.J., 23
Bidwell, H.E., 64
Bird, Seman L., 60
Bishop, Ellis, 84
Bishop, Maitland L., 34-35
Blaisdell, Joseph, 113
Booth, Ellen Warren Scripps, 81
Booth, George, 81
Booth, James Scripps, 81
Bosley, Edward R., 51

Brooks Art Stone Corporation, 100
Brown, Frank E., 103
Burnham, Daniel, 84
Burnham, John, 84-85
Bushnell, David and Nina, 86
Busch, Adolphus, 15

CHAMBERS, H.C., 25, 97
Chandler, Helen D., 86
Churriguera, Jose de, 74
Clark, Alson S. and Medora, 81
Clark, Robert Judson, 82
Clements, Stiles O., 2
Coate, Roland, 19
Comstock, H.O., 23, 24
Cornell University, Beaux Arts architectural tradition at, 11-12
Council, Lucile, 70
Cox, Amariah G., 27
Coxhead, Ernest, 71
Craftsman bungalows, 37-38
Cram, Ralph Adams; *The Substance of Gothic*, 106
Creller, W.F., 102
Culbertson, James A., 51

DONOVAN JOHN J., 7

EASON, WILLIS M., 34
Ellinger, William W., III, 97
Everett, Henry A., 62

Everett, Josephine, 62

FARQUHAR, ROBERT, 2
Fox, Rev. Daniel F, 35
French, H.C., Jr., 34

GARFORD, ARTHUR LOVETT, 76
Garner, Herman H., 113
Garnsey, Julian Ellsworth, 100, 103
Gates, Mrs. P.G., 92
Gaut, Helen Lukens, 31
Gebhard, David, 73
Gilbert, Cass, 73
Gill, Irving, 2, 5, 82
Gladding, McBean, 59, 86, 98, 99-100
Goodhue, Bertram G., 73, 85, 106
Greene and Greene, 2, 7, 32, 34, 39, 40, 41, 46, 49, 51
Greene, Charles Sumner, 3, 31
Greene, Henry Mather, 2
Grey, Elmer,1, 6, 16, 31-32
Griffith, W. Cady, 28

HALDEMAN, H.R., 65
Haldeman, Harry F., 65-66
Haldeman, Harry M., 65
Hamilton, J.E., 26
Hardy, F.A., 77
Hartman, C.S., 92
Haskell, Fitch, 97
Haver, June, 52
Hebbard, William S., 5
Hebrard, Jean, 12
Heineman Brothers, 45
Hewitt, Harwood, 2
Hinds, Joseph E., 39
Hinds, Samuel S., 55-56
Hogan, Frank G., 44-45, 97, 101
Hogan, Col. W.J., 44-45
Howard, John Galen, 7, 71
Hunt, George, 103
Hunt, Myron, 1, 5,19, 25, 97
Hunt, Sumner, 2

JAMES, G. WHARTON, 92
Jefferson, W.T., 81, 97
Jenks, S. Herbert, 27
Jewett, William K., 61
Johnson, Reginald, 2, 7
Johnson, Kaufman & Coate, 75
Julian, C.C., oil scandal, 65

KAMANSKY, DAVID, 93
Kendall-Curtis, 36
Krempel, John P., 5

LACEY, HENRY ROBERTS, 38-39
Lacey, W. DeWitt, 53
Linda Vista School, 1927, 109
Linnard, D.M., 17, 19, 20, 22, 23, 24, 48, 97
Los Angeles Architectural Club, 2
Los Angeles Pressed Brick Company, 95
Lummis, Charles F., 2
Lund, Ann Scheid, 98

MARSTON, ABBIE, sister, 9, 62
Marston (Hastings), Alice, sister, 9
  Writings on early Pasadena, 9, 10
Marston, Edith Hatfield, wife, 11, 13
Marston, Franklin Augustine (Frank), father, 9, 10
Marston, Keith Palmer, son, 3, 52, 99, 105
Marston, Phineas F., grandfather, 8-9
  Lighthouse building, 8-9
Marston, Sylvanus Boardman, great-uncle, 8
Marston, Sylvanus Boardman (1883-1946)
  Architectural credentials, 5
  Architectural education, 11-13
  Death, 115
  Early Pasadena days, 9-11
  Family background, 8-9
  Marriage, 13
  Place in Pasadena's architectural circles, 5-6
  Professional honors, 3
  World War I experiences, diary, 104-105

MARSTON, VAN PELT & MAYBURY
  Contributions to Arts and Crafts movement, 32, 45
  Country house style, 63
  French country style, 67
  Italian renaissance style, 57
  Overview of firm, 2-4
  Revival architecture, 49
  School designs, 110
  Small house designs, 69-70
  Spanish colonial revival architecture, 74-75

CIVIC AND COMMERCIAL COMMISSIONS:
  Abbey of the Psalms Mausoleum, Los Angeles, 1929, 108
  Arcade Building, 1927, 99
  Eliot Junior High School, Altadena, 1932, 110
  Hill Avenue Branch Library, 1924, 109
  Hollywood Memorial Park Cemetery, Los Angeles, 1917-1929, 107
  Hollywood Cathedral Mausoleum, Los Angeles, 1917, 1921, 107-108
  Home Laundry Company, 1922, 103-104
  Las Olas Beach Club, Venice, 1926, 114
  Don Lee Building, 1925, 99-100
  Linda Vista Park Gate, Santa Monica, 1911, 40-41
  Lincoln Avenue Church, 1916, 107

Mechanic Arts Building, UCLA, n.d., 111
Mission School, Dixon NM, 1910, 110-111
G.L. Morris Building, 1924, 98-99
Grace Nicholson Treasure House, 1924, 91-96
  Description of building, 95-96
  Design origins, 93-95
  Garden, 96
  Overview, 91-92
Orange County Fruit Exchange, Orange, 1921, 112
Pacific-Southwest Trust and Savings Bank, 1927, 100-101
Padua Hills Theater, Claremont, 1930, 112-114
Pasadena Athletic Club, 1925, 101-103
Pasadena National Bank, 1913, 100-101
Prospect Park Entrance Gate, n.d., 40
San Rafael Elementary School, 1929, 110
Scott Chapel, Methodist Episcopal Church, 1929, 106-107
Turner and Stevens Mortuary, 1922, 103, 115
Warner Building, 1927, 97-98
Westminster Presbyterian Church, 1927, 105-106
Westridge School, 1923, 111-112
William Wilson Building, 1927, 100

PASADENA RESORT HOTEL COMMISSIONS:
Hotel Maryland, 17-19, 92, 98
  Bungalows, 18
  Maryland Apartments, 18-19
Huntington Hotel, 19-21
  Cottages, 20-22
    Chance View Cottage, 1927, 22
    Clovelly Cottage, 1926, 21
    Ferncroft Cottage, 1926, 20
    Finleen Cottage, 1926, 20, 21
    Howard Cottage, 1927, 22
    Mariner Cottage, 1926, 22
Vista del Arroyo Hotel, 22-24, 29, 62
  Bungalows, 25-28
    B, C, and D Bungalows, 1920-21, 25, 26
    Cox Bungalow, 1935, 27
    Griffith Bungalow, 1935, 28
    Hamilton Bungalow, 1926, 26
    Jenks Bungalow, 1928, 26
    Maxwell Bungalow, 1929, 28
    Stuart Bungalow, 1925, 27

RESIDENTIAL COMMISSIONS:
599, 606, 623, 636 S. Mentor Avenue, 1910-1912, 36-37
Mrs. Robert Anderson, 1911, 34
Mark R. Bacon, 1923, 56
Ferdinand R. Bain, Palms, 1924, 53-54
Francis H. D. Banks, 1916, 49-50
Ella Barnes, 1909, 32-33
Herbert E. Bell, 1929, 69

H.E. Bidwell, 1913, 63-64
Seman L. Bird, 1920, 50-60
Ellis Bishop, Rancho Santa Fe, 1928, 82-85
Maitland L. Bishop, 1911, 34
James Scripps Booth, 1922, 81-82
Helen D. Chandler, Altadena, 1929, 85-86
Bertha Holt Clark, 1922, 87-88
E.S. Crawford, 1926, 70-71
Diggs House, 1926, 70-71
Willis M. Eason, 1911, 34
Nelson Eddy, Brentwood, 1939, 52
George B. Ellis, 1911, 35
Joseph B. Erkenbrecher, San Marino, 1931, 69
Josephine Everett, 1928, 61-62
Rev. Daniel F. Fox, 1910, 35
H.C. French, Jr., 1910, 34
Arthur Lovett Garford, 1916, 75-76
L.G. Haase, 1911, 33
Harry F. Haldeman, Beverly Hills, 1928, 65-66
Frances and Helen Hamilton, 1924, 53
F.A. Hardy, 1927, 77
Edward C. Harwood, San Marino, 1926, 69
William Hespeler, 1912, 46-47
Thomas E. Hicks, 1913, 51
Joseph E. Hinds, 1910, 39-40
Samuel S. Hinds, 1915, 54-56
George S. Hunt, 71-72
W.T. Jefferson, 1921, 79-81
William K. Jewett, 1915, 60-61
Henry Roberts Lacey, 1912, 38-39
W. DeWitt Lacey, 1917, 53
Sylvanus B. Marston, 1910, 33-34
Clinton P. McAlister, 1909, 37-38
J.J. McCarthy, 1929, 69
Jane E. Meeker, 1915, 36
John Henry Meyer, San Marino, 1920, 78-79
Douglas Morris, 1928, 65
Henry Newby, 1913, 47-48
Harry V. Ogden, 1930, 66-67
Charles Paddock, 1932, 66
William Henry Peters, 1923, 56, 88-90
William D. Peterson, 1912, 62-63
R.A. Pratt, 1924, 77-78
St. Francis Court, 1908, 41-44
Hannah Nevin Shaw, 1924, 79
E.S. Skillen, 1925, 85
William R. Staats, 1924, 67-68
Wiley W. Stephens, 1925, 86-87
Mrs. Francis E. Stevens, 1927, 86
Catherine G. Sturgis, 1926, 70
Robert A. Swink, 1911, 38
Thomas House, Ithaca N.Y., 1907, 12-13
G. Roscoe Thomas, 1911, 45-46
Dr. Roy Thomas, Hancock Park, 1923, 50
Joseph E. Tilt, 1920, 58
John N. Van Patten, 1922, 64-65

Herbert M. Vanzwoll, 1928, 56-57
Thomas W. Warner, 1924, 58-59

MARTIN, ALBERT C., 2
Martin, Albert C., Jr., 2, 3, 12
Martin, Clarence, 12
Maxwell, George H., 28
Maybury, Edgar Wood
  Personal and professional history, 7
  Work on Nelson Eddy house, 52
  Work on George S. Hunt house
McDonald, Marianne, 85
Meyer, John Henry, 79
Midwick Country Club, 5, 17, 53, 68
Miller, Joaquin, 9
Moore, Charles, 75
Morgan, Julia, 97
Morgan, Octavius, 2, 5, 15
Mullgardt, L.C., 2

NEFF, WALLACE, 6, 19, 45, 67, 75, 82
Newcomb, Rexford: *Mediterranean Domestic
  Architecture in the United States*, 74, 87
Newby, Henry, 48
Nicholson, Grace, history and character, 92-93, 96

OHRMUND BROTHERS, 95
On, F. Suie, 93
Orban, Paul, Jr., 5
Overland Club, 5, 45, 48, 55, 84, 101

PACIFIC ASIA MUSEUM, PASADENA, 93, 96. *See also*
  Marston, Van Pelt & Maybury, Grace Nicholson
  Treasure House
Paddock, Charles, 66, 101-102
Pan-Pacific Exposition, San Diego, 1915, 73, 74
Parkinson, John, 2
Parsons, William E., 71
Pasadena, California:
  As health resort, 16-17
  Central Business District, 97-98
Pasadena Playhouse, 55
Pasadena Presbyterian Church, 79, 104
Perkins, Jeanne, 91
Peters, William Henry, 90
Powell, Herbert J., 106
Prairie Style, 33-34

RANCHO SANTA FE, 82-85
Ranney, Mary Lowther, 111
Raymond Hotel, Pasadena, 24
Rea, Alfred W., 2
Regan, Phil J., 88
Requa, Richard S., 2
Richardson, Henry Hobson, 85
Ritchie, Ward, 55

Robinson, Jackie, 107
Roehrig, Frederick, 1, 5, 32, 97
Rose Bowl, 45
Royce, Stephen, 23
Rumney, Amie C., 111

SANDERS, F.C.S., M.D., 16
Scripps, James E., 81
Sears, M. Urmy, 95
Shakespeare Club, 62
Shaw, Roy and Hannah Nevin, 79
Smith, George Washington, 75, 82
Soule, Winsor, 2
Southern California Chapter of the American
  Institute of Architects (AIA), 1
Spanish colonial revival architecture in California,
  73-74
Spaulding, Sumner M., 2
Staats, William R., 68
Stahlhuth, Fred, Smith & Stahlhuth Stonemasons,
  40-41
Stanton, J.E., Gladding, McBean artist: *By Middle
  Seas*, 98
Stephens, Wiley W., 87
Stewart, Colin, 17
Stickley, Gustav, 31
Stuart, Holloway Ithamer, 27

THIENE, PAUL G., 79
Thomas, Carl C., 13, 46
Thomas, G. Roscoe, 45-46
Tilt, Joseph E., 58
Tregor, Nisson, 108

VALLEY HUNT CLUB, 79
Van Pelt, Garrett Beekman
  AIA Fellow, 3
  Old Architecture in Southern Mexico (1926), 7, 74
  Personal and professional history, 6-7
Vroman's Book Store, 98

WARNER, THOMAS W., 58-59
West & Company, 95
Wiemeyer, George, 24
Wheeler, James C., 108
White, Andrew D., 12
White, Charles E., 32
White, Walter, 6
William Smith Architectural Stone Company, 96
Wilson, William, 100
Winslow, Carleton M., 97
Winter, Robert, 91
Withey, Henry, 2
Wright, Frank Lloyd, 34

YOCH, FLORENCE, 70